Palm™
Programming

Symbol Support Center - 800-653-5350

comm-dev-forum@ news.palmos.com

Glenn Bachmann

002-4692391- 1964059

SAMS

A Division of Macmillan Computer Publishing
201 W. 103rd St., Indianapolis, IN 46290.

support@symbol.com

Palm™ Programming

Copyright © 1999 by Sams Publishing

International Standard Book Number: 0-672-31493-2

Library of Congress Catalog Card Number: 98-87631

Printed in the United States of America

First Printing: June 1999

00   4   3

Trademarks

Warning and Disclaimer

EXECUTIVE EDITOR
Brad Jones

ACQUISITIONS EDITOR
Chris Webb

DEVELOPMENT EDITOR
Matt Purcell

MANAGING EDITOR
Jodi Jensen

PROJECT EDITOR
Heather Talbot

COPY EDITOR
Kris Simmons

INDEXER
Rebecca Salerno

PROOFREADER
Donna Martin

TECHNICAL EDITOR
Ben Gottlieb

SOFTWARE DEVELOPMENT SPECIALIST
Michael Hunter

INTERIOR DESIGNER
Gary Adair

COVER DESIGNER
Aren Howell

COPY WRITER
Eric Borgert

LAYOUT TECHNICIANS
Brandon Allen
Stacey DeRome
Timothy Osborn
Staci Somers

Contents at a Glance

Contents

About the Authors

Lead Author

Glenn Bachmann is president of Bachmann Software and Services, LLC (www.bachmannsoftware.com), a leading provider of software products and professional software development services in the mobile computing and wireless communications industries. Among Bachmann Software's acclaimed software products are Bachmann Print Manager and Bachmann Report Manager for the Palm computing platform. Having developed business applications in everyday use on computers worldwide, Bachmann Software's clients and customers are among the world's leading corporations in and out of the computer industry.

Contributing Authors

Gregory P. Winton is a professional software architect with more than a decade of experience developing software for companies ranging from small startups to Chase Manhattan Bank. He is currently the director of software development at Bachmann Software and Services. Greg is the sole author of Chapter 19, "Shared Libraries: Extending the Palm OS," but Greg's presence is felt in practically every chapter because he provided both content and inspiration in many other areas of the book.

Frank Ableson is an expert in computer hardware/software communications, network programming, and image processing, and he relishes solving problems in general. Frank is the author of Chapters 20 and 21, which focus on serial and infrared communications. Frank is the resident communications guru at Bachmann Software and also runs his own consulting firm, CFG Solutions. His biggest fans are his wife, Nikki, and children, Julia and Tristan.

Acknowledgments

I'd like to thank Macmillan Publishing, and Chris Webb in particular, for being supportive during the writing of this book: You are a pleasure to work with.

I am grateful for the contributions of my esteemed co-authors, Greg Winton and Frank Ableson. I've known and worked with Greg for more than half of my career: I have the utmost respect for him as a software professional, a co-worker, a confidant, a company strategist, and a trusted friend. Frank Ableson is the ultimate "can-do" guy and has come through time and again in tight situations with solutions to the most vexing programming problems.

Most of all, I thank my wife, Joananne, and my children, Nicholas, Julianne, and Courtney, for giving me unquestioning support, patience, and understanding throughout the emotional highs and lows of running a business and writing a book. It's incredible how much exhaustion and stress can be wiped away by a child's smile.

Tell Us What You Think!

As the reader of this book, *you* are our most important critic and commentator. We value your opinion and want to know what we're doing right, what we could do better, what areas you'd like to see us publish in, and any other words of wisdom you're willing to pass our way.

As an Associate Publisher for Sams Publishing, I welcome your comments. You can fax, email, or write me directly to let me know what you did or didn't like about this book—as well as what we can do to make our books stronger.

Please note that I cannot help you with technical problems related to the topic of this book, and that due to the high volume of mail I receive, I might not be able to reply to every message.

When you write, please be sure to include this book's title and authors as well as your name and phone or fax number. I will carefully review your comments and share them with the authors and editors who worked on the book.

Fax: 317-581-4770

Email: adv_prog@mcp.com

Mail: Brad Jones
           Sams Publishing
           201 West 103rd Street
           Indianapolis, IN 46290 USA

Introduction

Who Should Read This Book?

This book is appropriate for software developers, system designers, quality assurance professionals, and technical writers who want to learn about software development for the Palm computing platform. It targets most those at an intermediate level in software development, having familiarity with tools such as compilers, editors, and debuggers as well as programming concepts such as variables and functions.

Although the book was written assuming the reader has little or no Palm programming experience, I do assume the user has at least a working knowledge of the C or C++ programming languages. Experience with another language such as Java is a reasonable substitute for this knowledge. For much of the book, experience with programming on an event-driven, graphical operating system such as Windows, Macintosh, or UNIX is helpful.

How to Use This Book

You can use this book in two ways: a beginning-to-end tutorial or a set of 24 standalone chapters that demonstrate how to work with specific areas of Palm programming. For beginning Palm developers, I recommend reading the first four chapters straight through, followed by the first few chapters on user-interface programming, followed by the first two chapters on database programming.

For those with some Palm programming experience, a brief review of chapters one through four might be all that is necessary, although I advise at least a quick refresher course in some of the basics of user interface and database programming before moving on to the advanced topics.

The remainder of the book consists of a series of single-chapter treatments of intermediate to advanced Palm programming topics. Given that you've mastered the basics of the Palm programming model as well as the basics of user interfaces and databases, you can pretty much attack the rest of the book in any order you want or as specific needs arise. For each chapter, you should make sure to build and run the examples as well as read the source code. It is the best way to learn!

How to Contact the Author

I have set up a public mailing list dedicated to providing a forum for discussing this book, asking questions, posting comments, and so on. To subscribe, send an email message to `bss-public-palmprogramming-subscribe@egroups.com`. To send a message to the group, address it to `Bss-public-palmprogramming@egroups.com`. In addition, look for corrections and changes to the content of the book, new programming examples, and other information that will be posted on my Web site, `www.bachmannsoftware.com`.

I welcome comments and questions from readers and will do my best to respond in a timely manner.

Conventions Used in This Book

This book uses different typefaces to differentiate between code and regular English, and also to help you identify important concepts.

Text that you type and text that should appear on your screen is presented in `monospace` type.

`It will look like this to mimic the way text looks on your screen.`

Placeholders for variables and expressions appear in `monospace italic` font. You should replace the placeholder with the specific value it represents.

This arrow (➥) at the beginning of a line of code means that a single line of code is too long to fit on the printed page. Continue typing all characters after the ➥ as though they were part of the preceding line.

NOTE

A Note presents interesting pieces of information related to the surrounding discussion.

TIP

A Tip offers advice or teaches an easier way to do something.

CAUTION

A Caution advises you about potential problems and helps you steer clear of disaster.

Getting Started with Palm Programming Using CodeWarrior

PART

I

IN THIS PART

CHAPTER 1

Introduction to Palm Programming and CodeWarrior

I have lived through three major computer-platform revolutions in my career: the move to personal computers from mainframes and minicomputers, the adoption of graphical user interfaces, and the rise of the Internet. I distinctly recall feeling a sense of wonder as I witnessed the adoption of new technology and the creation of entirely new market opportunities. During each of these periods of transition, new companies began, became successful, and, in some cases, displaced old companies that either weren't paying enough attention or couldn't make the transition to the new platform quickly enough.

There is no doubt in my mind that handheld and mobile computing is a fourth wave of change that is rippling through our industry. It is clearly changing the way that we work and live our lives and brings computing power to a whole new user community. Although at one time this technology was expensive, slow, and bulky and its capabilities were ridiculed in the press (including a well-known comic strip), a new breed of handheld devices captured the imaginations (and shirt pockets!) of consumers and business people worldwide. The Palm Connected Organizer is by far the most successful of these new devices and consequently is receiving a lot of attention from software developers looking to create new software applications that provide computing power for the mobile user.

In order to get you started creating those applications, this chapter provides

- A brief overview of the Palm Computing platform and how it came about
- What it's like to program for the Palm in C++
- What tools are involved in Palm Programming

Having used Chapter 1 to dispense with matters of housekeeping, I then get right into what this book is all about: teaching you how to write Palm applications.

The Palm Computing Platform

The Palm Connected Organizer, or Palm for short, is one of the biggest success stories in computer history. It is the first handheld computing device and operating system to achieve truly widespread acceptance in the workplace, having sold several million units in its first few years of existence.

This has significance for the software development community: For the first time, there is a single handheld platform available with a large enough installed base to capture the attention of large numbers of developers. In addition, Palm Computing is actively licensing the Palm OS to other hardware manufacturers, both encouraging the creation of a wide variety of devices that are suited for different markets as well as growing the installed base.

A quick survey of the devices supporting the Palm OS yields the following:

Palm Computing: PalmPilot Professional, Palm III, Palm IIIx, Palm V, Palm VII (scheduled to ship in 1999)

Symbol Technologies: SPT1500

IBM Corporation: IBM Workpad

Qualcomm: pdQ Smartphone (scheduled to ship in 1999)

Several other vendors have announced plans to create devices that support the Palm Computing platform as well.

The Palm Computing platform has five main pieces:

- A standard hardware design
- An interface for extending the Palm via add-on hardware components
- An operating system, Palm OS
- Data synchronization to and from host systems via hot-sync
- The Palm SDK and associated tools that enable programmers to develop applications

It is important to note that all the devices listed here run one common operating system: Palm Computing's Palm OS. You can reasonably expect that your Palm application will run on a wide variety of hardware devices. Developers such as you and me appreciate that, and as a result, Palm Computing is rapidly attracting new developers to the platform.

What Is a Palm Application?

A Palm application is in one sense a file with an extension of .PRC. (Executables are often referred to as .PRC files.) .PRCs are created on the desktop by writing code and creating resources using a development tool such as CodeWarrior and are then transferred to the Palm device using hot-sync. On the Palm device, a .PRC is actually a special kind of database called a resource database. (Resources and databases are discussed in detail later.) A .PRC contains all the elements of your application, including the code itself and user-interface elements.

Palm applications, like applications in other environments, are event-driven. This means that your application code interacts with and is notified by Palm OS as significant events happen, such as pushing a button or completing a pen stroke. Almost everything that occurs in the system which affects your application will be sent as an event.

Although internally Palm OS is multitasking, Palm applications do not multitask: If a user is running your application and he decides he needs to look up a friend's phone number, your application will exit when he invokes the Address Book. Also, note that Palm applications do not have the ability to create multiple threads of execution.

Aside from the program that runs on the Palm device, some applications require a conduit. A conduit is not a Palm application at all; it is a special Windows or Macintosh component, developed with standard Windows/Macintosh tools (Microsoft's Visual Studio or Metrowerks' CodeWarrior), that gets invoked when you perform a hot-sync. Conduits can provide special database synchronization between data on the Palm and the desktop. They can also be used to transfer files and perform other tasks requiring interaction with the desktop. Conduit development is a large, complex topic that, if explored thoroughly, could fill a book on its own. I provide a basic overview in this book, choosing instead to focus on the Palm side of things.

How Are Palm Applications Written?

Most Palm programs today are written in C++, although many of the recent extensions to C++ are not supported by the available Palm development environments. You will find that the essence of C++ (inheritance, polymorphism, and so on) is supported, but beyond that, things get dicey. Among other things, you will not find support for C++ templates or exceptions. If you are looking to port code from another platform to the Palm that relies on these features, you will unfortunately need to rewrite some of your code.

Many compilers today offer a built-in set of standard functions called the C runtime library. Functions such as `malloc`, `printf`, `memset`, and `strcpy` are old friends that as programmers we have come to rely on, even in new operating system environments. Unfortunately, the current Palm SDK does not support the standard runtime library. Instead, it offers its own set of memory and string routines. These routines are not as comprehensive nor as fully functional as their counterparts in the C runtime library, so many developers have resorted to writing their own functions as they need them.

> **NOTE**
>
> As developers, we debate the merits of taking extra time to write portable, compiler-independent, and operating-system–independent code. Well, the Palm is an instance where you will profit handsomely if you have been careful to write portable code that insulates you from dependencies on the underlying operating system interfaces. When you want to port some code to the Palm, you will also be rewarded for having shown patience and restraint in not jumping at the chance to take advantage of the latest C++ extensions or operating-system–specific frameworks. At my company, we are taking a conservative stance on new compiler and OS features for this very reason.

The CodeWarrior Tools

The official toolset is Metrowerks' CodeWarrior. (Palm Computing has announced plans to license and eventually distribute the Palm version.) Before I describe CodeWarrior, one other toolset that has achieved popularity among Palm developers is GCC. GCC is a name commonly used to refer to the GNU C tools that support cross-platform development. The GNU tools are a free download from the Internet, and they contain everything you need to create Palm applications with the exception of conduits. (You need to obtain the Conduit SDK from Palm for this.)

CodeWarrior is the name of the development environment created by Metrowerks. It runs on Windows 95, Windows NT, or Macintosh environments. Like GCC, it contains all the components you need to develop Palm applications. Unlike GCC, it contains a built-in IDE (interactive development environment) for managing and building projects.

It also contains a resource-creation tool called Constructor that allows you to develop the user interface for your program by dragging resource elements from a palette onto your forms.

Which toolset should you use? Here are some important areas where there are differences between the tools: Depending on your needs and style of programming, they might help you decide:

- Support
- Debugging
- Building your project
- Resource creation
- Price

Support

CodeWarrior is the official development environment recommended by Palm. Although this might never impact you, as time goes on, I expect Palm's developer support staff to assume you are using CodeWarrior. Of course, you can call Metrowerks if you have problems installing or using CodeWarrior. There is no company behind GCC, so you are dependent on peer support with that development tool.

Both environments enjoy a healthy and lively following in various discussion forums on the Internet, so for the time being, if you have a tool-specific problem, it is likely you will find peer support by searching the messages from their forums.

Debugging

CodeWarrior comes with a graphical, menu-driven source-level debugger. GCC comes with GDB, which uses EMACS to display the source code being debugged. In GDB, you must type commands to display the contents of variables, the stack, and so on.

Building Your Project

GCC assumes you will be using standard makefiles to build your Palm programs from the command line. Shareware, freeware, and commercial front ends to GCC provide an IDE for GCC users. CodeWarrior does not support command-line builds; you must go through the IDE to build your project. Also, depending on whether you come from a Macintosh or Windows development background, you might find the user interface for the CodeWarrior IDE confusing and awkward: Many people complain that the IDE does not conform to the standard look and feel of Windows tools.

Resource Creation

CodeWarrior comes with Constructor, a visual resource development tool that lets you interactively create the user interface for your program. What's more, CodeWarrior completely hides the source code for these resources and insists on managing things such as resource IDs; things go haywire if you manually change them yourself. GCC originated in the early days of Windows development, where resources were defined by typing scripts into text files, which then got compiled via a command-line tool into the final program. As with the IDE, there are third-party tools available to help you manage your GCC resources.

Price

Although essentially a non-issue for commercial software vendors, many hobbyists and part-time developers will balk at paying several hundred dollars for CodeWarrior. All other things being equal (and I just noted where they are not), you can't beat the price of GCC.

There is no right answer to the question of which development tool you should use. Aside from issues of support and price, in most of the areas I list, the factor is personal taste. Although these days it gets me slapped with the "Luddite" label, I personally prefer environments that let me do command-line builds because they offer me more control over the use of my development tools. I also find myself developing for many different computer platforms, and it is unproductive to keep changing from one IDE to another. I prefer instead to use a single editor and a good set of makefile scripts. Nevertheless, I have opted to use CodeWarrior, primarily because of the support issue and because of promises from Metrowerks that it will provide command-line builds with the next version. (I should also note that I do not use the CodeWarrior built-in editor.)

This book assumes you are using CodeWarrior, although I assure those who have chosen GCC that in almost all cases, the sample code provided will compile just fine in either environment. The only major differences are where I walk you through the steps required to create resources using CodeWarrior's Constructor tool. Under GCC, you use PilRC to create linkable resources from text files containing special commands to describe the resource's appearance. You should have no trouble looking up the PilRC equivalents for the examples.

The Palm SDK

If you purchase CodeWarrior, you get the Palm OS Software Development Kit (SDK) for free on the CodeWarrior CD. For GCC users, or for those who want to update their

CodeWarrior installations, the latest SDK is downloadable from the Palm Computing Web site.

The SDK contains headers, libraries, tools, a tutorial, sample code, and documentation on how to use the Palm SDK application programming interfaces (APIs) in your Palm programming. It also contains the source code for the built-in applications such as Address Book. Be aware that much of the documentation is in the form of reference material and function listings. Aside from the tutorial, most of the material answers the "what," but not much material is devoted to answering the questions "how" and "why."

The Palm SDK documentation is logically divided into interface management, system management, and memory and communication management.

"Interface Management" provides the closest thing to an overview and then provides a reference for the available user-interface resource types as well as functions used in managing your application's user interface. I refer to this manual the most.

"Memory and Communication Management" covers a wide territory, including how to allocate and manage memory chunks, the Palm database interface, serial and infrared communications subsystems, and the networking APIs.

"System Management" is kind of a catch-all, covering error handling, alarms, events, system and application preferences, string management, and other miscellaneous areas.

I highly recommend taking the time to walk through the tutorial. It is also a great idea to explore the source code for the built-in applications as well as the other examples. With an SDK as large as Palm's, there is nothing like looking at other people's code to gain an understanding of how to properly use the APIs.

The documentation until recently was available only as a series of separate PDF files, which was a source of many complaints. The docs are now available in printed format (see the Palm Web site for ordering instructions), and from what I can see of the new 3.1 SDK, the online documentation has been reorganized to make searches across the entire SDK much more manageable.

Summary

This chapter provided an overview of the Palm device, the Palm Computing platform, Palm programs, and the tools and languages used to develop Palm applications. One thing noticeably absent from our first chapter is source code. Don't panic! This is virtually the only chapter in the book that doesn't show you specifically how to program some aspect of the Palm. Let's get to it: Welcome to *Palm Programming*!

CHAPTER 2

Anatomy of a Palm Application

This chapter takes apart and examines a Palm version of the old "Hello World" program (I call it "Hello Palm"), the classic first program we all create when confronted with a new programming environment or development platform.

The "Hello Palm" program not only illustrates the basic structure of a Palm application, but it also serves as a template for practically every other sample program in this book. As you'll see when you walk through setting up a new CodeWarrior Palm project, getting all the settings just right can be tedious: What I've found to be easiest is to simply clone "Hello Palm" and change just a few settings rather than start from scratch.

PilotMain and the Smallest Palm Program Ever

I remember the first time I was confronted with a "Hello World" program written for Microsoft Windows on a 286. (Yes, I know that means I'm old....) Having seen my share of simple DOS programs that consisted of four or five lines of code in a single `main()` function, it was a shock to realize that I needed several hundred lines of code dealing with message loops, window procedures, and class registration just to get a window to display the text "Hello." It eventually became clear to me that for the most part, this code never changed; I simply copied and pasted the same boilerplate code from project to project.

Programming the Palm is similar. With the way I've structured "Hello Palm," you can learn about 300 lines of boilerplate code (including comments) in this chapter and then forget it. I would be remiss if I did not explain all that strange-looking code in every Palm program, but you should keep in mind that with only a few exceptions, it will not be necessary to revisit it.

Before you dive into the full "Hello Palm" program, take a quick look at the smallest Palm program ever. It does nothing, and aside from allowing you to try some functions in the debugger, I can't imagine what you would ever do with such an application. But it does give you a place to start:

```
/*
   PilotMain ()
   Main entry point into pilot application.
   Parms:   wCmd   - launch code.
            pInfo - struct associated w/ launch code.
            fuLaunch - extra info about launch.
*/
DWord
PilotMain (Word wCmd, Ptr pInfo, Word fuLaunch)
{
    return 0;
}
```

This is a very boring program because it ends as quickly as it starts—no user interface, nothing. However, it's a valid Palm program; you can build it and download it to your Palm.

Just as a standard DOS or UNIX program begins with `main()`, a Palm program begins with `PilotMain`. `PilotMain` is called when your program is launched by the operating system. Your application can be launched normally or in special modes using launch codes. This code is passed as the first parameter to `PilotMain`. (In the code segment, I've named it `wCmd`.)

Launch Codes

Launch codes can be issued by the system or by another application. Why would you receive a launch code? For example, many applications (such as the built-in ones) support the "find" interface. When the user wants to find a database record using the system find interface, the target application is launched using a special code, `sysAppLaunchCmdFind`, with the find parameters passed in the `pInfo` parameter to `PilotMain`. An application can also receive a non-normal launch code for a system reset, a time change, or a notification that a hot-sync has completed. An application can even define its own launch codes to let other programs interact with it. For a complete list of the standard Palm launch codes, refer to the Palm SDK documentation.

The third and final parameter to `PilotMain` contains optional launch flags that are dependent on the launch code and the data passed in `pInfo`.

Now that you know something about launch codes, you can check what launch code is passed to the little program and even do something about it:

```
switch (wCmd)
{
    case sysAppLaunchCmdNormalLaunch:
    {
        // Initialize application.
        break;
    }
    default:
    {
        err = 0;
        break;
    }
}
return err;
}
```

Here I put in a simple switch statement that for now only checks for the "normal" launch code. All other codes are ignored, so they fall into the default case.

Checking the Palm OS Version

Before you go too far in the program, a good thing to do is to make sure it is running on the required version of the Palm OS. As you saw in Chapter 1, "Introduction to Palm Programming and CodeWarrior," there are several different versions of the Palm device in the field. When the new devices were brought to market, Palm Computing occasionally updated the Palm OS. With each new revision of the OS came new functions and subsystems for the developer to take advantage of.

Although it's wonderful to get new functions, some users still have older devices that are running versions of the Palm OS which do not support those functions. For example, infrared support only became available with the Palm III device, which contained version 3.0 of the Palm OS. You need to decide the minimum version of the Palm OS that you want to support in your application and check for that version in your application's start-up code so that you end your application gracefully on older devices. For an application that uses the infrared library, you would make sure that the OS was at least version 3.0.

Listing 2.1 should be called first in any Palm application with a check for the minimum OS version the application is prepared to handle. In this case, I chose version 2.0.

LISTING 2.1 CHECKING THE APPLICATION'S VERSION FOR COMPATIBILITY

```
Err    err;

    // Check version compatibility.
    err = AppCheckVersion (0x02000000, fuLaunch);
    if (err)
    {
        // Incompatible - exit.
        return err;
    }

/*
    AppCheckVersion ():
    Check hardware compatibility.
    Parms:   dwReqVersion  - required ROM version.
             fuLaunch      - launch flags.
    Return:  0 if ROM is compatible or error code.
*/
Err
AppCheckVersion (DWord dwReqVersion, Word fuLaunch)
{
    // Assume the best.
    Err err = 0;

    // Get the ROM version.
    DWord dwRomVersion;

    FtrGet (sysFtrCreator, sysFtrNumROMVersion, &dwRomVersion);

    // Check if it's compatible.
    if (dwRomVersion < dwReqVersion)
    {
        // Version is too low, see what launch flags are.
        Word  wLaunchCheck = sysAppLaunchFlagNewGlobals |
        ➡sysAppLaunchFlagUIApp;

        if (wLaunchCheck & fuLaunch == wLaunchCheck)
        {
            // Tell user the problem.
            FrmAlert (RomIncompatibleAlert);

            // Pilot 1.0 will continuously relaunch this app unless we
            // switch to another safe one.
            if (dwRomVersion < osVersion20)
            {
                AppLaunchWithCommand(sysFileCDefaultApp,
                ➡sysAppLaunchCmdNormalLaunch, NULL);
            }
        }
```

```
        err = sysErrRomIncompatible;
    }
    return err;
}
```

This code calls the Palm SDK function `FtrGet` to obtain the ROM version and compares it against the minimum required version. If the ROM version is too old, I issue an alert and exit the program. (Alerts are covered in Chapter 5, "Interacting with the User: Forms." For now, it is enough to understand that it is a kind of pop-up message box.)

The Main Form

Of course, most Palm programs will display a user interface. On the Palm, you create a user interface by displaying one or more windows to the user. These windows are called forms. (See Chapter 5.) The main screen of a Palm application is commonly referred to as the main form.

> **NOTE**
>
> In this section, I present the basic code necessary to load your application's main form. You will need to create your form using CodeWarrior's Constructor tool. If you already know how to use Constructor to create a simple form resource, you might want to go ahead and do that now. Otherwise, I walk you through resource creation using Constructor in Chapter 4, "Creating and Managing Resources."

In the last section, I put in a switch statement to handle the `sysAppLaunchCmdNormalLaunch` launch code. Now, it's time to add some code that actually does something:

```
        case sysAppLaunchCmdNormalLaunch:
        {
            // Show the main form.
            FrmGotoForm (MainForm);
            AppEventLoop ();
            break;
        }
```

This code looks simple enough: If it is asked to launch the application, it shows the main "window" or form and then goes into what looks like an event loop. Both actions are interrelated. Let's take a closer look at what's happening.

FrmGotoForm is a Palm SDK function that, given a form's resource ID (as defined in Constructor), will attempt to load the associated form. This will cause the Palm OS to pass a special event to the application, indicating that a form is about to be loaded.

Events

An event is a structure defined in the Palm SDK that can carry information to an application from the Palm OS. How do you receive events? In an event loop! Listing 2.2 shows you how.

LISTING 2.2   USING AN EVENT LOOP TO RECEIVE EVENTS

```
/*
   AppEventLoop (void)
   Process events coming to application.
   Parms:   none
   Return:  none
   Note:    Application is in this function for majority
            of its execution.
*/
void
AppEventLoop (void)
{
   EventType   event;

   do
   {
      EvtGetEvent (&event, evtWaitForever);

      // Ask system to handle event.
      if (false == SysHandleEvent (&event))
      {
         // System did not handle event.

         Word        error;
         // Ask Menu to handle event.
         if (false == MenuHandleEvent (0, &event, &error))
         {
            // Menu did not handle event.
            // Ask App (that is, this) to handle event.
            if (false == AppEventHandler (&event))
            {
               // App did not handle event.
               // Send event to appropriate form.
               FrmDispatchEvent (&event);
            } // end if (false == AppEventHandler (&event))
         }    // end if (false == MenuHandleEvent (0, &event, &error))
```

```
      }          // end if (false == SysHandleEvent (&event))
   }
   while (event.eType != appStopEvent);
}
```

AppEventLoop is a do-while loop that continually calls the Palm SDK function EvtGetEvent until it receives an appStopEvent, which indicates the application is closing down. For each event it receives, it is your responsibility to follow a standard protocol in determining who should handle the event. First, you determine if the system wants to handle it by calling SysHandleEvent. Failing that, you check to see if the event belongs to the current menu (if any). If it does not, you have found an event that might be interesting to the application. Such events are passed to the AppEventHandler routine for closer scrutiny. If the AppEventHandler routine does not handle the event, it gets passed to the current form's event-handler function via the FrmDispatchEvent() call.

In AppEventHandler (outlined in Listing 2.3), I check the event type to see if it's something I am interested in. Because the primary job at this point is to get the main form loaded, I check whether the event is type frmLoadEvent, and if it is, I pass it to the AppLoadForm handler.

AppLoadForm performs three tasks that cause the main form to be properly loaded:

- It calls FrmInitForm to initialize the form resource.
- It calls FrmSetActiveForm to set the form to receive input from the user.
- It sets an "event handler" for the form.

In the next section, I explain form event handlers, but note that you check to see which form is being loaded, rather than just assume it's the one and only main form. This step might be overkill for this application, but it reminds you that an application can have more than one "main form." For example, the Appointments application has several main "views." If you were to do the same, you would have similar load-handling code for each form. Listing 2.3 shows how to implement an application event handler.

LISTING 2.3   THE APPLICATION EVENT HANDLER

```
/*
   AppEventHandler (EventPtr)
   Handle application-level events.
   Parms:   pEvent   - event to handle.
   Return:  true  - handled (successfully or not)
            false - not handled
*/
Boolean
```

continues

LISTING 2.3 CONTINUED

```
AppEventHandler (EventPtr pEvent)
{
   Boolean bHandled = false;

   switch (pEvent->eType)
   {
      case frmLoadEvent:
      {
         // Load the form resource.
         Word  wFormID = pEvent->data.frmLoad.formID;

         AppLoadForm (wFormID);
         bHandled = true;
         break;
      }

      default:
      {
         break;
      }
   }
   return bHandled;
}
```

The Main Form Handler

The main form's event handler in the "Hello Palm" program is largely a placeholder: At this point, it only needs to trap the form's frmOpenEvent event and respond by redrawing the form. That's it! So why did we need a form event handler for "Hello Palm?" Most main forms do a little more than the one in "Hello Palm," which at the moment only stubbornly sits there, staring at the user. As you'll see in Chapter 5, many events of significance, such as button taps, pass through the form handler. Given that almost all main forms eventually do at least one or two things, it's a good idea to set up the infrastructure up front because it's boilerplate anyway. See Listing 2.4.

LISTING 2.4 EVENT HANDLER FOR THE MAIN FORM

```
/*
   MainFormEventHandler:
   Parms:  pEvent   - event to be handled.
   Return: true  - handled (successfully or not)
           false - not handled
*/
Boolean
```

```
MainFormEventHandler (EventPtr eventP)
{
   Boolean  handled = false;

   switch (eventP->eType)
   {
      case frmOpenEvent:
      {
         // Main form is opening

         FormPtr formP = FrmGetActiveForm ();

         FrmDrawForm (formP);

         handled = true;
         break;
      }

      default:
      {
         break;
      }
   }
   return handled;
}
```

If you are familiar with event-driven programming on other computer platforms, this might look familiar, at least conceptually. An application is launched by the operating system in response to a user action. In response, the application does some initial house-keeping and setup, launches its main window, and then goes into an endless event loop until it receives an event indicating it's time to shut down. The main window, as well as each window created during the lifetime of the application, is responsible for handling its own events.

Hello Palm!

At this point, I've covered all the basic, boilerplate code elements that are a part of virtually every Palm program in existence. It's time to put all this together and create your first Palm application: "Hello Palm!"

"Hello Palm" contains all the elements I've covered so far, along with a few minor additions. In anticipation of writing many more programs beyond this one, I broke out the "boilerplate" code from the code that is likely to change over time and created two separate .CPP files: helo_app.cpp and helo_mai.cpp. helo_app.cpp contains the `PilotMain` function, the event loop, and the application's event handler. This code will largely remain the same no matter what kind of application uses it. I then took the main form event handler and moved it into helo_mai.cpp. Because the main form will be different from program to program, it follows that this source file will change often as I reuse it in other projects.

The other addition is a common header file, hello.h. I use hello.h to define common values and provide prototypes for functions that will be referenced by more than one source file. Among other things, hello.h defines the creator ID. Creator IDs must be unique among applications installed on a Palm device. The examples in this book all use the creator ID "TEST", but be aware that this means that you can install only one sample program on a device at a time. Palm Computing provides a service on its Web site to let you register unique creator IDs for your company and its products. Those IDs are guaranteed by Palm to be unique so your application will not collide with any other application when a user installs it.

The Source Code

Listing 2.5 shows the source code for Hello Palm's main header file, hello.h. Listings 2.6 and 2.7 represent the application's main startup code and the main form handler, respectively.

LISTING 2.5   HELLO.H

```
/*
   HELLO.H
   Hello application declarations.
   Copyright (c) 1999 Bachmann Software and Services, LLC
   Author: Glenn Bachmann
*/

// Prevent multiple includes
#ifndef HELLO_H
#define HELLO_H

#define  HELLO_FILE_CREATOR   ('TEST')

#define  PALMOS_VERSION_20 (0x02000000)

#define  PALMOS_VERSION    (PALMOS_VERSION_20)

   /*
      MainFormEventHandler (EventPtr)
```

```
    Parms:    pEvent    - event to be handled.
    Return:   true   - handled (successfully or not)
              false - not handled
*/


Boolean  MainFormEventHandler (EventPtr pEvent);

#endif
```

LISTING 2.6   HELO_APP.CPP

```
/*
    HELO_APP.CPP

    Hello application functions

    Copyright (c) 1999 Bachmann Software and Services, LLC
    Author: Glenn Bachmann
*/

// System includes
#include <Pilot.h>
#include <SysEvtMgr.h>

// Application-specific includes
#include "hello.h"
#include "helo_res.h"


// Private constants.
const unsigned long  appFileCreator = HELLO_FILE_CREATOR;
const unsigned short appFileVersion = HELLO_FILE_VERSION;
const unsigned short appPrefID      = HELLO_PREF_ID;
const unsigned short appPrefVersion = HELLO_PREF_VERSION;
const unsigned long  appOSVersion   = PALMOS_VERSION;
const unsigned long  osVersion20    = PALMOS_VERSION_20;



// Private structures.


// Private functions.
static Err     AppStart ();
static void    AppStop ();
static void    AppEventLoop (void);
static Boolean AppEventHandler (EventPtr);
```

continues

LISTING 2.6 CONTINUED

```c
static void    AppLoadForm (Word);
static Err     AppCheckVersion (DWord, Word);

/*
   PilotMain ()
   Main entry point into pilot application.
   Parms:  wCmd  - launch code.
           pInfo - struct associated w/ launch code.
           fuLaunch - extra info about launch.
*/
DWord
PilotMain (Word wCmd, Ptr /*pInfo*/, Word fuLaunch)
{
   Err   err;

   // Check version compatibility.
   err = AppCheckVersion (appOSVersion, fuLaunch);
   if (err)
   {
      // Incompatible - exit.
      return err;
   }

   switch (wCmd)
   {
      case sysAppLaunchCmdNormalLaunch:
      {
         // Initialize application.
         err = AppStart ();
         if (!err)
         {
            // Show the main form.
            FrmGotoForm (MainForm);
            AppEventLoop ();
            AppStop ();
         }
         break;
      }
      default:
      {
         err = 0;
         break;
      }
   }
   return err;
}

/*
   AppStart ():
```

```
      Initialize the application.
      Parms:    none
      Return:   0 if success, or error code.
*/
Err
AppStart ()
{
   return 0;
}


/*
   AppStop ():
   Save the current state of the application.
   Parms:    none
   Return:   none
*/
void
AppStop ()
{
}

/*
   AppEventLoop (void)
   Process events coming to application.
   Parms:    none
   Return:   none
   Note:     Application is in this function for majority
             of its execution.
*/
void
AppEventLoop (void)
{
   EventType    event;

   do
   {
      EvtGetEvent (&event, evtWaitForever);

      // Ask system to handle event.
      if (false == SysHandleEvent (&event))
      {
         // System did not handle event.

         Word         error;
         // Ask Menu to handle event.
         if (false == MenuHandleEvent (0, &event, &error))
         {
            // Menu did not handle event.
```

continues

LISTING 2.6 CONTINUED

```
                // Ask App (that is, this) to handle event.
                if (false == AppEventHandler (&event))
                {
                    // App did not handle event.
                    // Send event to appropriate form.
                    FrmDispatchEvent (&event);
                } // end if (false == AppEventHandler (&event))
            } // end if (false == MenuHandleEvent (0, &event, &error))
        } // end if (false == SysHandleEvent (&event))
    }
    while (event.eType != appStopEvent);
}

/*
    AppEventHandler (EventPtr)
    Handle application-level events.
    Parms:   pEvent   - event to handle.
    Return:  true  - handled (successfully or not)
             false - not handled
*/
Boolean
AppEventHandler (EventPtr pEvent)
{
    Boolean bHandled = false;

    switch (pEvent->eType)
    {
        case frmLoadEvent:
        {
            // Load the form resource.
            Word  wFormID = pEvent->data.frmLoad.formID;

            AppLoadForm (wFormID);
            bHandled = true;
            break;
        }

        default:
        {
            break;
        }
    }
    return bHandled;
}

/*
    AppLoadForm (Word)
    Load a form.
```

```
    Parms:    wFormID  - form to be loaded.
    Return:   none
*/
void
AppLoadForm (Word wFormID)
{
    FormPtr pForm = FrmInitForm (wFormID);

    FrmSetActiveForm (pForm);

    // Set the event handler for the form.
    //    The handler of the currently active form is called by
    //    FrmHandleEvent each time it receives an event.
    switch (wFormID)
    {
        case MainForm:
        {
            FrmSetEventHandler (pForm, MainFormEventHandler);
            break;
        }

        default:
        {
            break;
        }
    }
}

/*
    AppCheckVersion ():
    Check hardware compatibility.
    Parms:    dwReqVersion  - required ROM version.
              fuLaunch      - launch flags.
    Return:   0 if ROM is compatible or error code.
*/
Err
AppCheckVersion (DWord dwReqVersion, Word fuLaunch)
{
    // Assume the best.
    Err err = 0;

    // Get the ROM version.
    DWord dwRomVersion;

    FtrGet (sysFtrCreator, sysFtrNumROMVersion, &dwRomVersion);

    // Check if it's compatible.
    if (dwRomVersion < dwReqVersion)
    {
```

2

ANATOMY OF A
PALM
APPLICATION

continues

LISTING 2.6 CONTINUED

```
        // Version is too low, see what launch flags are.
        Word  wLaunchCheck = sysAppLaunchFlagNewGlobals |
     ➥sysAppLaunchFlagUIApp;

        if (wLaunchCheck & fuLaunch == wLaunchCheck)
        {
            // Tell user the problem.
            FrmAlert (RomIncompatibleAlert);

            // Pilot 1.0 will continuously relaunch this app unless
            // we switch to another safe one.
            if (dwRomVersion < osVersion20)
            {
                AppLaunchWithCommand(sysFileCDefaultApp,
             ➥sysAppLaunchCmdNormalLaunch, NULL);
            }
        }
        err = sysErrRomIncompatible;
    }
    return err;
}
```

LISTING 2.7 HELO_MAI.CPP

```
/*
   HELO_MAI.CPP
   Main form handling functions.
   Copyright (c) Bachmann Software and Services, 1999
   Author: Glenn Bachmann
*/

// System headers
#include <Pilot.h>
#include <SysEvtMgr.h>

// Application-specific headers
#include "hello.h"
#include "helo_res.h"

static void    MainFormInit (FormPtr formP);

/*
   MainFormEventHandler:
   Parms:   pEvent   - event to be handled.
   Return:  true   - handled (successfully or not)
            false  - not handled
*/
```

```
Boolean
MainFormEventHandler (EventPtr eventP)
{
    Boolean  handled = false;

    switch (eventP->eType)
    {
        case frmOpenEvent:
        {
            // Main form is opening

            FormPtr formP = FrmGetActiveForm ();

            MainFormInit (formP);

            FrmDrawForm (formP);

            handled = true;
            break;
        }

        default:
        {
            break;
        }
    }
    return handled;
}

/*
    MainFormInit:
    Initialize the main form.
    Parms:   formP - pointer to main form.
    Return:  none
*/
void
MainFormInit (FormPtr formP)
{
}
```

Creating a CodeWarrior Project for "Hello Palm"

All this code is nice, but it would be nicer if you could build it, wouldn't it? This section shows you how to create a CodeWarrior project to properly build a Palm application.

The CD-ROM that accompanies this book provides the source code, including a CodeWarrior project file, for each example. You are encouraged to use the project file for this chapter's "Hello Palm" example as the basis for your own projects. (Like the old story about makefiles, nobody ever writes a makefile from scratch; they just copy one that works from somebody else.) I take a moment here to explain how "Hello Palm's" project was created.

The way I see it, you essentially have two choices in creating a new CodeWarrior project: Create one from scratch from an empty project, or use one of the predefined Palm OS project types, which are called stationery by the folks at Metrowerks. The latter sounds like a sure winner, but in my experience, I've spent some unpleasant time fixing the undesirable side effects created by choosing these predefined projects as a template, so I now follow these steps to create a new project:

1. Start CodeWarrior, and choose New Project.

2. Choose Empty Project in the Select Stationery dialog, and check the Create Folder option.

3. Name your project, which will autocreate a folder and .MCP file of the same name.

4. Now, modify the project settings by selecting Edit, Hello Settings from the main menu.

5. Under Target, Target Settings, set the Target Name to Hello, the Linker to Mac OS 68K Linker, and the Post Linker to the PilotRez Post Linker, as in Figure 2.1.

FIGURE 2.1

Configuring project settings for "Hello Palm."

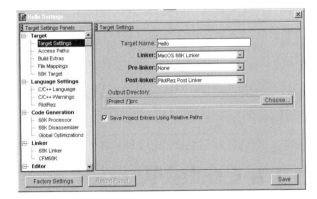

6. Specify the directory where you want your .PRC file to be placed as the Output Directory.

7. To enable your project to be moved to another directory on your computer, check the option to save using relative paths.

8. Under Target, Access Paths, you need to set the paths where CodeWarrior will look for your source and output components. Check the Always Check User Paths option, and set the project path to be a \SRC directory, and add another path to be your \PRC directory (or the directory you specified as the output directory).

9. Under System Paths, ensure that it points to the location of your Palm support files (usually "Palm *x.x* Support" where *x.x* is the version of the OS).

10. Under Target, 68K Target, set the project type to be a Palm OS application, and name the .TMP file.

11. In Language Settings, PilotRez, set Mac Resource Files to be the name of the .TMP file specified in the last step. Also, check Disable UI Resource.

12. Under Language Settings, Output options, set the name of your .PRC file (for example, hello.prc). Also, set your unique creator ID here. (Use "TEST".)

That's all the configuration necessary. Now, you add files to the project as follows:

1. From the main menu, choose Project, Add Files.

2. Add the appropriate runtime library by selecting MSL Runtime 2i.lib, located in the Palm OS x.x Support path.

3. Add your source files (helo_mai.cpp and helo_app.cpp).

4. Add your resource file (hello.rsrc).

When you've added your files, the "Hello Palm" project should look like Figure 2.2.

FIGURE 2.2

The main project view for "Hello Palm."

If this sounds unpleasant, I admit it; it is unpleasant. However, I think it's a good idea to know how to create a project without the stationery option, and this way, I have full control over how my project is set up. Unfortunately, using the pre-existing stationery

32

creates a project called "Starter," including template source files. It is (in my opinion) just as much work, and given that I have already identified the areas of the app that will be boilerplate and used from project to project, it is also unnecessary. You might want to experiment with both approaches and choose the one that works best for you.

Building and Running "Hello Palm"

To build "Hello Palm," access the Project menu in CodeWarrior and choose Make (F7 for short). Once you've addressed any compilation problems, you should see two new files in your output directory \PRC, hello.prc and hello.psym. hello.psym contains symbolic debugging information that will be used when tracing through your code with CodeWarrior's Debugger. hello.prc is the actual program.

Your program is transferred to the Palm device in the same manner as any program you might have purchased or downloaded off the Web: Use the Palm Install tool to locate and select the .PRC file, and use hot-sync to transfer the file. After the hot-sync is complete, you should see "Hello Palm" listed in your Palm's main application list.

Figure 2.3 is what "Hello Palm" looks like when running.

FIGURE 2.3

Hello Palm!

Summary

In this chapter you got your first look at actual Palm application code. Many of the topics covered will become standard elements in the sample applications used in the rest of *Palm Programming*, including PilotMain, launch codes, version checking, event loops, and the main form. You also created your first project using CodeWarrior, which you will also reuse throughout this book.

The next two chapters will round out the introductory section of the book, and complete our coverage of the basics of Palm programming.

CHAPTER 3

Rapid Development Using the Palm Emulator

In my experience, many books on programming either do not cover the topic of debugging at all or treat it as an afterthought. This is unfortunate because you can make huge productivity gains by investing just a little time up front in understanding your program's operating environment as well as the available development tools and techniques that can help you observe how your program is working in that environment.

Although debugging is often considered something you do after a program is written, the best time to make plans for how you'll debug an application is before you write the first line of code. If you don't understand how to effectively use the tools at your disposal now, you will be in deep trouble when you have a 100,000-line (or longer) program that does not work properly, and you have no idea how to tell what's wrong.

Unless you get a handle on how to efficiently locate and resolve some of the most common programming mistakes on the Palm, you will be doomed to a horribly long and frustrating compile-edit-debug cycle. Thankfully, there are tools and techniques available to shorten this cycle significantly.

In this chapter, we explore some of the best ways to achieve faster development times by making good use of these debugging tools and techniques. Specifically, we will cover

- What the factors are that make Palm debugging difficult
- Effective debugging techniques on the Palm
- The Palm Error Manager
- How to speed development using POSE, the Palm OS Emulator

Why Palm Development Is Slow

Programming for the Palm environment presents some unique problems to the developer in terms of program testing and debugging. Perhaps the most obvious difference from other development environments is that on the Palm, your code is written, compiled, and linked on a different host system from the target OS.

You typically develop your Palm application using the CodeWarrior tools, which are hosted on Windows, Macintosh, or whatever your chosen desktop environment. To be run or tested on the target device, your application's .PRC file must be installed via the Palm Install Tool and subsequently hot-synced to the device. If you're like me, you'd start looking for a better way to develop and test your application after only a few iterations of this process.

Some tried and true techniques can help this situation somewhat; I cover them in this chapter. More importantly, some thoughtful people have created what is perhaps the single most useful development tool available to Palm developers, the Palm OS Emulator (or POSE for short).

But First, a Short Detour...

Before proceeding, I want to take a moment to mention a development technique that at first might sound radical but in my own experience has proven to be extremely useful in Palm programming. I'm talking about writing code designed to be so portable that it can be compiled and run either on the Palm or on the development environment's host system.

A while back, my company was contracted to develop a large Palm application that would involve a lot of program logic, some database interaction, and serial communications. Before we started the project, we realized that debugging the complex program logic would be an extremely inefficient process. The program would tie up the Palm's serial communications port, effectively cutting us off from the ability to debug the device from the Windows-hosted CodeWarrior.

We decided to try an unusual approach: Proceed with the project as if it were a Windows application and only periodically recompile the program as a Palm application. Such an approach provided a sanity check on the portability of the code and an opportunity to drive the product to the release stage and introduce some quality assurance testing.

How did we achieve portable code when the programming interfaces to the Palm and Windows developer are so wildly different? In fact, it was not difficult at all. We developed a few thin layers of code on top of things such as the string management APIs so that a function such as StrCopy would conditionally compile to either the Palm or Windows equivalent. We even took the four or five Serial Manager APIs we needed and created a "Serial Manager Emulator" layer that mapped all of the Ser calls to their Windows equivalents! What we did not attempt, and what would have been a little more complex, was to create a portability layer for the Palm user-interface functions. As luck would have it, our application did not have much of a user interface, so we bit the bullet and created separate user-interface code for both Windows and Palm.

If you are thinking we spent a lot of time on this setup when we could have been coding our application, you are wrong. Over the course of four months, we saved a dramatic amount of time by being able to perform practically all of our development, testing, and debugging under Windows. When we neared the end of the project, we needed to put together and build as a Palm application all of the components we had developed. The few problems we did encounter (and there were only a few because most of the normal bugs and gaffes had surfaced and been resolved earlier) took what seemed like forever to find and fix.

Should you adopt this technique in your own Palm development? It's hard to give a general answer to that question because all programs are different. At our company, we value portable code because it is almost inevitable that the code we write will at some point need to be ported to some other platform. Our clients appreciate the fact that their products don't need rewriting to support new platforms. If these issues are not as important to you for whatever reason, then you might not realize as much of a benefit as we did. But it's something to think about.

Effective Debugging Techniques for the Palm

One of the best ways to debug your application is to use development practices that will minimize the time you have to spend in front of a debugger. It sounds odd, but the most efficient debugging you can do is performed without a debugger. Even with the best, state-of-the-art debugging tools, staring at your program as it executes line-by-line is slow and tedious at best. When you consider that the Palm platform has not been around long enough to have attracted the state-of-the-art tools found elsewhere, you can start to see that the debugger should be used as a last resort.

Seasoned software developers use several techniques that help expose problems with their programs early and isolate the problem to a single module, function, or even line of code. Some call this collection of techniques "debug scaffolding" because as you develop the "real" code, you simultaneously build up a growing framework of code designed to catch a wide variety of errors and give you visibility into the inner workings of your program.

The Palm Error Manager

The Palm Error Manager supports several useful macros that can help your program report unexpected conditions. These macros work on the same general principle as that of the well-known "assert" macro available on many other platforms. You give the macro a condition to test and a message to display if the condition triggers an error message. The error displayed includes not only the specified text but also the name of the source code module and the relevant line number.

Three macros are supported:

`ErrDisplay`	Always displays an error message
`ErrFatalDisplayIf`	Displays a fatal error message if the first argument is evaluated to be TRUE
`ErrNonFatalDisplayIf`	Displays a nonfatal error message if the first argument is evaluated to be TRUE

You can control the level of error checking by setting a special macro value `ERROR_CHECK_LEVEL` to either `ERROR_CHECK_FULL` (which enables all three error calls), `ERROR_CHECK_PARTIAL` (which enables `ErrDisplay` and `ErrFatalDisplayIf` calls), or `ERROR_CHECK_NONE` (which disables all `Err` calls).

It is important to understand that the level of alerts supported is determined at compile time, but the error condition check is performed at runtime.

Although similar to the assert macro in function, in actual usage `ErrFatalDisplayIf` and `ErrNonFatalDisplayIf` act like the reverse of assert in that the alert is triggered if the condition is TRUE rather than FALSE. For example, the following code tests to see whether a pointer is NULL. If the expression p == NULL evaluates to TRUE, the message `Null Pointer` is displayed:

```
ErrFatalDisplayIf ( p == NULL, "Null Pointer!");
```

The question of how much error checking should be left in your code when it is released to your users is the subject of a long-running debate that is not specific to the Palm platform. Different developers follow different schools of thought; some think that these checks are developer tools only, whereas others firmly believe that they are invaluable tools for determining system problems in the field.

Logging

Strictly speaking, no logging facility comes built-in to the Palm SDK. In many situations, however, message boxes and `ErrDisplay` macros are too obtrusive or awkward to employ in revealing your program's workings. For example, if your Palm is receiving data via the serial or infrared port from some other device or host, it is not acceptable to display a modal message requiring user intervention for every incoming message or packet of data.

What is really needed is an "error logger" window that can display a stream of events as they happen. This is actually pretty easy to code and involves simply using `WinDrawChars` to draw directly on the screen. Create a test program that exercises the functionality in question, and create a main form that devotes a section of its display area to your logging messages. This arrangement lets you see each event as it happens, but with a little work, you can actually create a scrolling list of events.

The CodeWarrior Debugger

When you finally need to sit down and step through your code line-by-line, you need a source-level debugger. CodeWarrior provides a source-level debugger that can let you control and observe your application's execution either on the Palm device itself or under the Palm OS Emulator. (I cover the Emulator later in the chapter.)

The debugger works with a special file generated during your project's build that has an extension .PSYM. This file appears in the same output location as your .PRC file. You need to specify this file when running the debugger. You can launch the CodeWarrior Debugger by double-clicking the .PSYM file (if you are using Windows Explorer), or you can launch the debugger and then navigate to the .PSYM file in response to the File, Open prompt. Finally, you can choose the Project, Debug menu option within the main CodeWarrior IDE. Note that this choice rebuilds your application prior to launching the debugger.

If you will be debugging against the Palm device itself, prior to starting a debugger session, you must ready your Palm device by placing it in the cradle and ensuring that the cradle is connected to your computer's serial port. Because the debugger communicates with the device via the serial port, you also need to make sure that the port is free.

If you will be debugging against the Emulator, you need to make sure the Emulator is running before launching the debugger; otherwise, you will receive errors.

Once your application is loaded in the debugger, you can set breakpoints, step through code, observe variable values, and perform most tasks that you do in other debugging environments. For more details on how to operate the CodeWarrior debugger, refer to the CodeWarrior documentation.

The Palm OS Emulator

The Palm OS Emulator, or POSE, is a wonderful piece of software that provides an emulation of the Palm OS on both Windows and Macintosh platforms so that you can run, test, and debug your application without downloading it to a Palm device.

As I write this, POSE is a rapidly evolving tool, and new versions are posted to the Palm developer Web site fairly frequently. You should make a habit of checking the site often for new releases. At present, I am using a "seed" version called 2.1d26 that is not officially released yet appears to be robust enough in my experience.

Figure 3.1 shows POSE in action.

FIGURE 3.1

POSE version 2.1d26, with menu options displayed after right-clicking the mouse.

To use POSE, you need a ROM just like the physical Palm device needs a ROM. You can obtain "debug" versions of the ROMs associated with the various Palm OS releases from the Palm developer zone Web site, `www.palm.com/devzone`. In the version of POSE I am using, you can choose from a menu of available ROMs when you start the Emulator. When the ROM is loaded, the Emulator displays the Palm startup screen just as you would normally see after a reset of the Palm device. In fact, in almost all respects, POSE will act and respond just like the real McCoy, right down to the built-in applications.

Even without using the CodeWarrior debugger, POSE offers you tremendous productivity gains by allowing you to run each build of your software without having to download it to the Palm device. In addition, the debug ROMs that POSE loads offer better, more robust checking against things such as memory overwrites and other error conditions. You might find yourself in a situation where your application fails under POSE but works fine on the device. You should believe POSE: It is almost certain that you are accidentally getting away with an error on the device that is being caught by POSE.

POSE also offers other nice features. It can detect invalid memory writes, stack overflows, leaks, and other memory-related errors. It also provides several types of logging and can even do profiling for you. Last but not least, it is a handy way to take screenshots of your application. (I make extensive use of this feature throughout this book.)

The most compelling use of POSE is in tandem with the CodeWarrior debugger. As I mentioned earlier in the chapter, you can set the debugger so that it controls an application running on either a serially connected Palm device or one running on the Emulator. The latter is easy to set up: Simply open the debugger's Preferences dialog, and under Palm OS, choose Emulator instead of Palm Pilot as the target environment. Make sure you have the Emulator running, and then launch the debugger as you normally would. You should be able to control and interact with your application as it runs on the Emulator.

Only a few kinds of programs are not supported well under the debugger/POSE combination. One of the more notable examples, infrared support, is still lacking under POSE, leaving the developer with few options other than roll-your-own logging and message boxes. (Been there; done that!) On the other hand, and as a credit to the POSE developers, POSE does a very nice job of redirecting serial communications to your PC's physical port, which makes serial debugging possible. I was also pleasantly surprised when it turned out that the latest version of POSE redirected the wireless networking layer of the Palm VII device to use an existing Internet connection if present.

Summary

By placing this chapter near the beginning of this book, it was my hope that I could emphasize the importance of understanding the debugging techniques and tools available to the Palm programmer at an early stage in the learning process. The compile-edit-debug cycle for Palm programming is so expensive that it is foolhardy to not take advantage of the help that is available.

An extensively detailed document that comes with the latest version of POSE gets into much more detail regarding POSE's features than I have here. I encourage you to read this document. A mailing list, `emulator-forum@ls.3com.com`, is also dedicated to questions and support related to the Emulator. Finally, it should be noted that POSE is an "open source" utility, with source code freely available to the developer community. Those developers with useful extensions to the tool are encouraged to make contributions.

CHAPTER 4

Creating and Managing Resources

In Chapter 2, "Anatomy of a Palm Application," you created your first Palm program, "Hello Palm." You walked through all the pieces of code that were involved in creating the program. You skipped one essential component in developing "Hello Palm": creating the main form's visual appearance. This chapter will make amends for that omission by explaining Palm OS resources and CodeWarrior's Constructor tool, which together allow you to define the visual elements of your Palm program outside of the actual code.

This chapter covers

- What resources are and why they are used
- The CodeWarrior Constructor tool
- How to create and manage resources in a CodeWarrior project

This chapter will not be an exhaustive tutorial or reference on using Constructor. Refer to the CodeWarrior documentation for more in-depth descriptions of how to use the Constructor tool. Rather, I focus on describing what resources are, as well as giving practical information above and beyond what is found in the Constructor user manual.

What Is a Palm Resource?

You can consider Palm resources special data structures, stored separately from your program code, which are included in your program's .PRC file by the CodeWarrior linker in your project's build. Although most often, we think of resources as relating to user-interface elements, Palm OS resources can be menus, forms, user-interface controls, menus, character strings, string lists, application info string lists, alerts, icons, or bitmaps.

Without resources, you would either hard-code these definitions in static or global program values, in which case you would need to recompile your application every time they changed, or you would store them in an external database, which creates programming and performance overhead. Resource files allow you to change many characteristics of your program without recompiling. They also encourage good separation of code and data using a standard format. Finally, because they are loaded at runtime by Palm OS, they reduce the footprint and memory requirements of your application.

I cover almost all the various resource types in one chapter or another as you encounter them throughout this book.

Why Use Constructor?

In CodeWarrior, you define all user-interface elements using the visual Constructor resource management tool. Right out of the box, Constructor is the only way to create and modify your resources so they are in the correct format expected by the linker; the resource file generated by Constructor is in a proprietary binary format, so all changes must happen through Constructor.

That said, a number of third-party utilities can help you manage your resources via text files and GCC. My personal preference (for what it's worth) is to keep the best of both worlds: have a visual tool for designing and prototyping, yet be able to browse and modify the actual resource tags in a text file as needed. If nothing else, the text-file version would be more suitable for tracking changes in your program with version control and source code management tools.

Creating a Resource Project File in Constructor

Constructor creates a single resource file that contains all the resources you've defined in your application. As with much of the code created in "Hello Palm," I've found that some parts of a resource file are pretty much boilerplate and do not change from project to project. Just as it is unnecessary to create a new CodeWarrior project file from scratch for each new Palm project, it is also unnecessary to create a new resource file for each new project.

Walk through the creation of a resource file, and as you go along, I note which settings you will need to modify specifically for each project.

To create a resource file, launch Constructor, and from the main menu, choose File, New Project File. You should see a window similar to the one in Figure 4.1, which represents your project. At the bottom of the window are the global settings for the resource file, and at the top are sections representing each possible type of resource. This interface might seem unusual to those used to navigating project hierarchies in other tools, but over time, you will become accustomed to the somewhat non-standard look and feel of Constructor.

FIGURE 4.1

Constructor's main project window.

A few global settings change from project to project. Specifically, you should

- Set your application's icon name from Untitled to the one you want the user to see in the Palm application list.
- Create an application icon by clicking the Create button, which invokes the icon editor.
- Make sure that Autogenerate Header File is checked.
- Specify a header filename where Constructor should place the definitions for the IDs associated with your resources.

After these project settings are complete, you can save your resource file. You should save it to the same location that stores your other source files.

4

CREATING AND MANAGING RESOURCES

What's a Resource Fork?

Saving your resource file causes a couple of interesting things to happen. First, a header file is created with the name you chose in the Header Filename setting. Given that you haven't yet created any individual resources, this header will be mostly empty, but eventually, all your resource IDs will be defined here. Be warned that you should not attempt to modify your resource definitions by directly editing this file! Changing the header definitions does not cause any changes to the corresponding binary resources in the resource file, so things will be out of sync if you make edits here. Also, any changes you make in the header will be overwritten the next time you save your resource in Constructor. If you need to make changes to your resources, relaunch Constructor and make the changes there.

The second thing that occurs is that your resource file is saved with a .RSRC extension. This is not terribly exciting until you notice (if you are working under Windows) that a new subdirectory called resource.frk is also created and it appears to contain a copy of your resource file.

To me, a long-time Windows developer, this was hopelessly confusing. Which file contained my resources? Which one should I add to my project file? Which one should I double-click to edit my resources? As it turns out, this is an attempt by CodeWarrior to mimic the storage behavior of Constructor under the Macintosh OS and to allow the transparent transfer of resources between Mac and Windows development environments. What CodeWarrior does is create a two-part file: a data fork and a resource fork. The resource fork, which actually contains your resources, will always be stored in the resource.frk subdirectory. Even though it shows up as a 0-byte length file, you can include the data fork file in your project and even re-edit your resources in Constructor by double-clicking the data fork file. The resource fork file will automatically be loaded.

Version Control Considerations

My company uses a version-control system, and I've noticed that CodeWarrior in some respects does not coexist peacefully with it:

- Most version-control systems will set the read-only attribute of a file after you check a file in to the depot. Unfortunately, Constructor and the IDE expect both resource files and project (.MCP) files to be read-write. In all fairness, this problem is common to other software development environments. A workaround is to always check out the project and resource files for editing prior to building or running Constructor.

- The dual nature of resources causes headaches in that you must remember to check out and check in both files to the version-control system.

Example: "Hello Palm" Revisited

Reopen the resource file you created earlier, and design the main form for "Hello Palm." (For an exhaustive treatment of how to define various types of forms in Constructor, see Chapter 5, "Interacting with the User: Forms.") You can open an existing resource file either via the File, Open command in Constructor or by double-clicking the data fork resource file (.RSRC).

To add a form, highlight the Forms section in the top half of the Constructor main project window, and choose Edit, New Form Resource from the Constructor main menu. Click once on the Untitled label, and give your form a name of Main. Press Enter when you are done. Now, you can invoke the Form Layout window by double-clicking the form. The Form Layout window is pictured in Figure 4.2.

FIGURE 4.2

The (initially empty) main form Layout window.

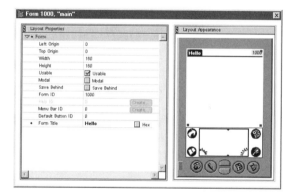

On the left are all the properties you can set for the form. On the right is a WYSIWYG representation of what your form will look like on the Palm. For main forms, about the only property you'll need to change from the default is the Form Title, which you can set to "Hello".

You add user-interface elements such as buttons and labels to a form by dragging them from the Catalog window. The Catalog window is not initially visible, so you have to load it by choosing Window, Catalog from the Constructor main menu.

Once the Catalog window is loaded, you can drag any supported user-interface resource type onto the form. For this simple form, you only need a label. Click the Label resource type, and drag it to the center of the form. A new form object of type Label is created, and the current properties pane changes from that of the form to that of the new label object. Because of the modest needs of this program, simply change the label Text property to read "Hello Palm". You might need to resize the label so that all the text shows.

At this point, you can save your work. (I've found it a good idea to save my work often during long Constructor sessions; there are few things more heartbreaking than experiencing a system crash after getting 25 teeny-weeny user-interface elements positioned just right on a form!) Return to the main CodeWarrior IDE to build your .PRC file, which will contain your new resource definitions.

Summary

This concludes the introductory section of Palm Programming. In the first four chapters, I've

- Described the Palm Computing platform and the tools involved in creating a Palm program
- Created the structure and code components required for most standard Palm applications
- Discussed the debugging environment and strategies for determining the cause of coding errors
- Examined the CodeWarrior toolset, including the IDE and Constructor
- Created the first Palm program, "Hello Palm"

At this point, you should be ready to dive into more specific subject matter. Where should you go from here? I recommend covering at least the first few chapters of the user-interface section, especially Chapter 5 and Chapter 6, "Button Controls." These chapters will give you some experience in creating more complex user interfaces, experience you can then apply as you learn about Palm databases, communications, and more advanced topics.

Programming the Palm User Interface

PART

II

IN THIS PART

CHAPTER 5

Interacting with the User: Forms

You can implement the most efficient algorithms, design the most elegant program architecture, or design the most flexible data storage system in the world. But if people running your application cannot quickly and easily learn how to effectively exploit those features, it is likely that they will discard your application in favor of one that is easier to use.

Creating an attractive, easy-to-use application that strikes just the right balance between providing all the features that customers want and maintaining an application's focus remains a difficult challenge. This is an especially daunting problem on handheld platforms such as the Palm, where the immediate temptation is to replicate the breadth of functionality and complex user interfaces found in desktop applications.

This chapter provides an introduction to programming the Palm user interface by presenting the most widely used building block in a Palm application's user interface: the form. You'll learn about the unique problems and constraints associated with Palm user-interface design and implementation. More specifically, you'll become familiar with how you can use the Palm form APIs to shape your application's interface. By the end of the chapter, you will have used the Palm form APIs along with the CodeWarrior Constructor tool to code several examples that use forms: a message box, an "about" box, and a rudimentary shopping-list form.

In this chapter, you'll learn about

- The unique characteristics of the Palm user-interface model
- The various types of forms and how they are applied in the Palm user interface
- How to use Palm development tools and the Palm APIs to program forms

The Palm User Interface

The Palm user interface is different from the one you might be used to working with on other computer platforms. Perhaps the most obvious difference is its size: The standard display dimensions today are 160 pixels wide by 160 pixels high. Although we might expect improvements in screen resolution, gray-scaling, and perhaps a modest increase in resolution, there is no indication from Palm Computing that we might expect Palm OS applications to run on devices with significantly larger screen real estate. As developers, we assume and even embrace this small form factor when designing our applications.

Aside from screen size, there are some other differences:

- Only one application is visible at a time.
- Application forms are not resizable or movable.
- The display features no color.
- There is limited gray-scale support.

Application developers must learn to live within these restrictions and design their user interfaces to work well on the Palm device.

Developers should also understand that users expect the Palm to provide information almost instantaneously. Keep in mind the following tenets:

- Place the most often used information on the main screen.
- Relegate lesser used information to secondary screens and pop-up screens.
- Provide fast and easy access to the most commonly needed information, with the minimum pen strokes required.
- Minimize the number of screens the user must navigate in your application.
- Avoid placing the user in difficult-to-escape modes such as nested dialogs.
- Do not make the user scroll through more than one or two screens to locate information.
- Consider moving complex or infrequently accessed data to the desktop and using conduits to get the information downloaded to the Palm.

For further guidelines, I encourage you to read the *Palm OS 3.0 Cookbook*, which is part of the Palm SDK.

What Is a Form?

A form can perhaps best be defined as a visual container for user-interface elements. Some of the user-interface elements commonly found on forms are labels, buttons, lists, and check boxes. For those familiar with user interfaces on other computer platforms such as Microsoft Windows, the most obvious parallel to a form is a window or a dialog box.

Palm applications generally have one or more forms, which together compose the user interface for the application. Forms are either full-screen or pop-up. Full-screen forms are sometimes called views because they usually provide different logical views of the data associated with the application. A view is similar to the concept of a window on other platforms, except that it cannot be moved or sized and can only appear one at a time. Views are said to be modeless because they do not force the user to complete a specific action in order to perform other application functions. Every application has at least one full-screen form: its main form.

Pop-up forms are closely related to the concept of modal dialogs. They occupy a portion of the screen and "pop up" over the currently active form. When an application displays a pop-up form, the user can resume using the rest of the application only after dismissing the pop-up form. Pop-up forms are often referred to as dialogs in the Palm SDK.

The Palm SDK has much to say about the standards and guidelines that application developers should follow in the process of designing their forms. Pop-up forms in particular should always be designed to fill the entire width of the screen and are justified to the bottom of the screen so that the top portion of the current form is still visible to the user.

Examples of Forms in Real Life

Figures 5.1, 5.2, and 5.3 show real-life examples of forms in the built-in Palm Address Book application.

FIGURE 5.1

The main form of the Address Book application.

FIGURE 5.2

The Address Entry Details pop-up form.

FIGURE 5.3

An alert confirming the deletion of a note entry.

Programming with Forms

The Palm SDK supports several different ways of incorporating forms into your application:

- Alerts
- Simple pop-up forms
- Complex pop-up forms
- Full-screen forms

The following sections explore these types of forms in depth.

Alerts

The simplest form of all is called an alert. Alerts are the closest thing Palm has to message boxes in that their general appearance and functionality is already handled for you. On the downside, for each different type of message you want to display, you must still use Constructor to create an alert resource. Unfortunately, there is no "standard" message box API that predefines a common resource (although we create one later in this chapter).

There are two kinds of alerts. The simplest is created entirely in Constructor and has fixed-text content that is hard-coded into the resource: If you want to change the text, you have to change the resource in Constructor and rebuild your application.

In the next section, we'll use the simplest type of alert to display a pop-up message on the Palm. As with many Palm programming tasks, this one has two components: using Constructor to create the resource and adding code to interact with the resource in your application.

Using Constructor to Create a Simple Alert Resource

As you saw in Chapter 4, "Creating and Managing Resources," CodeWarrior comes with a visual resource editor called Constructor. You use Constructor for creating any kind of form resource; it provides a quick way to manage and navigate all of your project's resources.

To create an alert in Constructor, follow these steps:

1. Open the main project window for your resources.
2. Select the Alerts resource type from the project window.
3. Add a new Alert resource by choosing Edit, New Alert Resource or pressing Ctrl+K.

    A new, untitled alert resource appears under the Alerts section. Note the ID of the Alert: We'll be using it soon.
4. Rename the new Alert resource from the default <untitled> to some name that is meaningful.
5. Double-click the new resource to open the Alert Properties window. (See Figure 5.4.)

FIGURE 5.4

Creating an alert resource in Constructor.

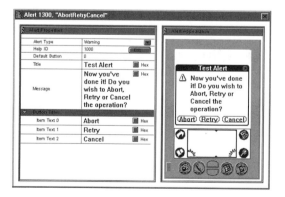

The Alert Properties Window appears with two panes: a property sheet on the left and a visual representation of how your new alert will appear on the Palm display. Note that the alert comes with some default properties, such as a title, message text, and OK button already filled in with placeholder values.

6. Enter each of the Alert Properties with the values described in Table 5.1.

TABLE 5.1 ALERT RESOURCE PROPERTIES

Property	Meaning
Alert Type	Choose from a set of available alert types: Information, Confirmation, Warning, and Error.
Help ID	The ID of an associate string resource containing help text. Palm recommends that each alert or form contain help text that is displayed when the user taps the "I" on the form. To define help text, create a new string resource from the main project window and type the text that should be associated with the alert or form. The ID of the string resource is the value that you should then set in the Help ID property.
Default Button	If there is only one button on the alert, this property is grayed out. If there are two or more buttons defined, set this property to the item ID of the button that should be the default button.
Title	The text that should appear in the title bar of the alert.
Message	The text that should appear in the client area of the alert.
Button Titles	For each button defined, enter the label shown on the surface of the button. Note that if you want to remove a button from an alert, highlight the button in the properties pane and choose Edit, Clear Button Text from the main Constructor menu.

When you are happy with the appearance of your alert resource, close the Alert Properties Window and choose File, Save from the main menu.

Adding Alert Handling to Your Application

Now that you've specified the appearance of your alert in Constructor, it is time to see it in action. Just as you would hope, it's easy: To display your alert in your application, all you need to do is add the following code:

```
err = FrmAlert (MyAlertID);
```

MyAlertID is the ID of the alert. The return code is simply the ID of the button the user taps to dismiss the alert. (If there is only one button, you can safely ignore the return code.)

Let's look at an example of handling an alert with three buttons—Abort, Retry, and Cancel:

```
Word wButton;
wButton = FrmAlert (AbortRetryCancel);
switch (wButton)
{
    case 0: // Abort
    case 1: // Retry
    case 2: // Cancel
}
```

Figure 5.5 shows what our simple alert looks like when called from an application.

FIGURE 5.5

*The Abort, Retry,
Cancel alert in
action.*

Custom Alerts

If you want to be able to customize the text of an alert during your program's runtime (for error messages, debugging purposes, and so on), you need to use a custom alert. You create custom alerts in the same way as regular alerts, but the item text can contain up to three special embedded replaceable characters, ^1, ^2, and ^3, which correspond to three parameters in the FrmCustomAlert API.

When your program runs, you pass the values you want to display in place of these characters, as in the following example:

```
err = FrmCustomAlert ( MyAlertID, "Error 21", "No item
➥   selected", "");
```

Note that the third parameter is an empty string; use an empty string if your alert resource does not define all three replaceable characters or if you simply do not need to supply text. The replaceable character will be changed to an empty character string in the alert display.

This might sound like an unreliable way to provide a generic message box capability in your application—we agree—but we're going to remedy that situation in the next section.

`PalmMessageBox`: a Reusable Message Box API

The basic flaw in using `FrmCustomAlert` to implement message box functionality in your application is that when you call the `FrmCustomAlert` function, you are trusting that the alert resource matches your call in terms of the number and meaning of the replaceable parameters. Imagine an alert resource defined with alert message text as follows:

```
"Warning: the database named ^1 already has ^2 records in it with
➥ that field value"
```

Unless you are very familiar with this resource, you could easily misuse the alert by making the following call:

```
FrmCustomAlert (MyAlertID, "Error", "Too many records", "Abort");
```

As you can see, the text passed in the first two parameters is inappropriate in the context of the alert resource. What's more, the third parameter value will never be seen by the user: The designer of the alert resource did not define a replaceable parameter with ^3. Unfortunately, this is not safe and is unnecessarily error-prone, especially in an application with a significant number of alerts.

What is needed here is a simple, reliable general-purpose message box API that lets you define its message text at runtime according to program conditions. Let's create one:

1. Define a new alert in Constructor with a title of "Information" and a message containing a single replaceable parameter ^1. See Figure 5.6 to see how the alert appears in Constructor.

FIGURE 5.6

Creating a custom alert with replaceable parameters in Constructor.

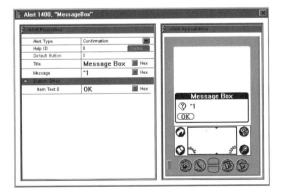

2. Create a function as follows:

```
Word PalmMessageBox (Word wAlertID, CharPtr pMessage)
{
    Word err;
    err = FrmCustomAlert (wAlertID, pMessage, "", "" );
    return err;
}
```

That's all there is to it: We now have a general-purpose message box API that we can use in a variety of program situations and to which we can always be assured we are passing the right parameters. With a little extra work, we could predefine a series of these message box APIs, one for each type of alert. We might even remove the need to pass the alert ID, instead simply asking the caller to select what type of alert he wants from a number of predetermined types.

Look at Figure 5.7 to see our message box function in action.

FIGURE 5.7

Our general-purpose message box alert.

Custom Forms

Obviously, alerts are somewhat limited in functionality and appearance: They may only contain a single text string and one or more buttons. For more complex user interactions, we will instead use Palm's Form Resource.

Although forms are more flexible and support a rich set of programming interfaces, you add forms to an application in a similar fashion as adding alerts. We will follow the two-step sequence established in the previous section, first defining a form resource in Constructor and then adding code to load and interact with the form in our application.

We'll start by adding a simple pop-up About box to our program. We'll then move on to a more complex example that begins to explore the power of the form API.

Using Constructor to Create a Form Resource

To create a form in Constructor, follow these steps:

1. Open the main project window for your resources.

2. Select the Forms resource type from the project window.

3. Add a new form resource by choosing Edit, New Form Resource or pressing Ctrl+K.

   A new, untitled form resource appears under the Forms section. Once again, note the ID of the Form: We'll be using it in our sample code later in this section.

4. Rename the new Form resource from the default <untitled> to "About."

5. Double-click the new resource to open the Form Properties window. (See Figure 5.8.)

FIGURE 5.8

The About box form in Constructor.

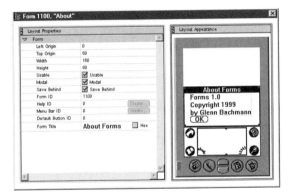

The Form Properties Window appears with two panes: a property sheet on the left and a visual representation of how your new form will appear on the Palm display. You will immediately notice that you have many options available in defining the appearance and behavior of your form.

6. Enter each of the form properties with the values described in Table 5.2.

TABLE 5.2 FORM RESOURCE PROPERTIES

Property	Meaning
Left Origin	Offset of the form, in pixels, from the left edge of the display.
Top Origin	Offset of the form, in pixels, from the top edge of the display.
Width	Width of the form, in pixels.

Property	Meaning
Height	Height of the form, in pixels.
Usable	The 3.0 Palm documentation states that this property is not currently supported.
Modal	Check this if you are defining a modal dialog. If it is checked, the operating system will refuse to process pen events that occur outside the form, effectively forcing the user to complete his interaction with the form before moving on to other program functionality.
Save Behind	Also checked generally for modal dialogs. If checked, the system will save the value of the pixels that are covered by the form and automatically restore them when the form is deleted.
Form ID	The unique ID of the form. This property is automatically set by Constructor but you can change it if you want.
Help ID	Refer to Help ID in Table 5.1.
Menu Bar ID	You can enter the ID of a menu bar resource here to associate a menu with the form.
Default Button ID	The ID of the button that you should assume is selected if the user switches to another application while the form is active.
Form Title	The title text to be displayed on the form.

Because this will be a modal pop-up form, we will need to make some adjustments to these properties:

1. Resize the form to take up the bottom one half of the screen. You do this by changing Left Origin, Top Origin, Width, and Height to 0, 80, 160, and 80. You can also use your mouse to directly drag the upper boundary of the form down by 80 pixels. In many cases, I find it to be more accurate to directly modify the numeric coordinates in the properties pane.

2. Check the Modal property.

3. Check the Save Behind property.

Note that you should check both the Modal and Save Behind properties for all modal dialogs.

Adding Elements to the Form

For our new form to look like the one in Figure 5.8, we need to add some form elements. Specifically, we will need an OK button and a label.

Constructor has a special window called the Catalog, which presents a palette from which you can add any supported element type to your form using drag and drop.

To use Constructor to add the missing elements to our form, follow these steps:

1. If the Catalog window is not showing, choose Window, Catalog from the menu or press Ctrl+Y.

2. Click the Button type and drag it onto your form. The main Constructor project window changes to display the properties of the new button. For now, leave the properties at their defaults. (I discuss button resources and their properties in more detail in Chapter 6, "Button Controls.")

3. Drag a label type onto the form. Position it in the upper part of the form and widen it to almost fill the width of the form. In the Properties pane, set the text to reflect your application's name and copyright information.

4. Save your form by closing the form properties window and choosing File, Save from the main menu. Your form resource is ready for integration into your application.

The Resource Header File

Before we integrate the new form into our program, let's take a short detour, peek under the covers, and see what is happening as we add resources to our project.

Two important files are created and updated during a Constructor session:

- A header file containing the IDs of each resource defined in the resource file. This file has an .H extension and is located in your project's SRC directory.

- The resource file itself. This file has a .RSRC extension.

CodeWarrior has some odd legacy behavior that results in two .RSRC files being created: one in the SRC directory of your project and one in a directory called RESOURCE.FRK off your SRC directory. You will notice that the copy in the SRC directory is size 0 bytes. The real resources are stored in the RESOURCE.FRK directory, but you should not mess with the size 0 bytes file. This seemingly bizarre behavior has its roots in CodeWarrior's Macintosh beginnings, and Palm has stated its intention to remove this behavior in a future version of CodeWarrior.

CAUTION

Do not directly edit the resource header file. It is regenerated by Constructor after every resource editing session, so you will lose any changes you make. Use Constructor to change resource IDs or define new resources.

Adding Form Handling to Your Application

If you look through the Palm SDK documentation, you will see a fairly large and sometimes confusing set of APIs for handling forms. There are more than 50 APIs dealing with various aspects of form handling. Most of these are related to either interacting with form elements or supporting behaviors associated with modeless, full-screen forms.

Modal, pop-up dialogs, involve three main functions:

- FrmInitForm
- FrmDoDialog
- FrmDeleteForm

Here's how we use them to display our new form resource:

```
/*
   AboutFormShow ():
   Show the about dialog box.
   Parms:   none
   Return:  none
*/
void AboutFormShow ()
{
   FormPtr   pForm = FrmInitForm (AboutForm);
   FrmDoDialog (pForm);
   FrmDeleteForm (pForm);
}
```

Outside of using an alert, this is the simplest way to invoke a form. You pass the ID of the form resource to FrmInitForm, which returns a form pointer. If you pass the form pointer to FrmDoDialog, the API does not return until the user clicks a button in the form. The ID of the button is returned to the caller as a result code. You are then responsible for deleting the form.

Note that if necessary, you should perform any initialization of form elements before calling FrmDoDialog. Likewise, any querying of the state of form elements must occur prior to calling FrmDeleteForm.

Figure 5.9 illustrates our about box.

FIGURE 5.9

*Our about box
form in action.*

Using Forms to Capture User Input

Now that we've seen how to initialize a form resource, display it as a modal dialog, and properly destroy it, let's look at how we capture user-entered values from form elements after the form is dismissed.

As an example, let's create a "shopping list" screen that asks the user to check off which items he will need at the grocery store. Note that although we will use check-box form elements in this example, I cover check boxes only to the extent necessary for this example. Chapter 6, "Button Controls," covers check boxes in depth.

Use Constructor to create another form called "Create Shopping List", and configure it so it resembles Figure 5.5. This time, carefully pay attention to giving your form elements IDs that reflect the elements' purposes. For example, change the ID of the OK button to "OK". Add a second button at the bottom of the form, and give it a label of "Cancel". Finally, add two check-box field resources with labels "Milk" and "Cookies". After you are satisfied with the layout of your form, save it.

Remember when we took a peek at the resource header file that Constructor created for our resources? Here's where it becomes important: Constructor takes some liberties in supplying IDs for your form elements. Basically, it takes your supplied ID (such as "OK") and appends the resource type. The ID for the OK button winds up OKButton, the ID for the Milk check-box field winds up MilkCheckbox, and so on. These are the IDs that you will need to use to obtain element values from your form.

> **TIP**
>
> If you are consistent in your naming system for your form elements, it will become easy to guess the resulting ID as Constructor defines it. Constructor's insistence on mucking with the name is just another odd behavior that we expect will be eliminated as the Palm tool set matures.

Now, let's add some code to capture the user's shopping list selections:

```
/*
   CreateShoppingList ():
   Displays the Create Shopping List dialog, allowing the user to select
   items to add to the shopping list.
   Parms:   none
   Return:  none
*/
void CreateShoppingList ()
{
   Boolean bGetMilk;
   Boolean bGetCookies;
   // Initialize the form
   FormPtr  pForm = FrmInitForm (CreateShoppingListForm);
   // Preset the check boxes for all items to be unchecked
   // Get the index of the check box form object
   Word wIDMilk = FrmGetObjectIndex (pForm,MilkCheckbox );
   // Given the object index, get a pointer to the control object
   // for the check box
   ControlPtr pCtlMilk = (ControlPtr) FrmGetObjectPtr (pForm, wIDMilk);
   // Use the object pointer, set the check box value to 0 (False)
   CtlSetValue ( pCtlMilk, 0 );
   ...
   // Display the dialog
   FrmDoDialog (pForm);
   // Get the values from the check box
   bGetMilk = CtlGetValue ( pCtlMilk );
// Destroy the form
   FrmDeleteForm (pForm);
}
```

This code uses some new APIs to initialize and query the form elements. I explore in depth the APIs that provide interaction with the various types of form elements as we dive into the details of each resource type. For now, it is sufficient to understand that given a form pointer, we can obtain a pointer to any given form element by supplying its resource ID. Once we have a pointer to a form element, we can use Palm SDK APIs to set and query the element's value.

More Complex Forms: Event Handlers

The methods used so far in form handling hide the complexity of what happens inside the form. The caller only knows what button was pressed and the state of the various controls. This capability satisfies the needs of a great many forms.

Some forms require some custom handling of events while the form is still visible on the screen. Perhaps the form supports a pop-up calendar date-picker. Maybe the form's display needs to change based on some user action such as a radio button selection. Each of these situations requires handling events that occur inside the form and taking action on the event.

To hook into the flow of events that are happening inside a form, a programmer must create an event handler for the form. If you have programmed for Windows, you can consider the form event handler a kind of dialog box or window procedure. It is a callback function that gets notified upon any significant event in the life of a form.

Continuing with our shopping-list example, let's add the ability for a user to select a date when the shopping list will be used. The standard way to handle date selection in a Palm application's user interface is to use a push button as a launching point into the Palm SDK's SelectDay function. Upon return, the push button's label is set to the selected date. Unless we somehow trap the push button event, we have no way of knowing when to show the calendar date-picker dialog. With the addition of an event handler, the task becomes straightforward.

The following is a minimal form event-handler procedure:

```
Boolean MyEventHandler (EventPtr pEvent)
{
    Boolean  bHandled = false;
    return bHandled;
}
```

As we've said, an event handler receives notification of any significant event in the life of a form. It receives this notification by way of the EventPtr parameter. For most forms, we are only interested in one kind of event: ctlSelectEvent. This event indicates that a control on the form has been tapped or selected or has somehow changed state. A form's event handler receives this notification and has an opportunity to take action on the event. If the application chooses to process the event, it should return TRUE in the event handler.

Let's modify our event-handler callback to handle the case in which a new push button DateButton is tapped:

```
Boolean CreateShoppingList_EventHandler (EventPtr pEvent)
{
    Boolean  bHandled = false;
    switch (pEvent->eType)
    {
        case ctlSelectEvent:
        {
```

```
        Word wCmd = pEvent->date.ctlSelect.controlID;
        // A control button was pressed.
        switch (wCmd)
        {
          case DateButton:
          {
            SWord mth, day, year;
            if ( SelectDay ( selectDayByDay, &mth, &day, &year,
            ➥ "Select a Shopping Day") )
            {
               FormPtr pForm = FrmGetActiveForm ();
               Word wIDDate = FrmGetObjectIndex (pForm,DateButton );
               // Given the object index, get a pointer to the control
               object
               ControlPtr pDate = (ControlPtr) FrmGetObjectPtr
               ➥ (pForm, wIDDate);
               char szDate[20];
               CStrPrintf ( szDate, "%d/%d/%d", mth, day, year );
               CtlSetLabel ( pDate, szDate );
          }

          bHandled = true;
          break;
        }
    return bHandled;
}
```

If we examine this code, we see that when we receive notification that
CreateShoppingListDateButton was tapped, we call the standard SelectDay function,
which pops up a familiar "date-picker" form. Upon return, we take the month, day, and
year of the selected date, format it, and set it as the new label of our push button.

The final step in adding an event handler to our form is to tell the Palm OS that it should
associate our event handler with our form. It's a single function call:
FrmSetEventHandler().

Now, let's hook the event handler into our CreateShoppingList function:

```
// As usual, we initialize the form
FormPtr  pForm = FrmInitForm (CreateShoppingListForm);

// We set an event handler for the form
FrmSetEventHandler (pForm, CreateShoppingList_EventHandler );

// Launch the dialog
FrmDoDialog (pForm)

// Clean up
FrmDeleteForm (pForm)
```

After you have entered the code, the form should look like Figure 5.10.

FIGURE 5.10

Our nutritionally challenged shopping list form.

Summary

You've seen that the Palm display imposes some significant and unique challenges to a user-interface designer. It is especially important to become familiar with the various types and proper usage of forms, the most common user-interface element on the Palm device. Forms provide a natural framework for your application and guide the user through the application's functionality.

You should now be comfortable with creating forms using CodeWarrior's Constructor tool and integrating them into your application. You should also be thinking about how to structure your application so that it uses forms to present functionality in a logical fashion, providing maximum ease of use and utility for the user.

The next few chapters build on the concepts presented here, expanding the use of forms and exploring the other user-interface elements available to the Palm developer.

CHAPTER 6

Button Controls

In our modern world, we are surrounded by knobs, dials, buttons, and switches. From ATMs to voting machines, automobiles to elevators, light switches to televisions, we are confronted with a myriad of ways in which we make selections, adjust our environment, and control the way we live and work.

As in the real world around us, computer programs also provide special visual elements that help us make selections, adjust behavior, or control the software's execution. The overall presentation of these elements on a computer program is called its user interface. The individual elements that help us navigate the user interface are commonly referred to as "user-interface controls" or simply "controls."

As on most other computer platforms that support graphical displays, the Palm platform supports a rich array of controls for a developer to use in designing and constructing an application's user interface. This chapter begins a tour of the various types of controls, explores their uses, presents guidelines for implementation, and walks you through several examples of how to incorporate them into your application.

What Is a Control Object?

Control objects allow for user interaction with your program. As we saw in Chapter 5, "Interacting with the User: Forms," forms are visual containers that often present groups of controls. Strictly speaking, Palm control objects fall into a larger family of objects called user-interface objects. User-interface objects encompass a wide range of types, covering buttons, menus, forms, list boxes, scroll bars, windows, and more. Control objects in the Palm SDK represent a subset of user-interface objects and as a group are generally variations on the push button concept.

This definition notwithstanding, I've found it easier to adopt a broader definition of a control as any reusable user-interface element that has a well-defined appearance and behavior and is supported as a user-interface element on a form.

This chapter explores most of the available types of buttons in depth, and subsequent chapters cover other types of user-interface elements that, at least in my book (and it is my book!), also fall under the broader definition of a user-interface control.

Types of Control Objects

The Palm SDK provides support for a rich array of control objects. Each object has a name, a resource type that identifies it as a Palm resource, and a well-defined appearance and behavior. Table 6.1 describes each control object.

TABLE 6.1   CONTROL OBJECTS

Control Object	Resource	Appearance	Behavior
Button	tBTN	A rectangle containing a text label. Corners are round by default but can be set to have a rectangular frame.	When the user taps with the pen, the button highlight (inverts) the button's display region.
Push button	tPBN	Same as a button but always has square corners.	Same as a button, but the push button remains inverted after the pen is lifted.
Repeat button	tREP	Same as a button.	When the user taps with the pen, the object is repeatedly selected while the pen remains down. The repeating action stops when the pen is lifted.

Control Object	Resource	Appearance	Behavior
Check box	tCBX	A square, either empty or containing a check mark, depending on the check box's setting. May have a text label associated with it, which appears to the right of the square.	When the user taps with the pen, the check box's setting is toggled on or off, either checking or unchecking the square on the display.
Pop-up trigger	tPUT	A text label to the right of a down-arrow graphic.	When tapped, the control initiates an associated pop-up list box.
Selector trigger	tSLT	A text label surrounded by a gray frame.	When tapped, the control initiates a user-interface event.

What Is a Button?

As you can see, although only one control object is actually called "button," all of the control objects have some button-like appearance or behavior. Buttons are one of the most prevalent types of user-interface elements in Palm applications, or indeed non-Palm applications.

Buttons are unique in that they provide simple, one-tap manipulation of the user interface. No other action is required by the user to complete a command or provide information: no graffiti, no multi-step sequence of taps. Thus, buttons provide unprecedented power and simplicity to any user interface. Assuming you have made your buttons large enough (as the user-interface guidelines recommend), your entire application could theoretically be run by a person using her finger to manipulate the user interface.

About the only downside in using buttons instead of some other form of user-interface element is that they take up valuable real estate on the display. It is important to design your application so that the primary commands and actions are supported via onscreen buttons and secondary or optional commands are invoked via some other method (such as a menu).

Types of Buttons

Let's explore the various button types in depth so that you understand why you would use each type in different situations. To illustrate each type, I present a screenshot of a built-in Palm application form that makes appropriate use of the type of button.

Button

Probably the most common user-interface element, in Palm parlance, a plain old "button" is usually employed to execute a command. On other platforms such as Windows, this type of button is called a push button. Push buttons are actually another type of button on the Palm. See Figure 6.1.

FIGURE **6.1**

A button on a form.

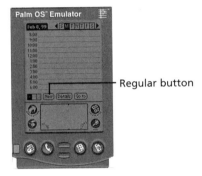

Regular button

Push Button

A push button on the Palm platform is what we are accustomed to calling a radio button. Due to screen real-estate considerations, these buttons are commonly grouped and placed directly adjacent to one another, but their behavior is essentially the same: You tap a single button to select a value from a set of possible values. Figure 6.2 below shows push buttons used to provide the user with the ability to choose one of five possible priorities.

FIGURE **6.2**

Push buttons providing a multiple-choice selection.

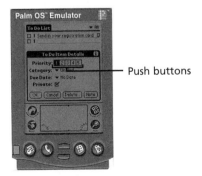

Push buttons

Repeating Button

A repeating button is most commonly used to create something called an increment arrow. (In Windows applications, this is referred to as a spin button.) An increment arrow is usually placed next to a label or field and is used to move forward or backward through a series of values. Getting a repeat button to look like an increment arrow takes some work, and I show you how to do this later in the chapter. Figure 6.3 shows repeat buttons being used as left and right arrows to control the week being viewed.

FIGURE 6.3

An increment arrow on the appointment day view form.

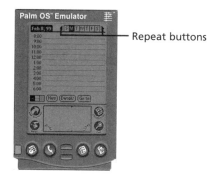

Repeat buttons

Check Box

Surprise! A check box is exactly what its name implies: A visual toggle for managing a value that can only have one of two states. Use a check box for yes/no or true/false values. In Figure 6.4, a check box is used to indicate a record as private or public.

FIGURE 6.4

A check box.

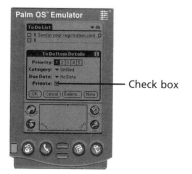

Check box

Pop-Up Trigger

A pop-up trigger is most commonly seen in conjunction with a list box resource. Together, they give the functionality of a drop-down combo box. I discuss pop-up triggers further in Chapter 8, "Giving the User a Choice: Lists and Pop-Up Triggers."

Selector Trigger

A selector trigger is best described as a "live" label; it displays a (noneditable) piece of text and also triggers an event when tapped. You can trap the event with a form handler and trigger some program options—such as a pop-up form. Upon return from the event, the text can change to reflect the user's action. The selector trigger saves precious screen real estate by combining a text label with the functionality of a push button. One of the most common uses of a selector trigger is to handle date selection with the help of the `SelectDay` API. In Figure 6.5, both the Date and Time values are in fact selector triggers.

FIGURE 6.5

A selector trigger used to select and display a date.

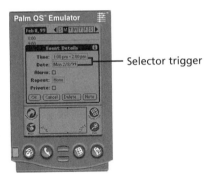

Selector trigger

Guidelines for the Use of Buttons

The Palm SDK provides guidelines for the use and display of buttons in your application.

You should use buttons for the most important commands; relegate secondary and optional commands to pop-up dialogs and menus. This rule stays in line with the recommendation that you keep high-frequency actions accessible with one tap.

Make command buttons large enough to support finger navigation. When placing command buttons on a form, leave at least three pixels between the edge of the dialog box and the buttons. Locate command buttons at the bottom of the screen, and align them evenly. When sizing command buttons, leave one pixel above and below the top and bottom of the text area, using the maximum height of the selected font as a measurement guideline. When sizing push buttons (a.k.a. radio buttons), leave two pixels to the left and right of the text label.

Using Buttons in Your Application

You will interact with the Palm SDK in four ways when putting buttons (and controls in general) in your application:

- Creating the visual representation of the buttons in your application resource with Constructor
- Calling the appropriate SDK functions to control the buttons' behavior and appearance within your program
- Trapping events triggered by pen interaction with buttons
- Reading values in control structures passed to you via control object events

Note that the last two items are only necessary if you need to use a form event handler to provide special event handling in your form. If this is not a requirement, you can easily place button controls and other user-interface elements by creating the resources in Constructor, setting the control values and states at form initialization time, and retrieving their values on the termination of the form.

Survey Says: A Simple Survey Application

To illustrate the use of each type of button, we'll create an application that presents a simple survey form. The form will ask the user to specify her marital status, age, date of birth, and whether she wants to be contacted. The form supports a reset button to set the form values back to defaults and a submit button, which for our basic application simply displays the user's current choices from the form in a message box.

Figure 6.6 shows what the survey form looks like.

FIGURE 6.6

Our survey application.

As you can see, we use command buttons, push buttons (radio buttons), a repeat button, a selector trigger, and a check box all in one form.

The first thing you'll need to do is create the main form resource and place each control on the form. I assume that by now you are familiar enough with Constructor, so I skip the detailed steps. However, I'd like to cover just a few subtle nuances in the creation of the form resource.

Grouped Push Buttons

Constructor allows you to assign a group ID to which a push button control belongs. All push buttons on the form that belong to the same group ID will behave, to the user at least, the way that radio buttons are expected to behave. Tapping on one button will automatically select that button and deselect the other buttons in the group. Leaving the push buttons assigned to group ID 0 does not give you this behavior. You need to identify a group ID that is nonzero and assign the same ID to each button that belongs to the group.

If you happen to put multiple groups of push buttons on a single form (for example, if we add a set of buttons to let the user choose a favorite color), assigning the groups different group IDs works just fine; each group operates independently.

Repeating Buttons and the Arrow Increment

Constructor does not offer built-in support for arrow-shaped repeating buttons. You have to manually tell Constructor what to use as the repeat button's label. To achieve an up-arrow and down-arrow look and functionality, you need to create two repeat buttons, one for up and one for down. The next part is not obvious: You need to set the label to a character code from a font that contains an arrow symbol. For up-down arrows, choose the Symbol 7 font in Layout Properties, and for the label, click the Hex checkbox (indicating the value you are entering should not be interpreted as a character string), and enter 01 for the up arrow and 02 for the down arrow. If you are like me and have not committed the character codes for the Symbol 7 font to memory, you might want to download a handy Palm utility called ASCIIChart by John Valdes, which displays all of the character codes and their values for each Palm font.

Listing 6.1 contains the code that implements the initialization and event handling for the main survey form.

LISTING 6.1 SOURCE CODE FOR THE MAIN SURVEY FORM

```
/*
   BTN_MAI.CPP
   Main form handling functions.
*/

// system headers
#include <Pilot.h>
#include <SysEvtMgr.h>

// Application-specific headers
#include "buttons.h"
#include "btn_res.h"

static void    MainFormInit (FormPtr formP);
static Boolean MainFormButtonHandler (FormPtr formP, EventPtr eventP);
static Boolean MainFormMenuHandler (FormPtr formP,
➥EventPtr eventP);

void ResetForm (FormPtr formP);
Word PalmMessageBox ( Word wAlertID, CharPtr pMessage );

static SWord s_Age = 35;

/*
   MainFormEventHandler:
   Parms:   pEvent   - event to be handled.
   Return:  true  - handled (successfully or not)
            false - not handled
*/
Boolean
MainFormEventHandler (EventPtr eventP)
{
   Boolean  handled = false;

   switch (eventP->eType)
   {
      case menuEvent:
      {
```

continues

LISTING 6.1   CONTINUED

```
            FormPtr formP = FrmGetActiveForm ();
            handled = MainFormMenuHandler (formP, eventP);
            break;
        }

    case ctlRepeatEvent:
        {
            FormPtr formP = FrmGetActiveForm ();
            handled = MainFormButtonHandler (formP, eventP);
            break;
        }
    case ctlSelectEvent:
        {
            // A control button was tapped and released
            FormPtr formP = FrmGetActiveForm ();
            handled = MainFormButtonHandler (formP, eventP);
            break;
        }

    case frmOpenEvent:
        {
            // Main form is opening

            FormPtr formP = FrmGetActiveForm ();

            MainFormInit (formP);

            FrmDrawForm (formP);

            handled = true;
            break;
        }

    default:
        {
            break;
        }
    }
    return handled;
}

/*
   MainFormInit:
   Initialize the main form.
   Parms:   formP - pointer to main form.
   Return:  none
*/
void
MainFormInit (FormPtr formP)
{
```

```
    // Set the controls to an initial state
    ResetForm ( formP );
}

/*
    ResetForm
    Resets each control on the form to a default state
*/
void
ResetForm (FormPtr formP)
{
    Word wIDContactMe = FrmGetObjectIndex (formP,
    ➥MainContactMeCheckbox );
    ControlPtr pCtlContactMe = (ControlPtr) FrmGetObjectPtr
    ➥(formP, wIDContactMe);

    Word wIDAge = FrmGetObjectIndex (formP, MainAgeLabel );
    ControlPtr pCtlAge = (ControlPtr) FrmGetObjectPtr (formP, wIDAge);

    Word wIDSingle = FrmGetObjectIndex (formP, MainSinglePushButton );
    ControlPtr pCtlSingle = (ControlPtr) FrmGetObjectPtr
    ➥(formP, wIDSingle);

    Word wIDMarried = FrmGetObjectIndex (formP, MainMarriedPushButton );
    ControlPtr pCtlMarried = (ControlPtr) FrmGetObjectPtr
    ➥(formP, wIDMarried);

    Word wIDDivorced = FrmGetObjectIndex (formP, MainDivorcedPushButton );
    ControlPtr pCtlDivorced = (ControlPtr) FrmGetObjectPtr
    ➥(formP, wIDDivorced);

    Word wIDDateofBirth = FrmGetObjectIndex (formP,
    ➥MainDateofBirthSelTrigger);
    ControlPtr pCtlDateofBirth = (ControlPtr) FrmGetObjectPtr (formP,
    ➥wIDDateofBirth);

    char szAge[5];
    CharPtr pszDate = CtlGetLabel (pCtlDateofBirth);

    // Set the marital status radio buttons to Single
    // Note that because this is grouped, user taps will automatically
    // turn off the untapped selections, but programmatically we have to
    // do it ourselves.
    CtlSetValue ( pCtlSingle, 1 );
    CtlSetValue ( pCtlMarried, 0 );
    CtlSetValue ( pCtlDivorced, 0 );

    // Set the label for age to 35
    s_Age = 35;
```

continues

LISTING 6.1 CONTINUED

```
    StrPrintF ( szAge, "%d", s_Age );

    // Try this - but you can still write past the end of a label
    FrmHideObject (formP, wIDAge);
    FrmCopyLabel (formP, MainAgeLabel, szAge);
    FrmShowObject (formP, wIDAge);

    // Or use an edit field that has editable and underline turned off

    // Set the date of birth label on the selector button to be 12/31/63
    SWord mth, day, year;
    mth = 12;
    day = 31;
    year = 1963;


    StrPrintF ( pszDate, "%d/%d/%d", mth, day, year );
    CtlSetLabel ( pCtlDateofBirth, pszDate );

    // Set the check box for "contact me" to no
    CtlSetValue ( pCtlContactMe, 0 );


}

/*
    MainFormMenuHandler:
    Handle a command sent to the main form.
    Parms:   formP     - form handling event.
             command   - command to be handled.
    Return:  true   - handled (successfully or not)
             false  - not handled
*/
Boolean
MainFormMenuHandler (FormPtr /*formP*/, EventPtr eventP)
{
    Boolean handled = false;

    switch (eventP->data.menu.itemID)
    {
        default:
        {
            handled = false;
            break;
        }
    }
```

```
        return handled;
}

/*
    MainFormButtonHandler:
    Handle a command sent to the main form.
    Parms:    formP    - form handling event.
              eventP   - event to be handled.
    Return:   true  - handled (successfully or not)
              false - not handled
*/
Boolean
MainFormButtonHandler (FormPtr formP, EventPtr eventP)
{
    Boolean handled = false;

    switch (eventP->data.ctlEnter.controlID)
    {
        case MainAgeUpRepeating:
        {
            // Decrement the age
            if ( s_Age > 22 )
            {
                Word wIDAge = FrmGetObjectIndex (formP, MainAgeLabel );
                ControlPtr pCtlAge = (ControlPtr) FrmGetObjectPtr
                ➥(formP, wIDAge);
                char szAge[5];

                s_Age--;
                StrPrintF ( szAge, "%d", s_Age );
                FrmHideObject (formP, wIDAge);
                FrmCopyLabel (formP, MainAgeLabel, szAge);
                FrmShowObject (formP, wIDAge);
            }
            break;
        }
        case MainAgeDownRepeating:
        {
            // Increment the age
            if ( s_Age < 65 )
            {
                Word wIDAge = FrmGetObjectIndex (formP, MainAgeLabel );
                ControlPtr pCtlAge = (ControlPtr) FrmGetObjectPtr
                ➥(formP, wIDAge);
                char szAge[5];

                s_Age++;
                StrPrintF ( szAge, "%d", s_Age );

                FrmHideObject (formP, wIDAge);
                FrmCopyLabel (formP, MainAgeLabel, szAge);
```

continues

LISTING 6.1 CONTINUED

```
            FrmShowObject (formP, wIDAge);
        }
        break;
    }
    case MainDateofBirthSelTrigger:
    {
        // Tapped the selector trigger button control
        // Show the selectday dialog, and update the date of
        // birth label upon return
        SWord mth, day, year;
        mth = 12;
        day = 31;
        year = 1963;

        if ( SelectDay ( selectDayByDay, &mth, &day, &year,
        ➥"Date of Birth") )
        {
            ControlPtr pCtlDateofBirth = (ControlPtr)eventP->
            ➥data.ctlEnter.pControl;
            CharPtr pszDate = CtlGetLabel (pCtlDateofBirth);

            StrPrintF ( pszDate, "%d/%d/%d", mth, day, year );
            CtlSetLabel ( pCtlDateofBirth, pszDate );
        }
        handled = true;
        break;
    }

    case MainSubmitButton:
    {
        char szMessage[100];

        // Get the values from the survey form
        Word wIDContactMe = FrmGetObjectIndex (formP,
        ➥MainContactMeCheckbox );
        ControlPtr pCtlContactMe = (ControlPtr) FrmGetObjectPtr
        ➥(formP, wIDContactMe);

        Word wIDAge = FrmGetObjectIndex (formP, MainAgeLabel );
        ControlPtr pCtlAge = (ControlPtr) FrmGetObjectPtr
        ➥(formP, wIDAge);

        Word wIDSingle = FrmGetObjectIndex (formP,
        ➥MainSinglePushButton );
        ControlPtr pCtlSingle = (ControlPtr) FrmGetObjectPtr
        ➥(formP, wIDSingle);

        Word wIDMarried = FrmGetObjectIndex (formP,
        ➥MainMarriedPushButton );
```

```
ControlPtr pCtlMarried = (ControlPtr) FrmGetObjectPtr
➥(formP, wIDMarried);

Word wIDDivorced = FrmGetObjectIndex (formP,
➥MainDivorcedPushButton );
ControlPtr pCtlDivorced = (ControlPtr) FrmGetObjectPtr
➥(formP, wIDDivorced);

Word wIDDateofBirth = FrmGetObjectIndex (formP,
➥MainDateofBirthSelTrigger);
ControlPtr pCtlDateofBirth = (ControlPtr) FrmGetObjectPtr
➥(formP, wIDDateofBirth);

CharPtr pAge = CtlGetLabel ( pCtlAge );
CharPtr pDateofBirth = CtlGetLabel ( pCtlDateofBirth );

char szContactMe[20];
char szMarital[50];
char szAge[20];
char szDateofBirth[50];

StrPrintF ( szAge, "Age = %s", pAge );
StrPrintF ( szDateofBirth, "DOB = %s", pDateofBirth );

if ( CtlGetValue ( pCtlContactMe ) )
{
   StrCopy ( szContactMe, "Contact me" );
}
else
{
   StrCopy ( szContactMe, "Do not contact me" );
}
if ( CtlGetValue ( pCtlSingle ) )
{
   StrCopy ( szMarital, "Marital Status = Single" );
}
else if ( CtlGetValue ( pCtlMarried ) )
{
   StrCopy ( szMarital, "Marital Status = Married" );
}
else
{
   StrCopy ( szMarital, "Marital Status = Divorced" );
}


StrPrintF ( szMessage, "%s, %s, %s, %s", szMarital, szAge,
➥szDateofBirth, szContactMe );

PalmMessageBox (MessageBoxAlert, szMessage);

handled = true;
```

continues

LISTING 6.1 CONTINUED

```
        break;
    }

    case MainResetButton:
    {
        ResetForm (formP);
        handled = true;
        break;
    }

}
return handled;
}
```

The main form's event handler (amazingly enough, called `MainFormEventHandler`) is where all the action begins.

Initializing the Form

As you saw in earlier chapters, if you want to be able to trap events that happen while a form is active, you have to supply a form event handler. All main application forms have an event-handler function, and this event handler also processes form initialization. (Contrast this with a modal pop-up dialog, in which form initialization happens before the form event handler receives notification.) The event that signals that the form is coming to life is `frmOpenEvent`. We trap this event and pass control to `MainFormInit`.

`MainFormInit`'s job is to set the initial display state of the various controls on the form. There are two times in the life of the survey form when we want to do this: During form initialization and when the reset button is tapped. We saved ourselves some work and created a single function `ResetForm` to handle both instances.

`ResetForm` is where for each control, we obtain a `ControlPtr`, which is then used in various SDK control functions to set the controls' values. For push buttons and check boxes, we use `CtlSetValue` to set each control's state to 1 or 0. You'll note that we have to explicitly set each push button (radio button) to on or off, even though this behavior is automatic for the user. The programmer has no such luxury. You must set each button manually so that only one button in a group is selected; otherwise, it is possible to select multiple buttons at the same time.

For controls whose values are reflected by their labels, we use `CtlSetLabel`. The two different kinds of user-interface elements in use here are a label (technically not a control at all) and a selector trigger. It is perfectly legal to set a selector trigger's label using

CtlSetLabel. For label objects, you actually cannot use CtlSetLabel. You should use form functions such as FrmCopyLabel and FrmGetLabel to manipulate label objects. Even then, there is some weirdness when trying to change label objects at runtime. I cover fields and labels in depth in Chapter 7, "Labels and Fields."

Trapping Control Events

In MainFormEventHandler, you'll see that we are interested in two events generated by controls: ctlRepeatEvent and ctlSelectEvent. Both events are passed to a common routine MainFormButtonHandler for processing.

ctlRepeatEvent is generated by repeat buttons (and scroll bars) for every half second that the pen remains within the bounds of the control. Because we have two repeat buttons (one each for incrementing or decrementing the age count), we check which one is being tapped by examining the controlID member of the event structure. Then, we simply increment or decrement our age counter, format it as a string, and reset the age label.

CtlSelectEvent is generated when the pen is lifted after having been tapped inside the bounds of a button. We have three buttons for which we care to trap this message: the date-of-birth selector trigger, the submit button, and the reset button. (The marital status radio buttons and the check box also generate these events, but the automatic handling of the events by Palm is sufficient for our purposes.) The selector trigger simply launches into the standard SelectDay API and, upon return resets the label with the new date. The reset button, as we've said, maps to our common ResetForm function.

The submit button requires us to obtain the value for each of the controls on the form and display them to the user in a message box. (We will reuse the PalmMessageBox function that we wrote in Chapter 5, "Interacting with the User: Forms.") This processing is the reverse of what happened at initialization time. Given a ControlPtr to each control, we call either CtlGetValue or CtlGetLabel to obtain the controls' values.

One final note before I close this treatment of buttons: If you're like me, you'll quickly tire of writing the same two lines of code over and over again to obtain a ControlPtr. You might want to add the following function to your (ever-growing) toolbox of utility functions:

```
ControlPtr PalmGetControlPtr (FormPtr formP, Word objID)
{
    ControlPtr p;
    Word wID = FrmGetObjectIndex (formP, objID);
    P = (ControlPtr)FrmGetObjectPtr (formP, wID);
    Return p;
}
```

Summary

This chapter provided a focused look at how the various types of buttons are incorporated in a form. I covered some of the areas in which you must take some not-so-obvious steps to achieve some common user-interface goals. The next chapter moves on to the subject of labels and fields.

CHAPTER 7

Labels and Fields

In many ways, the Palm, and indeed most handheld computers, is best suited for applications that involve simple user transactions. The truth is that although handwriting recognition has come a long way, and Palm's graffiti capability is better than most implementations, entering data directly into the Palm is not something you want to do a whole lot.

The most well-designed Palm applications tend to minimize data entry as a required activity for the user, relying instead on single-tap access and navigation through the application's data. Where the user must create data on the Palm, providing predefined choices via pop-up lists and tables goes a long way toward avoiding unnecessary and cumbersome data entry. It is also worth considering moving the data entry portion of your application to the desktop and providing a conduit that can exchange the data with the Palm.

That said, some situations still call for the ability to record data in the field. Quickly jotting down a memo, scribbling a to-do task before it slips your mind, or adding some notes regarding a client appointment are all compelling needs for the mobile computer user and provide a legitimate reason to include some simple data entry in an application.

This chapter focuses on the primary means for directly accepting textual or numeric user input in a Palm application: the field user-interface object. I also briefly cover the use of label resources as a complementary companion to field objects in forms.

What Is a Label?

I'll tackle the easiest topic first. A label displays noneditable text on a form. Labels are used in a variety of ways, but most labels provide a cue about the user-interface element (field, list, and so on) directly to the right or below the label. For example, on the Expense application's edit form, the Vendor and City fields have labels to their left. There are other uses for labels: a short bit of instruction at the top of a form or a way to get text to the left of a check box (although it will not respond to a tap).

The Palm style guidelines dictate that labels should be right justified and displayed using a bold font. It is also customary to use a colon at the end of the label.

What Is a Field?

A field object is akin to an edit control on Windows: It displays one or more lines of text and provides editing capability via either graffiti strokes in the special graffiti area or direct pen manipulation within the field. Fields are typically distinguished visually from labels by underlines, although it is possible to create a field that is not underlined.

Figures 7.1 and 7.2 show a single-line field and a multiline field in action within a Palm application.

Fields support some fairly advanced features, such as proportional fonts, left and right justification, single-line or multiline editing, cut, copy, and paste, and scrolling. (Note that only vertical scrolling for multiline fields is supported; there's no horizontal scrolling within a single line of text.)

Like a control object, a field object has an associated resource type and a set of SDK functions that let you interact with it in your application. Field objects also handle pen and other system events and pass those events to your code as field events.

FIGURE 7.1

The Expense edit form. The Vendor and City fields show labels and single-line fields.

FIGURE 7.2

The Memo application's New Memo form. Most of the form is devoted to one large multiple-line field.

Using Constructor to Create Labels and Fields

Labels and fields are created in Constructor and are fairly straightforward to define. Labels in particular are almost completely lacking in configurability other than setting the position, size, ID, and text.

Fields are slightly more complicated. Figure 7.3 displays a Constructor session for the Prescription application that we create later in this chapter.

FIGURE 7.3

Creating a field in Constructor.

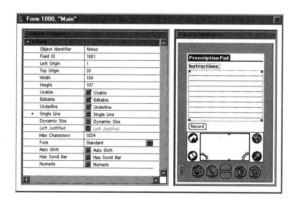

Let's quickly scan the unique attributes for a field resource in Table 7.1.

TABLE 7.1 FIELD RESOURCE ATTRIBUTES

Attribute	Meaning
Editable	If checked, sets the field to be editable. (Makes sense, right?) Although you usually will want to set this attribute, leaving it unchecked can be a handy way to create a programmatically changeable label that is less cumbersome to program than a regular label.
Underline	Also usually checked. If checked, each displayed line of text has a gray underline.
Single Line	Fields can be single line or multiline. Single-line fields do not allow the user to enter text beyond the visible extent of the field. They also do not accept tab or return characters. Multiline fields expand visually as the user enters more text.
Dynamic Size	If this is checked, the number of lines in a multiline field is increased or decreased as characters are added or removed. This setting is only applicable to multiline fields.
Left Justified	It is recommended for consistency that single-line fields be set as left justified. This setting has no effect on multiline fields.
Max Characters	This is the maximum number of characters that a field will accept. Multiline fields will continue to expand in size until they reach this limit. Single-line fields will beep if the limit is reached before the visually displayed field is filled with characters. The maximum possible number of characters in a field is 32,767.
Auto Shift	If this is checked, the field will automatically change the graffiti you enter so that an uppercase letter is substituted after an empty line in a multiline field, after a period or other sentence-terminating punctuation, and after two spaces are recorded.

Using Labels and Fields in Your Application

In many respects, incorporating fields into your application forms is just like the process for any other user-interface object: Create the field as a resource using Constructor, and use the SDK functions to initialize and interact with the field object within your form logic. Although it's not a typical thing that you need to do, you can also respond to events that are passed to you by the field.

Probably the trickiest development issue associated with using fields is that if you want to set the text to be displayed in a field, you actually are responsible for allocating a memory block handle, copying the desired text to the memory block, and passing it to the field. You cannot simply write

```
FldSetText(myfield, "Hello There");
```

Let me qualify that statement. You can actually do something like this, but the consequences are not attractive: The field will not be able to resize the field object's memory if the user changes the text in the field. In this case, the field does not even make a copy of the text; it simply retains the pointer that you pass in. Although it is more cumbersome to deal with memory handles, the downsides of not doing so are too undesirable to consider.

The proper way to set the text for a field object is by calling the field function `FldSetTextHandle()`. Once set, this memory handle is managed by the field object and will even get resized automatically as is necessary based on the user's input (which is subject to the maximum character length set in the field's resource attributes). Keep in mind that if you pass a memory handle to a field object, you are responsible for freeing the field's previously associated memory handle. Confused? Think of it this way: A field object comes with its own memory handle. If you replace it, you should clean up the old one. When the field object is destroyed (usually by the form when it is itself destroyed), the field knows enough to clean up after itself by destroying its own memory handle. One lesson to be learned here is to not intermix memory handles that are passed to fields with memory handles that have a purpose and expected lifetime outside the scope of a field.

When the time comes that you need to get the current text associated with a field object, you can obtain the handle by calling `FldGetTextHandle()`. Again, be careful about ownership of this handle; the field will dispose of it when the field is destroyed.

If you want a specific field object to automatically get the input focus when a form opens, you can use `FrmSetFocus` with the index of the field.

There are many other field behaviors and attributes that you can set using the field functions, but in most applications, it is sufficient to be able to set and get the field value when a form opens and closes.

Just What the Doctor Ordered

To illustrate the use of fields, we'll create a simple form that allows a doctor to write a prescription for a patient on the Palm using the pen stylus and graffiti. (We've all seen how unreadable some handwritten prescriptions are. With our application, as long as our fictional doctor can manage graffiti, we should have no problem reading the doctor's orders!)

Figure 7.4 shows our form in action.

FIGURE 7.4

Sage advice from the good doctor!

Listing 7.1 contains the code for the main form.

LISTING 7.1 THE SOURCE FOR THE MAIN FORM IN "PRESCRIPTION PAD"

```cpp
/*
   FLD_MAI.CPP
   Main form handling functions.
   Copyright (c) Bachmann Software and Services, 1999
   Author: Glenn Bachmann
*/

// System headers
#include <Pilot.h>
#include <SysEvtMgr.h>

// Application-specific headers
#include "fields.h"
#include "fld_res.h"

static void    MainFormInit (FormPtr formP);
static Boolean MainFormButtonHandler (FormPtr formP, EventPtr eventP);
static Boolean MainFormMenuHandler (FormPtr formP, EventPtr eventP);

Word PalmMessageBox ( Word wAlertID, CharPtr pMessage );

/*
   MainFormEventHandler:
   Parms:   pEvent   - event to be handled.
```

```
     Return:   true  - handled (successfully or not)
               false - not handled
*/
Boolean
MainFormEventHandler (EventPtr eventP)
{
   Boolean   handled = false;

   switch (eventP->eType)
   {
      case menuEvent:
      {
         FormPtr formP = FrmGetActiveForm ();
         handled = MainFormMenuHandler (formP, eventP);
         break;
      }

      case ctlRepeatEvent:
      {
         FormPtr formP = FrmGetActiveForm ();
         handled = MainFormButtonHandler (formP, eventP);
         break;
      }
      case ctlSelectEvent:
      {
         // A control button was tapped and released
         FormPtr formP = FrmGetActiveForm ();
         handled = MainFormButtonHandler (formP, eventP);
         break;
      }

      case frmOpenEvent:
      {
         // Main form is opening

         FormPtr formP = FrmGetActiveForm ();

         MainFormInit (formP);

         FrmDrawForm (formP);

         handled = true;
         break;
      }

      default:
      {
         break;
      }
   }
```

7

LABELS AND
FIELDS

continues

LISTING 7.1   CONTINUED

```
    return handled;
}

/*
   MainFormInit:
   Initialize the main form.
   Parms:   formP - pointer to main form.
   Return:  none
*/
void
MainFormInit (FormPtr formP)
{
    // Set the controls to an initial state
}

/*
   MainFormMenuHandler:
   Handle a command sent to the main form.
   Parms:   formP    - form handling event.
            command  - command to be handled.
   Return:  true  - handled (successfully or not)
            false - not handled
*/
Boolean
MainFormMenuHandler (FormPtr /*formP*/, EventPtr eventP)
{
    Boolean handled = false;

    switch (eventP->data.menu.itemID)
    {
       default:
       {
          handled = false;
          break;
       }
    }
    return handled;
}

/*
   MainFormButtonHandler:
   Handle a command sent to the main form.
   Parms:   formP    - form handling event.
            eventP   - event to be handled.
   Return:  true  - handled (successfully or not)
            false - not handled
*/
Boolean
```

```
MainFormButtonHandler (FormPtr formP, EventPtr eventP)
{
   Boolean handled = false;

   switch (eventP->data.ctlEnter.controlID)
   {
      case MainRecordButton:
      {
         Word wIDField = FrmGetObjectIndex (formP, MainNotesField );
         FieldPtr pCtlField = (FieldPtr) FrmGetObjectPtr
         ➥(formP, wIDField);

         // check to make sure there's something in it.
         If (FldGetTextLength(pCtlField>0)
         {
               Handle hText = FldGetTextHandle (pCtlField);
      CharPtr pText = (CharPtr)MemHandleLock (hText);
               PalmMessageBox ( MessageBoxAlert, pText );

                  MemHandleUnlock (hText);
         }
         handled = true;
         break;
      }

   }
   return handled;
}

/*
   PalmMessageBox:

   Toolbox API providing a general-purpose message box function

   Parms: wAlertID = ID of alert to show
          pMessage = ptr to message text to display

   Returns: ID of button chosen by user
*/
Word
PalmMessageBox ( Word wAlertID, CharPtr pMessage )
{
   Word err;

   err = FrmCustomAlert (wAlertID, pMessage, "", "" );

   return err;
}
```

Summary

In this chapter you learned how to deal with labels and fields in a Palm application. Although not the most exciting user interface element, labels and fields are found in almost all applications. With some of the nuances of these elements in mind, you should now have the information you need to quickly add field and label support to your program.

CHAPTER 8

Giving the User a Choice: Lists and Pop-Up Triggers

In the spirit of providing the user with the ability to navigate an application's user interface with a minimum of pen strokes, it is a good idea to present the user with short, predefined choices rather than make them use graffiti to make a choice. Doing so can make using your application a breeze; all the users have to do is tap a few times, and they have the information they need.

Lists are an excellent way of organizing choices for the user. You saw in Chapter 6, "Button Controls," that push buttons are one way to provide a multiple-choice, radio-button–like facility in situations where there are a few, easily recognizable choices (such as the days of the week). Obviously, there are limitations in the number of choices that can be offered using push buttons and the extent to which you can describe each choice in the label area.

In this chapter, you will explore how to use list user-interface elements in your Palm applications. I cover

- Behavior and appearance of lists on the Palm
- Guidelines for the use of lists in your application
- How to create list resources
- How to create pop-up list resources
- How to add list and pop-up list handling to your application code

Lists in the Palm Environment

Lists, or list boxes, are user-interface elements that present the user with a list of choices. The user can select any item in the list with the pen, resulting in that item's display being inverted. List boxes have built-in scrolling, with up and down arrows appearing to the right of the list if the number of items in the list exceeds the displayable area.

Examples of Lists in Action on the Palm

Figure 8.1 shows a list being used in the Palm Set Time form in the Appointments application. The hours and minutes selectors are both list boxes.

FIGURE 8.1

The Set Time form in the Appointments application.

Pop-Up Lists

When combined with a pop-up trigger, a list box becomes a pop-up list. Under Windows, this functionality is bundled as a single unit, called a combo box control. When programming the Palm, you have to put the two pieces together yourself. The initial display of a pop-up list is a single displayed item representing the current selection and a down arrow indicating the availability of more choices. When any part of the pop-up list is tapped (either the arrow or the text), the full list of available choices "drops down." The list stays visible until either an item from the list is tapped or another area of the form is tapped.

Figures 8.2 and 8.3 show a pop-up list in the address book application's edit form before tapping and after the list is popped up.

FIGURE 8.2

The Address Book edit form has a pop-up list for each phone number field that allows you to choose the type of number represented in each field (work, home, fax, and so on).

FIGURE 8.3

The Number Type pop-up list in "popped up" state.

8

GIVING THE USER
A CHOICE

Guidelines for Using Lists in an Application

You should use lists in situations where there are a predefined number of static options. The number of items in your list should be more than one or two; otherwise, consider using push buttons instead.

At the other end of the spectrum, ideally your list will not contain more items than are visible on the list display at one time. Scrolling is a nuisance for the user, and lists also have a shortcoming in the scroll department; they do not automatically scroll when the user chooses the hard scroll button located in the bottom middle row of buttons on the device.

Also note that lists do not provide for advanced features such as in-place editing, nor are they designed to contain other types of user-interface elements such as buttons or bitmaps. This functionality is available with a different type of user-interface element, a table. Tables are covered in Chapter 14, "Tables."

Creating List Resources

List resources are created with the help of Constructor, and if all you need is a simple list, the operation is pretty straightforward. Other than sizing and positioning, the attributes you need in the layout properties pane are Usable, Visible Items, and List Items.

Usable

For normal lists, leave the Usable box checked. For lists to be associated with pop-up triggers, you should uncheck this box so that the list does not draw until triggered.

Visible Items

Set Visible Items to the desired height of the list box display, expressed in terms of the number of items. This attribute is used to vertically size the list on the form, rather than explicitly specify the height in pixels.

List Items

If you know the possible values for your list ahead of time, it can be convenient to directly type them in to the list's resource definition. Highlight the List Items attribute, and choose Edit, New Item Text from the Constructor menu to add a new item. Tab over to the item text, and type in the text for the item. Repeat this process until you have all the items entered. Note that it is perfectly fine to leave List Items blank. Depending on how you will use your list, it might be preferable to set the list items at runtime or at resource design time. Figure 8.4 shows Constructor being used to create a list resource.

FIGURE 8.4

Creating a list resource in Constructor.

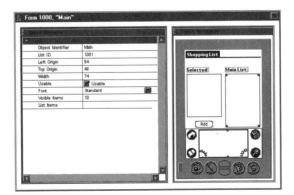

One thing you should know is that there is no built-in sorting capability associated with lists, so you might want to define the list items in the most desirable sort order.

Creating Pop-Up List Resources

Creating a pop-up list requires adding two resources to a form and connecting them: a pop-up trigger button and a list.

First, add a pop-up trigger resource to your form. Give it an object identifier because you will be referring to the pop-up trigger in your application code. Leave the List ID field blank for the moment.

Next, add a list resource to your form, and position it so that its upper-left border corresponds to the upper-left border of the pop-up trigger. Set the Usable attribute to false, type in the list items to be displayed, and set the Visible Items attribute to exactly match the number of items. Also, give the list an object identifier. (It is okay to use the same ID as the one for the pop-up trigger because Constructor will append the object type to your chosen identifier.) Note the List ID attribute for the list resource.

Assign the List ID to the pop-up trigger's list ID attribute. You will find that it is awkward (or impossible) to select the pop-up trigger once the list resource is located on top of it. To get around this, Constructor provides another way to get at resource properties: Under the Layout menu, choose Show Object Hierarchy. This displays a list of resources that are associated with the current form. Clicking a resource brings up the resource's properties just as if you had clicked it on the visual display. Figure 8.5 shows Constructor being used to create a pop-up list resource.

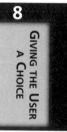

FIGURE 8.5

Creating a pop-up list resource in Constructor.

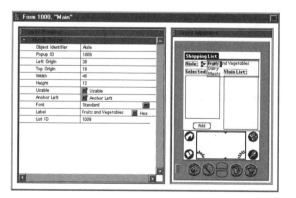

Adding List and Pop-Up List Handling to Your Application

The effort required for supporting lists in your application can range from almost none to moderately extensive. For a list or pop-up list that has a predefined set of items associated with the resource, your only real task is to determine the currently selected item at the proper time in your form's event handling (for example, when the OK button is tapped).

To obtain the currently selected item in a list, you call `LstGetSelection`, passing it the pointer to your list object. This pointer is obtained in the usual way:

```
Word wIDList = FrmGetObjectIndex (pForm, MyList );
ListPtr pList = (ListPtr) FrmGetObjectPtr (pForm, wIDList);
```

Given the list pointer, you obtain the zero-based index of the currently selected item:

```
uIndex = LstGetSelection (pList);
```

Given the index of any item on the list, you can obtain its text:

```
CharPtr pText = LstGetSelectionText (pList, uIndex);
```

This function is somewhat poorly named because it will give you the text associated with the item at index `uIndex`, regardless of whether it is selected.

One shortcoming of the list object is that there is no provision for setting a programmer-defined value to be associated with each list item. You must actually compare the item's text value in order to understand the item selected. This unfortunately results in code such as the following:

```
if (0 == StrCompare (pText, "Red"))
{
    // Item chosen was the red item;
}
else if (0 == StrCompare (pText, "Blue"))
{
    // Item chosen was the blue item
}
else if (0 == StrCompare (pText, "No Color"))
{
    // Item chosen was no color
}
```

If the text in the list item changes, you have to change your code. Keeping this in mind, you might want to isolate this type of comparison code to a helper function that returns a numeric value representing the chosen item. This way, you will have to change only one place in your code. I use this technique in the sample application that you will examine in a moment.

More Complex Handling—Drawing Your Own List

For situations where you want to control the appearance and behavior of lists at runtime, you have a little more work to do. Contrary to what you might expect, there are no `LstAddItem` and `LstRemoveItem` functions that allow you to manipulate list contents on a granular basis. Rather, you must supply the entire list at once using

```
LstSetListChoices (pList, ppItemText, itemCount);
```

`pList` is a pointer to the list object, `ppItemText` is a pointer to an array of text strings, and `itemCount` is the number of items you are passing.

If you hadn't gotten the idea that lists were designed with predefined choices in mind as the primary goal, it should now be crystal clear. It would be a lot of work to create a special array of text pointers and reset the list items every time a dynamic list changed. This type of interface is not terribly conducive to displaying a variable number of database records, for example.

That said, there is a way to work around this problem using a technique called a draw function. In this scenario, you pass `NULL` to `LstSetListChoices` and pass it the number of items you want in the list. Because the list will not know how to draw your list's items without any text, it is up to you to draw it yourself. If you set a draw function using `LstSetDrawFunction`, the list object will call it every time each list item needs to be drawn, passing the zero-based index of the item. You can use this item as an index into your own data storage, which can be an in-memory list, an indexed array of object pointers, a database, or anything you want. This is the technique I adopt in the sample application, and because of its flexibility, I recommend it for any implementation of lists beyond the most basic.

More Complex Handling—Trapping List Events

If you need to trap pen down or up events in a list box, you can do so. `LstSelectEvent` is generated when an item is selected (a pen down followed by a pen up). For more granular control, a `LstEnterEvent` is generated on a pen down, and a `LstExitEvent` is generated on a pen up. Most applications do not need this control, but it's nice to know it's there if you need it.

Pop-Up List Handling

Pop-up lists are slightly different in terms of event handling. For the most part, you will want to know when the user has changed the item selection in the pop-up trigger's associated list. To trap this event, you don't look for an event from the list object. Rather, you look for a popSelectEvent, which is generated each time the user selects an item from a pop-up list. The IDs of both the trigger that generated the event and the associated list object are passed along with the event. You will need the ID of the list object in order to query the new selected item.

A Shopping List Revisited

Back in Chapter 5, "Interacting with the User: Forms," we built a rudimentary shopping list form that allowed the user to use check boxes and push buttons to select items. Unfortunately, the only items this application allowed you to shop for were milk and cookies (hardly the type of diet your doctor would recommend).

Here, you will take another pass at a shopping list application, and in doing so, you will rely heavily on lists and pop-up lists to provide a more extensive set of choices to the user. The user interface for the new version is shown in Figure 8.6. The Selected and Main lists are list boxes that you draw yourself. The Aisle control is a pop-up list.

FIGURE 8.6

The new shopping list application.

As you can see, the application supports different classes of items based on the aisle in which they are located. All available items for the currently selected aisle are displayed in the "main" list on the right side of the form. If you want to add an item to your shopping list, you highlight it and tap the Add button.

The source code that implements the form shown is in Listing 8.1.

LISTING 8.1 THE CODE FOR THE MAIN FORM IN THE SHOPPING LIST APPLICATION

```cpp
/*
    LIST_MAI.CPP
    Main form handling functions.
    Copyright (c) Bachmann Software and Services, 1999
    Author: Glenn Bachmann
*/

// System headers
#include <Pilot.h>
#include <SysEvtMgr.h>

// Application-specific headers
#include "lists.h"
#include "list_res.h"

static void    MainFormInit (FormPtr pForm);
static Boolean MainFormButtonHandler (FormPtr pForm, EventPtr eventP);
static Boolean MainFormMenuHandler (FormPtr pForm, EventPtr eventP);

// Description of a single shopping item
typedef struct
{
    char    szItem[50];
} ShoppingItem;

// Predefined arrays of available shopping items
static ShoppingItem FruitsAndVegetables[] =
{
    { "Apples" },
    { "Lettuce" },
    { "Oranges" },
    { "Strawberries" },
    { 0 }
};

static ShoppingItem Dairy[] =
{
    { "Cheese" },
    { "Milk" },
    { "Orange Juice" },
    { "Yogurt"},
    { 0 }
};

static ShoppingItem Meats[] =
{
    { "Beef" },
    { "Chicken" },
```

8

GIVING THE USER
A CHOICE

continues

LISTING 8.1 CONTINUED

```
     { "Fish"  },
     { "Turkey"},
     { 0 }
};

// Array to hold selected items
static ShoppingItem s_Selected[13];

// Count of how many items are selected thus far
static int s_iNumSelected;

// Local helper functions
void MainFillMainList (FormPtr pForm);
void MainListDrawFunction (UInt itemNum, RectanglePtr bounds,
➥CharPtr *pUnused);

void MainFillSelectedList (FormPtr pForm);
void SelectedListDrawFunction (UInt itemNum, RectanglePtr bounds,
➥ CharPtr *pUnused);

CharPtr MainGetAisleSelection (FormPtr pForm);
CharPtr MainGetMainSelection (FormPtr pForm);

CharPtr MainGetMainText (FormPtr pFrom, Word wSelect);

/*
   MainFormEventHandler:
   Parms:  pEvent   - event to be handled.
   Return: true  - handled (successfully or not)
           false - not handled
*/
Boolean
MainFormEventHandler (EventPtr eventP)
{
    Boolean  handled = false;

    switch (eventP->eType)
    {
       case menuEvent:
       {
          FormPtr pForm = FrmGetActiveForm ();
          handled = MainFormMenuHandler (pForm, eventP);
          break;
       }

       // Note we grab popSelectEvent here to trap the pop-up trigger
       case popSelectEvent:
       case ctlSelectEvent:
       {
```

```
        // A control button was tapped and released
        FormPtr pForm = FrmGetActiveForm ();
        handled = MainFormButtonHandler (pForm, eventP);
        break;
    }

    case frmOpenEvent:
    {
        // Main form is opening

        FormPtr pForm = FrmGetActiveForm ();

        MainFormInit (pForm);

        FrmDrawForm (pForm);

        handled = true;
        break;
    }

    default:
    {
        break;
    }
  }
  return handled;
}

/*
   MainFormInit:
   Initialize the main form.
   Parms:    pForm - pointer to main form.
   Return:   none
*/
void
MainFormInit (FormPtr pForm)
{
    // Get a ptr to the main list
    Word wIDMainList = FrmGetObjectIndex (pForm, MainMainList );
    ListPtr pCtlMainList = (ListPtr) FrmGetObjectPtr (pForm,
    ➥ wIDMainList);

    // Get a ptr to the selected list
    Word wIDSelectedList = FrmGetObjectIndex (pForm, MainSelectedList);
    ListPtr pCtlSelectedList = (ListPtr) FrmGetObjectPtr (pForm,
    ➥ wIDSelectedList);

    // Get a ptr to the aisle (pop-up) list
    Word wIDAisleList = FrmGetObjectIndex (pForm, MainAisleList );
```

8

GIVING THE USER
A CHOICE

continues

LISTING 8.1 CONTINUED

```
    ListPtr pCtlAisleList = (ListPtr) FrmGetObjectPtr (pForm,
    ➥wIDAisleList);

    // Set the combo box to select the first item
    LstSetSelection ( pCtlAisleList, 0 );

    // Fill the main list based on the current aisle
    MainFillMainList (pForm);

    // Set the drawing function for the main list
    LstSetDrawFunction ( pCtlMainList, MainListDrawFunction );

    // Fill the selected list
    MainFillSelectedList (pForm);

    // Set the drawing function for the selected list
    LstSetDrawFunction ( pCtlSelectedList, SelectedListDrawFunction );
}

/*
    MainFillMainList:
    Fills the main list based upon the currently selected aisle
    Parms: pForm - pointer to main form
    Returns: none
*/
void
MainFillMainList (FormPtr pForm)
{
    // Get a ptr to the main list
    Word wIDMainList = FrmGetObjectIndex (pForm, MainMainList );
    ListPtr pCtlMainList = (ListPtr) FrmGetObjectPtr (pForm,
    ➥ wIDMainList);

    int iNumMainChoices = 0;

    // Determine the current aisle
    CharPtr pAisle = MainGetAisleSelection (pForm);

    // Get the count of available main list items from the selected aisle
    if (0 == StrCompare (pAisle, "Fruits and Vegetables"))
    {
        iNumMainChoices = sizeof ( FruitsAndVegetables ) / sizeof
        ➥( ShoppingItem ) - 1;
    }
    else if (0 == StrCompare (pAisle, "Dairy"))
    {
```

```
        iNumMainChoices = sizeof ( Dairy ) / sizeof ( ShoppingItem ) - 1;
    }
    else if (0 == StrCompare (pAisle, "Meats"))
    {
        iNumMainChoices = sizeof ( Meats ) / sizeof ( ShoppingItem ) - 1;
    }

    // Fill the main list based on the combo selection
    LstSetListChoices ( pCtlMainList, NULL, iNumMainChoices );

    // Redraw the list
    LstDrawList (pCtlMainList);

    return;
}


/*
    MainFillSelectedList:
    Fills the shopping selection list
    Parms: pForm - pointer to main form
    Returns: none
*/
void
MainFillSelectedList (FormPtr pForm)
{
    // Get ptr to selected list
    Word wID = FrmGetObjectIndex (pForm, MainSelectedList);
    ListPtr pList = (ListPtr) FrmGetObjectPtr (pForm, wID);

    // Fill the selected list based on how many have been selected so far
    LstSetListChoices ( pList, NULL, s_iNumSelected );

    LstDrawList (pList);

    return;
}


/*
    MainListDrawFunction:
    Draws a single item in the main list
    Parms: itemNum = 0 based index of item to draw
           bound = ptr to rectangle providing drawing bounds
           pUnused = ptr to char string for item to draw. In this app, we
           never give the actual item data to the list, so we ignore
           this parm
    Returns: none
*/
void
MainListDrawFunction (UInt itemNum, RectanglePtr bounds, CharPtr *pUnused)
{
```

8

GIVING THE USER
A CHOICE

continues

LISTING 8.1   CONTINUED

```
    FormPtr pForm = FrmGetActiveForm ();

    // Get the text to be drawn by looking it up in the appropriate
    // aisle
    CharPtr pText = MainGetMainText (pForm, itemNum);

    if ( pText )
    {
        // Draw it
        WinDrawChars (pText, StrLen (pText), bounds->topLeft.x, bounds->
        ➥topLeft.y);
    }
    return;
}

/*
    SelectedListDrawFunction:
    Draws a single item in the selected list
    Parms: itemNum = 0 based index of item to draw
           bound = ptr to rectangle providing drawing bounds
           pUnused = ptr to char string for item to draw. In this app, we
               never give the actual item data to the list, so we ignore
               this parm
    Returns: none
*/

void
SelectedListDrawFunction (UInt itemNum, RectanglePtr bounds,
➥ CharPtr *pUnused)
{
    FormPtr pForm = FrmGetActiveForm ();
    CharPtr pText = NULL;

    // Get the text to be drawn by looking it up in our selected list
    pText = s_Selected[itemNum].szItem;

    if ( pText )
    {
        // Draw it
        WinDrawChars (pText, StrLen (pText), bounds->topLeft.x, bounds->
        ➥topLeft.y);
    }
    return;
}

CharPtr
```

```
MainGetAisleSelection (FormPtr pForm)
{
   Word wID = FrmGetObjectIndex (pForm, MainAisleList);

   ListPtr pList = (ListPtr) FrmGetObjectPtr (pForm, wID);

   Word wSelect = LstGetSelection (pList);

   CharPtr pszSelect = LstGetSelectionText (pList, wSelect);

   return pszSelect;
}

/*
   MainGetMainSelection:
   Gets a ptr to the text representing the currently selected main list
   shopping item
   Parms: pForm
   Returns: ptr to selected item (can be null)
*/
CharPtr
MainGetMainSelection (FormPtr pForm)
{
   CharPtr pText = NULL;

   // Get the selection index from the main list
   Word wID = FrmGetObjectIndex (pForm, MainMainList);
   ListPtr pList = (ListPtr) FrmGetObjectPtr (pForm, wID);
   Word wSelect = LstGetSelection (pList);

   // Get the text at that index in the currently selected aisle
   pText = MainGetMainText (pForm, wSelect);

   return pText;
}

/*
   MainGetMainText:
   Gets a ptr to the text representing an item at index wSelect
   in the main list
   Parms: pForm, wSelect
   Returns: ptr to item (can be null)
*/

CharPtr
MainGetMainText (FormPtr pForm, Word wSelect)
```

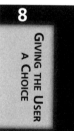

continues

LISTING 8.1 CONTINUED

```
{
   CharPtr pText = NULL;

   // Get the selected aisle
   CharPtr pAisle = MainGetAisleSelection (pForm);

   // Get the selected text based upon the aisle and index
   if (0 == StrCompare (pAisle, "Fruits and Vegetables"))
   {
      pText = FruitsAndVegetables[wSelect].szItem;
   }
   else if (0 == StrCompare (pAisle, "Dairy"))
   {
      pText = Dairy[wSelect].szItem;
   }
   else if (0 == StrCompare (pAisle, "Meats"))
   {
      pText = Meats[wSelect].szItem;
   }
   return pText;
}

/*
   MainFormMenuHandler:
   Handle a command sent to the main form.
   Parms:   pForm     - form handling event.
            command   - command to be handled.
   Return:  true  - handled (successfully or not)
            false - not handled
*/
Boolean
MainFormMenuHandler (FormPtr /*pForm*/, EventPtr eventP)
{
   Boolean handled = false;

   switch (eventP->data.menu.itemID)
   {
      default:
      {
         handled = false;
         break;
      }
   }
   return handled;
}

/*
   MainFormButtonHandler:
   Handle a command sent to the main form.
```

```
   Parms:   pForm    - form handling event.
            eventP   - event to be handled.
   Return:  true  - handled (successfully or not)
            false - not handled
*/
Boolean
MainFormButtonHandler (FormPtr pForm, EventPtr eventP)
{
    Boolean handled = false;

    switch (eventP->data.ctlEnter.controlID)
    {
        case MainAislePopTrigger:
        {
            // The aisle might have changed - refill the list
            MainFillMainList (pForm);

            break;
        }

        case MainAddButton:
        {
            // Get a ptr to the main list
            Word wIDMainList = FrmGetObjectIndex (pForm, MainMainList );
            ListPtr pCtlMainList = (ListPtr) FrmGetObjectPtr (pForm,
            ➥ wIDMainList);

            // Get the text from the main list
            CharPtr pszSelect = MainGetMainSelection (pForm);

            if (pszSelect)
            {
                // Add the item to the selected list
                StrCopy ( s_Selected[s_iNumSelected].szItem, pszSelect);

                // Increment the number of selections
                s_iNumSelected++;
            }

            // Refill selected list
            MainFillSelectedList (pForm);

            handled = true;
            break;
        }

    }
    return handled;
}
```

To make life easier, I created several helper functions that are called from various places in the code:

`MainFillMainList`	Fills the main list box with all the items that are available in the current "aisle"
`MainFillSelectedList`	Fills the shopping list "selected" list with all the items that have been chosen thus far
`MainGetAisleSelection`	Returns the text of the currently selected aisle in the aisle pop-up list
`MainGetMainSelection`	Returns the text of the currently selected item in the main list

Armed with these functions, the rest of the form handling becomes much easier. Let's walk through the main areas of the code that support the shopping list form.

When the form is initialized, I take the opportunity to set the current aisle to the first one ("Fruits and Vegetables"), and then, I call `MainFillMainList`, which proceeds to determine the current aisle and fill the main list with available items. For the demonstration purposes of this simple application, the available items for each aisle are stored in static arrays at the top of the source file. `MainFillMainList` does not pass the text of the items into `LstSetListChoices`. Rather, it passes `NULL` and the total item count. As I've said, if you do this, you will then be responsible for drawing the items yourself. I take care of that by setting the main list's draw function as `MainListDrawFunction`. For completeness, I do the exact same initialization for the selection list (which starts out empty).

Take a look at the two draw functions, `MainListDrawFunction` and `SelectedListDrawFunction`. Each receives an item number representing the item to be drawn and a rectangle that serves to bound the drawing. For the main list, the item number serves as a lookup into the array of available items associated with the currently selected aisle. For the shopping list, the item number is a direct index into the array `s_Selected`. Given the text to draw, I simply call `WinDrawChars`, passing it the text string and the bounds rectangle. (I cover window drawing in more depth in Chapter 9, "Menus.") Again, observe that I could have done anything I wanted with the item number; given how easy it is to code a draw function, I'll take the flexibility of making my own storage decision any day.

Now that the two lists know how to draw themselves (recall that the pop-up aisle list was prepopulated with items in the form resource and thus requires no special draw handling), the only work that remains is to handle changing the selected aisle and tapping the Add button.

Handling a change in aisle selection is easy, now that I've taken the trouble to code a generic routine that re-fills the main list based upon the current aisle. All I have to do is trap the `popSelectEvent` event and call `MainListFillList`. The old list contents are blown away and the list is re-filled.

Handling the Add button is not much more difficult. I trap the button event in the button handler and obtain the text associated with the currently selected main list item. I copy the text into the next available slot in the `s_Selected` array and increment the number of selected items. Then, I call `MainFillSelectedList` to blow away the previous list contents and re-fill from `s_Selected`.

Summary

In this chapter, you were able to review a fairly complex user interface using lists and pop-up lists. With a little bit of effort, you can put the ability to draw your own lists to work for you, resulting in a flexible display that changes based upon the user's selections.

The example presented here, although it's certainly more functional than the earlier button-based version, is still far from complete, and I obviously took some design shortcuts for the sake of clarity and brevity. Adding more functionality (a remove button, a more dynamic means of storing a list, and so on) is left as an exercise for you.

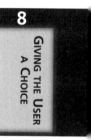

CHAPTER 9

Menus

On most modern graphical user interfaces, menus are one of the primary means of providing the user with the ability to control a program's execution. One of the reasons this is so is that menus are generally ubiquitous: Virtually every application has at least a main menu.

On the Palm, things are a bit different. Palm users place a premium on being able to control their applications with a minimum of pen tapping and user-interface navigating. Tapping a command button once with a pen (or a fingertip) is infinitely preferable to tapping on a menu to have it drop down, finding the menu command you want, and tapping again to execute it.

Nonetheless, menus do have an important role to play in many Palm applications, and there is support in the Palm developer toolset to create simple menu systems. In this chapter, you will come to understand

- How menus are used in the Palm environment
- Guidelines for menu usage in your application
- How to create menu resources
- How to respond to menu events within your application

What Is a Menu?

In general, menus provide a means for a user to control an application's execution by exposing a number of commands corresponding to individual menu items. As I've said, on most platforms menus are one of the main ways to provide this capability through the user interface. The Palm user interface de-emphasizes the importance of the menu system, preferring onscreen buttons as the main command interface. In fact, the menu system is not even visible on Palm applications unless the special menu icon is tapped.

The menu system is usually not visible. Combine that with the fact that it requires multiple pen taps to navigate to a menu item, and it becomes clear that you should design your user interface so that the most important commands in your application are available using one-tap methods, such as buttons, lists, and so on. Good candidates for options that should be placed on menus are preferences dialogs, clipboard commands, and database operations.

The first time you tap a menu button to display an application's menu, the Palm OS automatically displays the top-level menu bar. Every time the menu button is tapped subsequently, it will return to the last displayed menu. This is a helpful convenience that aids in executing the most common commands. Note that once you switch to a different application, Palm OS once again reverts back to displaying only the top-level menu names. After a menu command is executed, or the pen is tapped outside the menu area, the menu bar is dismissed.

Menus in Action on the Palm

Figure 9.1 shows the main menu for the To Do application on the Palm in response to a tap of the menu button.

FIGURE 9.1

The To Do main menu.

Menu Nomenclature

Before you go further, it is important to understand the terms used in the Palm documentation to refer to various menu constructs. This will be especially crucial as you walk through how to create menus in Constructor, which relies heavily on understanding these terms. As you've seen in other chapters, some of the Palm terms can be confusing. Furthermore, some of the terms have different meanings from the same names on other platforms, which I view as significant because most of us come to Palm programming from programming on other computer platforms.

The following definitions should help clarify the main concepts used in the Palm documentation (see Figure 9.2 for an example of each term):

- Menu bar—The menu bar displays the names of each available drop-down menu for the current application view. Note that applications may define different menu bars for different views or forms.

- Menu name—A menu name is the text that appears in the menu bar. When a menu name is tapped, the associated drop-down menu is displayed.

- Menu—This is what drops down below the menu name when it is tapped. The menu is a container for a list of menu items.

- Menu item—A menu item is what is mapped to an actual application command. Menu items can have optional graffiti shortcuts associated with them.

- Shortcut—Although not unique to menus, shortcuts are special graffiti strokes that provide quick access to an application function. You invoke a shortcut by using the special graffiti command stroke (a diagonal move, starting at the bottom left and ending at the top right of the graffiti area), followed by the unique letter associated with the command. The application then responds just as if you chose a menu item.

FIGURE 9.2

The elements of a menu.

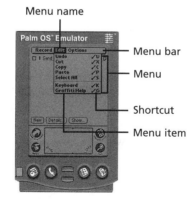

Guidelines for Menu Usage

The Palm user-interface design guides make several recommendations regarding the use of menus in an application. Where applicable, strive for consistency with the built-in applications by using the same menu structure, menu item names, and shortcuts. Provide shortcuts for each menu item. If you have a menu command in common with other applications, use the same shortcut for consistency.

A quick survey of the Palm built-in applications yields the following common menu items shown in Table 9.1.

TABLE 9.1 COMMON MENU ITEMS AND THEIR SHORTCUTS

Menu	Item Name	Shortcut
Record	New	N
	Delete	D
	Beam	B
Edit	Undo	U
	Cut	X
	Copy	C
	Paste	P
	Select All	S
	Keyboard	K
	Graffiti Help	G
Options	Font	F
	Preferences	R

Do not gray out unusable menu items; remove them instead. This rule requires some explanation because there is no way to dynamically add or remove items from a menu. Instead, if your application has modes in which certain commands become unavailable, you need to define multiple versions of your menu resource, one that has the command and one that doesn't, and then manually swap them in and out within your program. An easier alternative is to keep one menu system that contains all the possible commands and simply pop up an alert to the user explaining why the command is unavailable in the current mode.

Use separators to logically group related menu items and distinguish them from other menu items in the same menu. Make the standard copy, cut, and paste clipboard commands available whenever you have a form containing editable fields. In a form with editable fields, you should also make the standard system keyboard dialog and graffiti reference available from your Edit menu. Do not use your menu system to replicate commands that are available onscreen via buttons.

Using Constructor to Create Menus

Constructor is criticized (sometimes unfairly) for having an awkward user interface. When creating menu resources, I am forced to agree with the critics: Creating menu resources in Constructor is an awkward, error-prone adventure for the developer. Fortunately, you will not often edit menu resources during the development life cycle.

Figure 9.3 shows the main Constructor windows involved in creating a menu resource.

FIGURE 9.3

Creating a menu bar in Constructor.

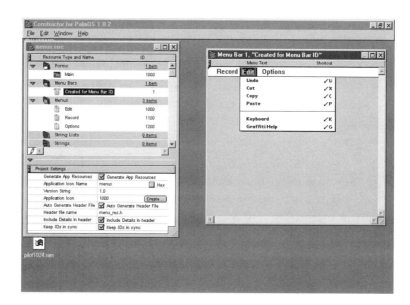

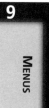

The following steps outline how you use Constructor to create a menu bar and associate it with a form:

1. Open your application's resource in Constructor.

2. Create a new menu bar resource in one of two ways:

   • Click the menu bar's resource type in the main project and choose Edit, New Menu Bar Resource from the main Constructor menu. Type a name for the menu bar resource, and double-click it to open the menu bar resource window.

   • Edit the form you want to associate the menu bar with, and in the Layout Properties Menu Bar ID field, type a unique ID (such as 1). When you press Enter or click outside of the ID field, the Create button to the right of the ID field activates. Click the Create button to open the menu bar resource window.

3. The initial display of the menu bar resource window is not terribly helpful in guiding you to your next step. What you need to do is define your first menu, which will have a menu name—the top-level text that will appear on your menu bar. To do this, choose Edit, New Menu from the Constructor menu. Recall that the entire menu system is called a menu bar, and the individual drop-down lists are called menus.

4. Enter a menu name for the new menu created in Step 3.

5. Create the first menu item for the current menu by choosing Edit, New Menu Item from the Constructor menu. Type the text that should appear on the menu item.

6. Repeat Step 5 for each menu item you want to be associated with the current menu. If you want to create a separator to logically group items, choose Edit, New Separator Item.

7. Repeat Steps 3–6 for each drop-down menu that should appear on your menu bar.

8. For each menu item that you want to associate with a shortcut, you can double-click the menu item to open the Property Inspector window. In the Shortcut key field, enter the single letter to be associated with the menu item.

9. When you are happy with the menu bar, save your resource file.

10. If you created your menu bar resource by starting from a form, your work is done; the new menu bar is associated with the form. If you created your menu bar resource as a standalone menu bar, you should edit the form you want to associate with the menu bar and enter the ID of the menu bar in the Menu Bar ID field.

It's been my experience during this process that it is easy to make mistakes that are not so easily fixed. I am in the habit of saving my work in Constructor often, so I can always abort my current session and return to the last correct version.

I've also learned that it is prudent to design your menu system on paper first and use Constructor to enter the final design once it is solid, rather than interactively play with the menu appearance in Constructor.

If you look at the main project window in Constructor, you will notice that Constructor creates two kinds of resources as a result of your session. The first is a menu bar resource, the ID that you associate with the form. The individual drop-down menus are created as separate menu resources under the menus resource type. If you need to change any part of your menu system, you can either navigate down from the menu bar resource or go directly to the menu resource.

Handling Menu Events in Your Application

You handle menus in your application in much the same way as buttons or other user-interface objects. Like most user-interface objects, menus generate events that are routed to your form's event-handler procedure. Specifically, when the user selects a menu item (via a pen tap or a shortcut), you receive an event of type `menuEvent`.

If you determine in your event handler that you have received a menu event, you can examine the event's `data.menu` pointer to see which menu item was selected. The menu structure has many data members, but the main item of interest is the `itemID` field, which contains the ID of the menu item that was selected by the user. The IDs for your menu system, like all other application resources, are created and stored automatically in your application's resource header file.

Given the selected menu ID, you can take the appropriate action from your event handler and return `TRUE` to the Palm OS, indicating that you have handled the event.

To understand this process, examine a sample application that traps menu selections and simply displays a message box indicating which selection was made. For the vast majority of applications, this is the only type of programming you need to add to handle menus. Figure 9.4 shows an application in action.

FIGURE 9.4

The menus application.

Listing 9.1 shows the code for the application's main form.

LISTING 9.1 THE MAIN FORM CODE FOR THE MENUS APPLICATION

```
/*
   MENU_MAI.CPP
   Main form handling functions.
   Copyright (c) Bachmann Software and Services, 1999
   Author: Glenn Bachmann
*/

// System headers
#include <Pilot.h>
#include <SysEvtMgr.h>

// Application-specific headers
#include "menus.h"        // common app header
#include "menu_res.h"     // resource ids

static void    MainFormInit (FormPtr formP);
static Boolean MainFormButtonHandler (FormPtr formP, EventPtr eventP);
static Boolean MainFormMenuHandler (FormPtr formP, EventPtr eventP);

Word PalmMessageBox ( Word wAlertID, CharPtr pMessage );

/*
   MainFormEventHandler:
   Parms:  pEvent  - event to be handled.
   Return: true  - handled (successfully or not)
           false - not handled
*/
Boolean
MainFormEventHandler (EventPtr eventP)
{
   Boolean  handled = false;

   switch (eventP->eType)
   {
      case menuEvent:
      {
         FormPtr formP = FrmGetActiveForm ();
         handled = MainFormMenuHandler (formP, eventP);
         break;
      }

      case ctlSelectEvent:
      {
         // A control button was tapped and released
         FormPtr formP = FrmGetActiveForm ();
         handled = MainFormButtonHandler (formP, eventP);
```

```
            break;
        }

        case frmOpenEvent:
        {
            // Main form is opening

            FormPtr formP = FrmGetActiveForm ();

            MainFormInit (formP);

            FrmDrawForm (formP);

            handled = true;
            break;
        }

        default:
        {
            break;
        }
    }
    return handled;
}

/*
   MainFormInit:
   Initialize the main form.
   Parms:   formP - pointer to main form.
   Return:  none
*/
void
MainFormInit (FormPtr formP)
{
    // Set the controls to an initial state
}

/*
   MainFormMenuHandler:
   Handle a command sent to the main form.
   Parms:   formP     - form handling event.
            command   - command to be handled.
   Return:  true  - handled (successfully or not)
            false - not handled
*/
Boolean
```

continues

LISTING 9.1 CONTINUED

```c
MainFormMenuHandler (FormPtr /*formP*/, EventPtr eventP)
{
    Boolean handled = false;

    switch (eventP->data.menu.itemID)
    {
        case RecordNew:
        {
            PalmMessageBox (MessageBoxAlert, "New Record");
            break;
        }
        case RecordDelete:
        {
            PalmMessageBox (MessageBoxAlert, "Delete Record");
            break;
        }
        case RecordPurge:
        {
            PalmMessageBox (MessageBoxAlert, "Purge");
            break;
        }
        case EditUndo:
        {
            // Get the currently active field object, and call the FldUndo
            // API
            PalmMessageBox (MessageBoxAlert, "Undo");
            break;
        }
        case EditCut:
        {
            // Get the currently active field object, and call the FldCut
            // API
            PalmMessageBox (MessageBoxAlert, "Cut");
            break;
        }
        case EditCopy:
        {
            // Get the currently active field object, and call the FldCopy
            // API
            PalmMessageBox (MessageBoxAlert, "Copy");
            break;
        }
        case EditPaste:
        {
            // Get the currently active field object, and call the FldPaste
            // API
            PalmMessageBox (MessageBoxAlert, "Paste");
            break;
        }
```

```
      case EditKeyboard:
      {
         // Invoke the keyboard dialog, with the default keyboard
         // NOTE: this only works if there is a field object with
         // the focus!
         // SysKeyboardDialog (kbdDefault);
         PalmMessageBox (MessageBoxAlert, "Keyboard");
         break;
      }
      case EditGraffitiHelp:
      {
         // Invoke the graffiti ref dialog, with the default reference
         SysGraffitiReferenceDialog (referenceDefault);
         break;
      }
      case OptionsAboutMenus:
      {
         // Invoke the graffiti ref dialog, with the default reference
         PalmMessageBox (MessageBoxAlert, "About");
         break;
      }
      default:
      {
         handled = false;
         break;
      }
   }
   return handled;
}

/*
   MainFormButtonHandler:
   Handle a command sent to the main form.
   Parms:   formP     - form handling event.
            eventP    - event to be handled.
   Return:  true  - handled (successfully or not)
            false - not handled
*/
Boolean
MainFormButtonHandler (FormPtr formP, EventPtr eventP)
{
   Boolean handled = false;

   switch (eventP->data.ctlEnter.controlID)
   {
      default:
      {
         handled = false;
         break;
      }
   }
```

9

MENUS

continues

LISTING 9.1   CONTINUED

```
    return handled;
}

/*
    PalmMessageBox:

    Toolbox API providing a general purpose message box function

    Parms: wAlertID = ID of alert to show
           pMessage = ptr to message text to display

    Returns: ID of button chosen by user
*/
Word
PalmMessageBox ( Word wAlertID, CharPtr pMessage )
{
    Word err;

    err = FrmCustomAlert (wAlertID, pMessage, "", "" );

    return err;
}
```

The action starts in MainEventHandler, where I trap events of type menuEvent. I route these events to the menu event handler MainFormMenuHandler, passing it a pointer to the form object as well as a pointer to the event itself.

Inside MainFormMenuHandler, I switch on the menu object's itemID field and trap each menu item ID that I am interested in. In this basic application, for the most part, I simply call the handy PalmMessageBox function to alert the user about which menu item was selected.

I have also provided some placeholders for handling common menu items related to the clipboard and field objects. If you have editable field objects on your form, you should support an undo operation, cut, copy, and paste clipboard operations, and the keyboard dialog and graffiti help.

Although you do have to write specific code to handle undo and clipboard operations, the code is boilerplate and easy to write. Built-in Palm functions directly correspond to each operation. When you receive an undo, cut, copy, or paste menu item, you should determine the form object that currently has the input focus (if any) by performing the following calls:

```
FrmGetActiveForm
FrmGetFocus
```

If an object on the form has the input focus (in which case, FrmGetFocus returns something other than noFocus), you can determine the object's type by calling FrmGetObjectType. If the object type is frmFieldObj, then call FrmGetObjectPtr to obtain the currently active field object.

If a field object has the input focus, you pass the object's pointer to the corresponding Palm field function as in Table 9.2.

TABLE 9.2   CLIPBOARD-RELATED FIELD FUNCTIONS

Operation	Field Function
Undo	FldUndo
Cut	FldCut
Copy	FldCopy
Paste	FldPaste

It's even easier to handle a request for the onscreen keyboard: Call the Palm function SysKeyboardDialog(). Note that this function will only work if it senses there is an active field object to type into.

To handle a request for graffiti help, once again Palm provides the function: SysGraffitiReferenceDialog().

Summary

This chapter essentially provides all the information most developers will ever need to know to incorporate menus into their applications. Although some aspects of designing the user interface can be cumbersome, menu handling is fairly straightforward once you work out all of the naming conventions and tool usage issues.

Although the Palm developer toolkit features more advanced techniques to manually load menus from resources and dispose of them, the built-in applications do not use them, and the vast majority of developers can get what they need without ever calling them.

9

MENUS

CHAPTER 10

Drawing Graphics

Most Palm applications take advantage of forms and other Palm user-interface resource types in presenting and managing their appearance. However, for whatever reason, some developers need to create new resource types of their own. Some graphics-oriented programs also need to use what we often refer to as "graphics primitives." In many situations, it is more convenient to bypass fields, labels, and such and render text output directly on the device display.

This chapter covers

- The characteristics of the Palm display
- Graphics primitives such as lines, rectangles, and bitmaps
- The Palm OS windowing model
- Multiple window issues

The Palm Display

As I emphasize many times throughout this book, the Palm display imposes unique restrictions on what you can do with your user-interface designs. Let's start by reviewing the physical characteristics of the Palm display:

- The current Palm display is limited to 160 pixels wide by 160 pixels high.
- There currently is no color support on any Palm device.
- Grayscale is not officially supported as of this writing, although headers in the Palm SDK indicate this support is coming. For now, your safest bet is to assume a pure monochrome display where each pixel is either black and white.

If you ponder these characteristics for a minute or two, you'll quickly realize that many of the attributes of modern graphical user interfaces are either not possible or (at best) are not well supported on the Palm device. There is simply not enough screen real estate to warrant support for sophisticated multiple-window handling, 3D graphics, or realistic icons and bitmaps.

Although the Palm's display support has not changed much since the device's introduction, you should be careful not to design your application so that it depends on the aforementioned screen characteristics of the currently shipping Palm devices. Things are moving extremely fast in the handheld device market: Battery and display technology continues to improve, and competitive pressures and customer demands will only increase.

Although Palm Computing has continued to stress simplicity and battery life over fancy screen technologies, there can be no doubt that at least some of the future Palm devices will improve upon the current screen support. The "unofficial" grayscale support in the current SDK is certainly evidence that the current display is not the final word from Palm Computing.

Lest you despair, I'll stop talking about what the device doesn't support and move on to examine the support that is there.

Graphics Primitives

The Palm OS supports a set of basic, raw functions for rendering graphics on the Palm display. Before you get all excited, let me warn you: Don't look for functions that draw circles, curved lines, polygons, or triangles. They don't exist, although you could certainly (with some effort) build these capabilities yourself.

Basically, you can use the Palm SDK to draw lines, rectangles, text, and bitmaps. Let's examine how to use each of these capabilities.

Lines

The following functions provide line-drawing support:

```
WinDrawLine

WinDrawGrayLine

WinEraseLine

WinFillLine
```

WinDrawLine is the most basic function. You pass WinDrawLine the x,y coordinates of two points: the start of the line and the end of the line. Lines drawn using WinDrawLine are a single pixel in width and are drawn in black. In fact, lines drawn by any of these functions are a single pixel in width. If you need to draw thicker lines, you must call WinDrawLine twice, shifting the coordinates for the second call by one pixel.

WinDrawGrayLine accepts the same parameters as WinDrawLine and draws a line that appears "gray." This gray appearance is achieved by alternating each pixel along the length of the line, producing a dotted line.

WinEraseLine will "erase" lines by drawing a line using the screen background "color" as the drawing color.

WinFillLine is the most flexible, but correspondingly hardest to use, line-drawing function. WinFillLine takes the same parameters as the other line functions but uses the current fill pattern to render the line. You will encounter patterns again in the discussion of rectangles, so it's worth examining what it means to set the current pattern.

Fill Patterns

You can set the current pattern on the Palm by calling the function WinSetPattern. WinSetPattern takes one parameter, a CustomPatternType. You might be disappointed (as I was) when you realize that a custom pattern type is simply an array of four words. Because a word is 2 bytes long, you wind up with a structure that represents 8 bytes, or 64 bits. Interpreted visually as a set of eight bytes stacked vertically, you get a binary pattern eight bits (pixels) wide by eight bits (pixels) high.

Because you can define any pattern you want in this 8×8 matrix, this is obviously a flexible drawing mechanism. Unfortunately, that flexibility comes with a cost: You might spend an inordinate amount of time doing binary math with a pencil and paper in coming up with the four words that represent your pattern. Other graphics systems provide common predefined values that map to either well-known colors or patterns. One could argue it would have been nice for the folks at Palm Computing to have defined such qualities as gray, light gray, and dot-dash-dot, but they didn't, so you have to.

Once you've determined the magic four-word sequence that will produce the desired pattern, you set it by calling WinSetPattern. To be a good citizen, you should first call WinGetPattern to obtain the current pattern so that you can restore it after you are done drawing.

Rectangles

You draw rectangles by calling one of the following functions:

```
WinDrawRectangle
WinEraseRectangle
WinFillRectangle
```

These functions are parallel to those that support line drawing. Instead of a set of x,y coordinates, the rectangle functions take a pointer to a `RectangleType` structure. Rectangles contain a "top-left" member, which defines the upper-left x,y coordinate, and an "extent" member, which defines how many pixels the rectangle extends in the vertical and horizontal directions. Be careful not to confuse the extent member with an absolute coordinate that defines the bottom-right corner of the rectangle; it's not.

Rectangles are always drawn filled with no border. Thus, `WinDrawRectangle` draws a solid black-filled rectangle. `WinFillRectangle`, as is the case with `WinFillLine`, fills the rectangle with the current pattern as set by `WinSetPattern`.

If you want to draw a rectangle without filling the rectangle's interior, use the `WinDrawRectangleFrame` function.

Drawing Text

Palm OS has basic character-drawing support in the Windowing functional area. This support is supplemented by functions in the Font function family.

To render text on the display, you use `WinDrawChars`, which takes a character string, a string length, and an x,y coordinate as parameters. The x,y coordinate represents the upper-left corner of the first character to be drawn.

There is no out-of-the-box support for advanced features such as text justification or word-wrapping, although again, you can use the existing Palm functions to build this capability. The Font function family will give you what you need to develop this kind of support by providing such information as the width in pixels of text represented in a given font.

Bitmaps

You draw bitmaps using the function `WinDrawBitmap`. `WinDrawBitmap` expects a pointer to a bitmap and an x,y coordinate representing the top-left corner of the display area where the bitmap should be drawn.

Bitmaps are defined as resources, so you create them using Constructor (or a compatible third-party resource utility). Given a bitmap resource, you must first load the bitmap using DmGetResource (*bitmapRsc, resourceID*), where *bitmapRsc* tells Palm that you want a resource of type bitmap and *resourceID* is the ID assigned to your bitmap by Constructor. If successful, DmGetResource returns a valid bitmap handle, which can be turned into a pointer via MemHandleLock. (More on the memory and database managers later in Chapter 17, "Palm OS Memory Management.")

The Palm OS Window Model

You will not find sophisticated windowing support in the Palm SDK. Rather, you will find a set of windowing primitives that, with a little bit of work and understanding, can provide the foundation for whatever windowing you want to support in your application.

What Is a Window?

Although I haven't made a point of it, I've already covered some forms of windowing: Forms are actually based on the windows API! Simply put, a window in the Palm OS is an object that has a rectangular dimension and is positioned either directly on the screen or offscreen. A form can be considered a window that has a lot of extra action, but you can use the windowing APIs to interact with the display area of a form.

Assuming you have any user interface at all in your program, there is always at least one window associated with the display. Usually, this window is both the "active" window and the "draw" window.

The draw window is the window to which all graphics-drawing functions render their output. The coordinate system of the draw window is window-relative, meaning that if two windows divide the screen in half vertically, each window has a coordinate space that begins at 0,0.

An active window has been set to respond to user actions such as pen strokes; it receives all user input. No other window can receive user input while another window is currently active. By default, setting the active window also sets the draw window.

Why would you create one or more windows in your application? Windows simplify your drawing logic by allowing you to use a window-specific coordinate system without worrying about drawing outside the bounds of the window (although there is a bug in the 3.0 implementation of the window-clipping functionality that can cause drawing to occur outside the window).

10

DRAWING GRAPHICS

Creating a Window

You create a window by calling the function `WinCreateWindow`. You place windows on the display by setting the Bounds parameter. The Frame parameter allows you to set whether your window will have a visible frame and, if so, how thick it will be. The Modal parameter indicates that the window is, well, modal (sorry!). If you were building up your own modal dialog-like window, you might set the Modal parameter to `TRUE`. The Focusable parameter indicates that the window is capable of being the active window and thus can receive user input.

In contrast to most other Palm functions, the `WinCreateWindow` function contains an Out parameter that receives an error value, if any. (Most Palm functions pass back errors via the return code.)

One "gotcha" in creating a window is that the window will not automatically draw its own frame: You must manually call `WinDrawWindowFrame` after creating your window if you want to immediately see a border on your window.

Also, note that the coordinate system associated with a window does not automatically omit the width of the window frame. You must offset your drawing within the window by the width of the frame, or else you will draw on top of your frame.

Speaking of coordinates, you can obtain the width and height of the current draw window by calling `WinGetWindowExtent`. It is highly recommended that if you are going to do any graphics drawing on the display, you do not rely on the current 160×160 scheme, but rather, you retrieve the extent of the screen display via `WinGetDisplayExtent`. This feature allows you to write code that will work on future Palm devices that might have larger screens.

Multiple Windows

You can create multiple windows, each having separate (or overlapping) locations on the screen. You can also use `WinCreateOffscreenWindow` to create an offscreen window for rendering graphics offscreen and quickly swapping display bits in and out (which is useful for such things as animation).

In a multiple-window display, you must manually set each window to be the draw window before drawing on it by calling `WinSetDrawWindow`.

PalmDraw: A Graphics-Drawing Demonstration Program

Now that I've covered the majority of the graphics and windowing functionality in Palm OS, I put some of that knowledge to work in a demonstration program. PalmDraw demonstrates the use of graphics and multiple windows by dividing the Palm display into four quadrants, each containing a window. Each of the four windows demonstrates one of the areas of graphics drawing that I've covered in this chapter: lines, rectangles, text, and bitmaps.

Figure 10.1 illustrates PalmDraw's four-quadrant display.

FIGURE 10.1

Multiple windows on the Palm display.

The code for implementing the main form's windowing and drawing functionality appears in Listing 10.1.

LISTING 10.1   THE MAIN FORM CODE FOR PALMDRAW

```
/*
   DRAW_MAI.CPP
   Main form handling functions.
   Copyright (c) Bachmann Software and Services, 1999
   Author: Glenn Bachmann
*/

// System headers
#include <Pilot.h>
#include <SysEvtMgr.h>

// Application-specific headers
#include "draw.h"
```

continues

LISTING 10.1 CONTINUED

```c
#include "draw_res.h"

static void    MainFormInit (FormPtr formP);
static Boolean MainFormButtonHandler (FormPtr formP, EventPtr eventP);
static Boolean MainFormMenuHandler (FormPtr formP, EventPtr eventP);

static void  DrawLines ( void );
static void  DrawRectangles ( void );
static void  DrawBitmap ( void );
static void  DrawText ( void );

/*
   MainFormEventHandler:
   Parms:   pEvent   - event to be handled.
   Return:  true  - handled (successfully or not)
            false - not handled
*/
Boolean
MainFormEventHandler (EventPtr eventP)
{
    Boolean  handled = false;

    switch (eventP->eType)
    {
       case menuEvent:
       {
          FormPtr formP = FrmGetActiveForm ();
          handled = MainFormMenuHandler (formP, eventP);
          break;
       }

       case ctlSelectEvent:
       {
          // A control button was tapped and released
          FormPtr formP = FrmGetActiveForm ();
          handled = MainFormButtonHandler (formP, eventP);
          break;
       }

       case frmOpenEvent:
       {
          // Main form is opening

          FormPtr formP = FrmGetActiveForm ();

          MainFormInit (formP);

          FrmDrawForm (formP);
```

```
            handled = true;
            break;
        }

        default:
        {
            break;
        }
    }
    return handled;
}

/*
   MainFormInit:
   Initialize the main form.
   Parms:   formP - pointer to main form.
   Return:  none
*/
void
MainFormInit (FormPtr formP)
{
    // Set the controls to an initial state
    // Create the windows: two on top, one below
    RectangleType rect;
    Word wErr;
    WinHandle whUpperLeft, whUpperRight, whBottomLeft, whBottomRight,
    ➥whOrig;
    SWord dwWidth = 160;
    SWord dwHeight = 160;

    WinGetDisplayExtent ( &dwWidth, &dwHeight );

    // Upper left
    rect.topLeft.x = 1;
    rect.extent.x = ( dwWidth / 2 ) - 1;
    rect.topLeft.y = 20;
    rect.extent.y = 60;
    whUpperLeft = WinCreateWindow ( &rect, simpleFrame, false, false,
    ➥&wErr );

    whOrig = WinSetDrawWindow ( whUpperLeft );
    WinDrawWindowFrame ( );
    WinSetDrawWindow ( whOrig );

    // Upper right
    rect.topLeft.x = dwWidth / 2;
    rect.extent.x = ( dwWidth / 2 ) - 1;
    rect.topLeft.y = 20;
    rect.extent.y = 60;
```

continues

10

DRAWING GRAPHICS

LISTING 10.1   CONTINUED

```
whUpperRight = WinCreateWindow ( &rect, simpleFrame, false, false,
➥ &wErr );
WinSetDrawWindow ( whUpperRight );
WinDrawWindowFrame ( );
WinSetDrawWindow ( whOrig );

// Bottom left
rect.topLeft.x = 1;
rect.extent.x = ( dwWidth / 2 ) - 1;
rect.topLeft.y = 80;
rect.extent.y = 60;
whBottomLeft = WinCreateWindow ( &rect, simpleFrame, false, false,
➥ &wErr );
WinSetDrawWindow ( whBottomLeft );
WinDrawWindowFrame ( );
WinSetDrawWindow ( whOrig );

// Bottom right
rect.topLeft.x = dwWidth / 2;
rect.extent.x = ( dwWidth / 2 ) - 1;
rect.topLeft.y = 80;
rect.extent.y = 60;
whBottomRight = WinCreateWindow ( &rect, simpleFrame, false, false,
➥ &wErr );
WinSetDrawWindow ( whBottomRight );
WinDrawWindowFrame ( );
WinSetDrawWindow ( whOrig );

WinSetDrawWindow ( whUpperLeft );
DrawLines ();

WinSetDrawWindow ( whUpperRight );
DrawRectangles ();

WinSetDrawWindow ( whBottomLeft );
DrawText ();

WinSetDrawWindow ( whBottomRight );
DrawBitmap ();

WinSetDrawWindow ( whOrig );
}

/*
   DrawLines:
   Draws sample lines
   Parms: none
   Returns: none
*/
```

```
void
DrawLines ( void )
{
   SWord wX, wY;

   // Get the bounds of the current draw window
   WinGetWindowExtent ( &wX, &wY );

   // Single solid line
   // Draw from one point to another
   WinDrawLine ( 1, 10, wX -2, 10 );

   // Double solid line
   WinDrawLine ( 1, 20, wX -2, 20 );
   WinDrawLine ( 1, 21, wX -2, 21 );

   // Single gray line
   WinDrawGrayLine ( 1, 30, wX -2, 30 );

   // Patterned lines
   CustomPatternType patternOld;
   CustomPatternType patternDotted = { 0xAAAA, 0xAAAA, 0xAAAA,
 ➥ 0xAAAA };
   CustomPatternType patternDashed = { 0xCCCC, 0xCCCC, 0xCCCC,
 ➥ 0xCCCC };

   WinGetPattern ( patternOld );

   // Single dotted line
   WinSetPattern ( patternDotted );
   WinFillLine ( 1, 40, wX -2, 40 );
   WinSetPattern ( patternOld );

   // Single dashed line
   WinSetPattern ( patternDashed );
   WinFillLine ( 1, 50, wX -2, 50 );
   WinSetPattern ( patternOld );

   return;
}

/*
   DrawRectangles:
   Draws sample rectangles
   Parms: none
   Returns: none
*/
void
```

continues

10

DRAWING GRAPHICS

LISTING 10.1   CONTINUED

```
DrawRectangles ( void )
{
    SWord wX, wY;
    RectangleType rect;

    // Get the bounds of the current draw window
    WinGetWindowExtent ( &wX, &wY );

    // Black Rectangle
    rect.topLeft.x = 1;
    rect.extent.x = wX - 2;

    rect.topLeft.y = 10;
    rect.extent.y = 20;
    WinDrawRectangle ( &rect, 0 );

    // Filled pattern rectangle
    CustomPatternType patternOld;
    CustomPatternType patternDotted = { 0xAA55, 0xAA55, 0xAA55, 0xAA55 };

    rect.topLeft.y = 35;
    rect.extent.y = 20;
    WinGetPattern ( patternOld );
    WinSetPattern ( patternDotted );
    WinFillRectangle ( &rect, 0 );
    WinSetPattern ( patternOld );

    return;
}

/*
    DrawBitmap:
    Draws sample bitmaps
    Parms: none
    Returns: none
*/
void
DrawBitmap ( void )
{
    VoidHand hBitmap;

    hBitmap = DmGetResource ( bitmapRsc, HappyBitmap );

    if ( hBitmap )
    {
```

```
      BitmapPtr pBitmap;
      SWord wX, wY;

      // Get the bounds of the current draw window
      WinGetWindowExtent ( &wX, &wY );

      pBitmap = (BitmapPtr)MemHandleLock ( hBitmap );
      WinDrawBitmap ( pBitmap, wX / 2 - 8, 22 );
      MemHandleUnlock ( hBitmap );

      DmReleaseResource ( hBitmap );
   }

   return;
}

/*
   DrawText:
   Draws sample text
   Parms: none
   Returns: none
*/
void
DrawText ( void )
{
   WinDrawChars ( "Hello Palm!", StrLen ( "Hello Palm!" ), 10, 30 );

   return;
}

/*
   MainFormMenuHandler:
   Handle a command sent to the main form.
   Parms:   formP    - form handling event.
            command  - command to be handled.
   Return:  true   - handled (successfully or not)
            false  - not handled
*/
Boolean
MainFormMenuHandler (FormPtr /*formP*/, EventPtr eventP)
{
   Boolean handled = false;

   switch (eventP->data.menu.itemID)
   {
      default:
      {
```

continues

10

DRAWING GRAPHICS

LISTING 10.1   CONTINUED

```
            handled = false;
            break;
        }
    }
    return handled;
}

/*
    MainFormButtonHandler:
    Handle a command sent to the main form.
    Parms:    formP    - form handling event.
              eventP   - event to be handled.
    Return:   true  - handled (successfully or not)
              false - not handled
*/
Boolean
MainFormButtonHandler (FormPtr formP, EventPtr eventP)
{
    Boolean handled = false;

    switch (eventP->data.ctlEnter.controlID)
    {
        default:
        {
            handled = false;
            break;
        }
    }
    return handled;
}
```

The code for PalmDraw is fairly simple: Step through the most interesting areas of the code to see how things are done.

Setting Up for Multiple Windows

Things get set up in the main form handler's Init handler. The first thing I do is call WinGetDisplayExtent to obtain the width and height of the display for safety:

```
SWord dwWidth = 160;
   SWord dwHeight = 160;

   WinGetDisplayExtent ( &dwWidth, &dwHeight );
```

I then create four windows, representing four quadrants within the display's region, by setting up a structure for the bounding rectangle and calling `WinCreateWindow`:

```
// Upper left
RectangleType rect;
WinHandle whUpperLeft, whUpperRight, whBottomLeft, whBottomRight,
➡ whOrig;

   rect.topLeft.x = 1;
   rect.extent.x = ( dwWidth / 2 ) - 1;
   rect.topLeft.y = 20;
   rect.extent.y = 60;
```

Finally, I force Palm to draw the windows' frames by setting the current draw window, drawing the frame, and then restoring the draw window to what it was:

```
   whOrig = WinSetDrawWindow ( whUpperLeft );
   WinDrawWindowFrame ( );
   WinSetDrawWindow ( whOrig );
```

The Line-Drawing and Rectangle-Drawing Windows

Once the windows are set up, I set each window in turn to be the current draw window, and I render the appropriate graphics on the window. The following segment is from the `DrawLines` function for handling the upper-left window:

```
SWord wX, wY;

   // Get the bounds of the current draw window
   WinGetWindowExtent ( &wX, &wY );

   // Single solid line
   // Draw from one point to another
   WinDrawLine ( 1, 10, wX -2, 10 );

   // Double solid line
   WinDrawLine ( 1, 20, wX -2, 20 );
   WinDrawLine ( 1, 21, wX -2, 21 );

   // Single gray line
   WinDrawGrayLine ( 1, 30, wX -2, 30 );

   // Patterned lines
   CustomPatternType patternOld;
```

```
CustomPatternType patternDotted = { 0xAAAA, 0xAAAA, 0xAAAA, 0xAAAA };
CustomPatternType patternDashed = { 0xCCCC, 0xCCCC, 0xCCCC, 0xCCCC };

WinGetPattern ( patternOld );

// Single dotted line
WinSetPattern ( patternDotted );
WinFillLine ( 1, 40, wX -2, 40 );
WinSetPattern ( patternOld );

// Single dashed line
WinSetPattern ( patternDashed );
WinFillLine ( 1, 50, wX -2, 50 );
WinSetPattern ( patternOld );
```

You can see that I obtain the window's width and height and adjust the draw calls as appropriate to account for the single pixel frame width. The patterned line drawing illustrates the use of SetFillPattern. (The dashed line pattern values came from using good old pencil and paper and a binary layout of a two-byte word structure.)

The logic for the rectangle-drawing window is similar to the line-drawing logic, so I won't bother to review it as well.

The Text-Drawing Window

The text window is handled by a single WinDrawChars call:

```
WinDrawChars ( "Hello Palm!", StrLen ( "Hello Palm!" ), 10, 30 );
```

I wasn't looking to get fancy for this demonstration application, but you could certainly spend some time with the Fnt functions and attempt to properly center the text within the window.

The Bitmap-Drawing Window

The bitmap-drawing window is a bit more complicated, but only because it requires us to manually load a bitmap resource and deal with memory handle locking and unlocking:

```
VoidHand hBitmap;

    hBitmap = DmGetResource ( bitmapRsc, HappyBitmap );

    if ( hBitmap )
    {
```

```
      BitmapPtr pBitmap;
      SWord wX, wY;

      // Get the bounds of the current draw window
      WinGetWindowExtent ( &wX, &wY );

      pBitmap = (BitmapPtr)MemHandleLock ( hBitmap );
      WinDrawBitmap ( pBitmap, wX / 2 - 8, 22 );
      MemHandleUnlock ( hBitmap );

      DmReleaseResource ( hBitmap );
   }
```

If I were to do a lot of bitmap manipulation, I would cut myself a break and whip up some helper functions:

```
Void
PalmDrawBitmap (Word wBitmapID, Sword x, Sword y)
{
   VoidHand hBitmap;

   hBitmap = DmGetResource ( bitmapRsc, wBitmapID );

   if ( hBitmap )
   {
      BitmapPtr pBitmap;

      pBitmap = (BitmapPtr)MemHandleLock ( hBitmap );
      WinDrawBitmap ( pBitmap, x, y );
      MemHandleUnlock ( hBitmap );

      DmReleaseResource ( hBitmap );
   }
   return;
}
```

There—no more worrying about resource loading or the possibility of not locking or unlocking memory!

Summary

Palm OS provides a basic set of graphics primitives that let you render lines, rectangles, text, and bitmaps on the display. A similar set of windowing functions are useful for creating drawing regions on or offscreen but are somewhat awkward to use.

Nevertheless, it is my expectation that as time goes on, the graphics and windowing model for at least some future Palm devices will grow and gain support for more advanced constructs. In the meantime, if you need to add drawing to your application, Palm provides enough raw tools for you to build your own utility functions.

10

DRAWING GRAPHICS

CHAPTER 11

Handling Pen Events

This chapter takes a look at how to directly handle pen events as they occur on the Palm display. Most applications never need to look at pen events, but developers of drawing programs, graphics applications, or games probably want to be able to take action based on events generated by pen movements.

I examine the events that are associated with pen strokes and then create two sample applications that demonstrate what you can do with these events.

What Is a Pen Event?

The three pen events are penDownEvent, penMoveEvent, and penUpEvent. These events are sent by the Event Manager to your form when the pen is tapped, moved, or lifted on the palm display.

The penDownEvent event is generated by the user touching the pen down in the display area. It passes to you the x/y coordinates of the pen relative to the current window. (Windows and coordinate spaces are discussed in Chapter 10, "Drawing Graphics.")

The penUpEvent event is sent when the user lifts the pen from the display. As with penDownEvent, you are passed the x/y coordinates of the pen. In addition, you are also passed the x/y coordinates of the beginning of the pen stroke (which should be the same as the coordinates passed in the last penDownEvent). Note that the start and end coordinates are in display coordinates and are not window-relative.

The penMoveEvent event is sent when the pen is down and it is moved on the display. You are passed the x/y coordinates relative to the current window.

How Pen Events and Control Events Coexist

It might have occurred to you that if you attempt to trap all the pen events that occur on the display, any controls or other user-interface elements on your form will not be able to process the pen events for their own purposes. Well, you are correct. If your form's event handler traps penDown events and returns TRUE, the penEvent will never be translated into a ctlSelectEvent (or other user-interface event). It is your responsibility to be aware of the location of the user-interface elements on your form, and to return false from your event handler if you detect a pen event in those locations.

The best advice I've seen in this situation is to divide the screen into regions, some of which contain user-interface elements that need to process their own pen events. Track the coordinates of those regions you should process pen events for and others for which you should pass the event back to the event dispatcher. If you carefully check the x/y coordinates passed to you in the event handler, your pen movements should be able to coexist peacefully with other user-interface elements.

What About Graffiti?

Although they are both driven by pen strokes, pen events actually have nothing to do with graffiti. Graffiti occurs when the user performs pen strokes in the special graffiti area on the Palm device. Capturing pen events does not interfere with the Palm's ability to perform graffiti handwriting recognition, nor will graffiti pen strokes generate pen events on your form.

Graffiti activity is handled directly by the Graffiti Manager, which translates pen strokes into key events. These key events are then passed into your application via the normal event loop mechanism.

Palm SDK functions allow you to interact in some ways with the Graffiti Manager and its dictionary handling. For instance, it is possible to trap a penUpEvent from the application display area and ask Graffiti Manager to process the stroke (see GrfProcessStroke) and "manually" translate it into a key event. This is in fact what the Graffiti tutorial does when it needs to recognize your strokes.

Doodle: A Pen-Drawing Program

The amount of paper wasted every day by idle doodlers in meetings around the world is abominable. Let's do something about that, and create an electronic doodle pad that doesn't waste precious trees.

Our program is called doodle, and it does its magic with very little coding. If by now you have guessed that we will implement doodle by taking advantage of pen events, you have guessed right.

Figure 11.1 shows what doodle looks like after a few pen strokes; the code for the main form appears in Listing 11.1.

FIGURE 11.1

Doodling away.

LISTING 11.1 SOURCE CODE FOR THE MAIN FORM OF DOODLE

```
/*
   DRAW_MAI.CPP
   Main form handling functions.
   Copyright (c) Bachmann Software and Services, 1999
   Author: Glenn Bachmann
*/

// System headers
#include <Pilot.h>
#include <SysEvtMgr.h>

// Application-specific headers
#include "draw.h"
#include "draw_res.h"

static void    MainFormInit (FormPtr formP);
static Boolean MainFormButtonHandler (FormPtr formP, EventPtr eventP);
```

continues

LISTING 11.1   CONTINUED

```
static Boolean MainFormMenuHandler (FormPtr formP, EventPtr eventP);

// Variables to track the last known pen position
static UInt s_x = 0;
static UInt s_y = 0;

static Boolean s_bPenDown = false;

/*
   MainFormEventHandler:
   Parms:   pEvent   - event to be handled.
   Return:  true   - handled (successfully or not)
            false - not handled
*/
Boolean
MainFormEventHandler (EventPtr eventP)
{
   Boolean  handled = false;

   switch (eventP->eType)
   {
      case menuEvent:
      {
         FormPtr formP = FrmGetActiveForm ();
         handled = MainFormMenuHandler (formP, eventP);
         break;
      }

      case penDownEvent:
      {
         if ( eventP->screenY < 130 )
         {
            s_x = eventP->screenX;
            s_y = eventP->screenY;

            s_bPenDown = true;
            return true;
         }
         else
         {
            return false;
         }
      }

      case penUpEvent:
      {
         if ( s_bPenDown && eventP->screenY < 130 )
         {
            UInt xNew = eventP->screenX;
```

```
      UInt yNew = eventP->screenY;

      WinDrawLine ( s_x, s_y, xNew, yNew );

      s_x = 0;
      s_y = 0;

      s_bPenDown = false;
   }

   break;
}

case penMoveEvent:
{
   // Only do something if the pen is down
   if ( s_bPenDown && eventP->screenY < 130 )
   {
      UInt xNew = eventP->screenX;
      UInt yNew = eventP->screenY;

      WinDrawLine ( s_x, s_y, xNew, yNew );

      s_x = xNew;
      s_y = yNew;
   }
   break;
}

case ctlSelectEvent:
{
   // A control button was tapped and released
   FormPtr formP = FrmGetActiveForm ();
   handled = MainFormButtonHandler (formP, eventP);
   break;
}

case frmOpenEvent:
{
   // Main form is opening

   FormPtr formP = FrmGetActiveForm ();

   MainFormInit (formP);

   FrmDrawForm (formP);

   handled = true;
```

continues

LISTING 11.1   CONTINUED

```
          break;
      }

      default:
      {
          break;
      }
  }
  return handled;
}

/*
   MainFormInit:
   Initialize the main form.
   Parms:   formP - pointer to main form.
   Return:  none
*/
void
MainFormInit (FormPtr formP)
{
   // Set the controls to an initial state
}

/*
   MainFormMenuHandler:
   Handle a command sent to the main form.
   Parms:   formP     - form handling event.
            command   - command to be handled.
   Return:  true  - handled (successfully or not)
            false - not handled
*/
Boolean
MainFormMenuHandler (FormPtr /*formP*/, EventPtr eventP)
{
   Boolean handled = false;

   switch (eventP->data.menu.itemID)
   {
      default:
      {
         handled = false;
         break;
      }
   }
   return handled;
}

/*
   MainFormButtonHandler:
```

```
   Handle a command sent to the main form.
   Parms:    formP    - form handling event.
             eventP   - event to be handled.
   Return:   true  - handled (successfully or not)
             false - not handled
*/
Boolean
MainFormButtonHandler (FormPtr formP, EventPtr eventP)
{
   Boolean handled = false;

   switch (eventP->data.ctlEnter.controlID)
   {
      case MainEraseButton:
      {

         RectangleType rect;
         rect.topLeft.x = 0;
         rect.topLeft.y = 16;
         rect.extent.x = 159;
         rect.extent.y = 136 - rect.topLeft.y;

         WinEraseRectangle ( &rect, 0);
         handled = true;
         break;
      }
      default:
      {
         handled = false;
         break;
      }
   }
   return handled;
}
```

Let's take a look at how doodle does its thing.

To draw on the screen as we move the pen around, we need to know when the pen is down, when it moves, and when it is up, as well as the pen's coordinates in all of these situations. As we've seen, this information is available via the pen events.

The following code processes the penDown event:

```
case penDownEvent:
{
   if ( eventP->screenY < 130 )
   {
      s_x = eventP->screenX;
      s_y = eventP->screenY;
```

```
          s_bPenDown = true;
          return true;
    }
    else
    {
       return false;
    }
}
```

Because we have a button at the bottom of our form, we want to avoid processing penDown events that occur in that region of the screen. We give the button a healthy buffer zone of 30 pixels, hence the test to see if the screenY value is less than 130.

If we care about the penDown event, we set a flag indicating that the pen is down, and we also store the current coordinates in some static variables. No drawing yet—the user has to move the pen first.

Here's our penMove handling:

```
case penMoveEvent:
     {
          // Only do something if the pen is down
          if ( s_bPenDown && eventP->screenY < 130 )
          {
             UInt xNew = eventP->screenX;
             UInt yNew = eventP->screenY;

             WinDrawLine ( s_x, s_y, xNew, yNew );

             s_x = xNew;
             s_y = yNew;
          }
          break;
     }
```

Here, we again check to see whether the y coordinate is less than 130 to avoid conflicts with the push button. If we want the event, we get the new coordinates and draw a line from the last saved pen coordinates to the new coordinates using the window function WinDrawLine. We finish up by again saving the new coordinates in our static variables.

Our penUp event is virtually identical to penMove, except that we also set our pen down flag to FALSE.

A quick word about the pen down flag. As it happens, it is possible to get spurious penUp events when the user taps the buttons located below the bottom of the display area. To combat this problem, we simply refuse to do anything on a penUp if our flag is not set.

All that's left to do is to provide the ability for our electronic doodler to erase his artwork (a handy feature if the boss happens to walk by the old cubicle!). We do this with a normal button event handler, which defines the rectangular region we want to erase (again leaving clearance for the button) and calling the `WinEraseRectangle` function.

Even More Fun: Tic-Tac-Toe

If doodling isn't enough of a time waster for you, not to worry. Now that we understand how to trap pen events, there's no end to the fun we can have. If we add just a little bit more drawing logic to our main form, we can have ourselves a fine game of Tic-Tac-Toe.

We hold on to all of the same pen-handling logic we saw in the last application, so I won't bother to repeat it here. All that's new is the following function, which paints the game board:

```
/*
   DrawGameBoard:
   Redraws the tic tac toe display
   Parms: none
   Returns: none
*/
void
DrawGameBoard ( void )
{
   // Our game area is 120 pixels high,  starts after the title area,
   // And ends above the button area on the bottom
   WinDrawLine ( 53, 16, 53, 136 );
   WinDrawLine ( 106, 16, 106, 136 );

   // Horizontal lines
   WinDrawLine ( 0, 56, 159, 56 );
   WinDrawLine ( 0, 96, 159, 96 );
   return;
}
```

To render the initial game board, we call this function from our form's initialization routine:

```
/*
   MainFormInit:
   Initialize the main form.
   Parms:   formP - pointer to main form.
   Return:  none
*/
void
MainFormInit (FormPtr formP)
{
   // Set the controls to an initial state
   DrawGameBoard ();
}
```

Finally, when we erase the form in response to the button, we are obligated to redraw the board as well.

Figure 11.2 shows what our game looks like. (I'm X, in case you hadn't guessed.)

FIGURE 11.2

Tic-Tac-Toe: We have a winner!

Summary

For those developers who want to allow users to draw freehand on the display, or for whatever reason require interaction with the user that the standard user-interface controls do not provide, pen events are worth examining.

Some important gotchas come with the territory, such as being aware of the location of your form's controls. But that's typical for software development: The lower you delve into what goes on behind the scenes, the more power you have to control and react to things, but along with that power comes responsibility and the need to be a well-behaved citizen in the use of system resources such as the display.

Databases

IN THIS PART

CHAPTER 12

Understanding Databases

If you've been reading the chapters in this book sequentially, you might have been wondering just how long I was going to put off discussing the topic of databases. The database support on the Palm is one of the most interesting and unique features of the Palm. It is also a topic that sooner or later most application developers need to understand because databases are one of the few ways for a developer to retain information across program invocations. Without databases, all information entered on the Palm would be lost as you switch from application to application.

The focus of this book, however, is giving Palm programmers the knowledge they need to use the Palm SDK in creating real-world applications. Although it is certainly informative to learn about the behind-the-scenes architecture, my feeling is that such a level of detail is not really required for you to begin working with databases. If you really want to learn more, the Palm SDK documentation, as well as a raft of articles and other resources, do a better and more accurate job of presenting that information than I ever could.

The next series of chapters cover various aspects of Palm database programming. I start in this chapter by laying down what I hope is a firm foundation for understanding what databases are on the Palm and how the Palm Data Manager works.

This chapter covers

- The underlying database model for the Palm
- An overview of the Palm Data Manager

- How to create, open, and delete a database

- How to browse the databases on your Palm

- How to obtain information on installed databases

The Palm Database Model

If you are unfamiliar with handheld architectures, you might find the data storage system on a Palm device to be wildly different from anything you've experienced on desktop systems. In reality, if you understand how file systems are implemented on desktop systems, you'll realize that the Palm system is not so far off from those systems. The Palm SDK does expose a bit more of the actual storage model, but essentially, it is similar.

The first surprise is that there is no file system per se. On the Palm, there is no such thing as a generic binary or ASCII file that can be read from and written to as a stream of bytes. Rather, any nonvolatile information is stored in databases.

What Is a Database?

A database is a collection of related records that are read from and written to by one or more Palm applications. A database is not a contiguous file of records; rather, it is a way to organize any number of individual records that can be distributed anywhere in the Palm's nonvolatile memory. The records themselves are actually chunks of memory in the Palm's storage.

Databases are opened, closed, created, and deleted as files are on traditional file systems. For the most part, there is no need for the Palm programmer to be overly concerned with the actual distributed nature of Palm's databases. Simply use the Data Manager's functions and structures to interface with the database, and you should be okay.

What Is a Record?

The Palm Data Manager organizes all the records associated with a database and provides functions that allow the programmer to create, query, update, and delete those records. The notion of a record on the Palm is fairly loosely defined. Simply stated, a record is a memory chunk that has no implicit structure. The Data Manager has no data dictionary support and has no concept that corresponds to a "field." It is up to the programmer to write application code that correctly interprets the layout of a record. In fact, each record in a database is created according to the size specifications passed by the programmer. It is up to the programmer to correctly size the record according to the requirements of the parent database.

The Palm Data Manager

As you might expect, the Palm Data Manager presents a helpful layer of functionality on top of the physical storage of the data itself. Through approximately 30 functions, the Data Manager helps you create, open, close, delete, and browse databases. It also provides functions for creating, modifying, and deleting records.

Based on this description, you can consider the Data Manager akin to the single-tier or flat-file database systems commonly found on today's PC systems. Perhaps the most well-known examples of such database systems are dBase and Btrieve. Like those systems, the Data Manager gives a Palm application direct access to the database itself and deals with records one at a time. Contrast this system with more advanced systems that support the relational model, referential integrity, SQL access, and set-oriented query and update operations.

Although vendors have announced the intention to bring some of the features of relational database management systems to the Palm, the limitations of the platform make the overhead imposed by these more advanced systems an undesirable tradeoff when the benefits are measured against the speed and memory gains to be made by direct access. One of the costs (there's always a cost!) of this tradeoff is that the responsibility for maintaining the data's integrity lies with each application that manipulates the database.

Using the Data Manager to Create and Manipulate Databases

If your application will need to track and manage data across program executions, you need to create a database.

How Do I Create a Database?

Due to the lack of any data-dictionary–like knowledge, creating a database is actually a simple affair. You effectively create only a database header with which records will later be associated. The Palm function that creates a database is DmCreateDatabase. Take a look at what you have to give DmCreateDatabase for it to work its magic:

```
Err DmCreateDatabase (UInt cardNo, CharPtr nameP, Ulong creator,
➥ Ulong type, Boolean resDB);
```

Each of these parameters requires some explanation:

- cardNo—Today's Palm devices support one and only one memory card. Palm Computing has anticipated the potential need for multiple memory cards, so it has exposed a way for the developer to specify which memory card a database will reside on. Because there is currently only one possible card, you should always pass 0 as the card number.

  Note: It is unclear at this writing how the application developer will be expected to deal with the possibility of multiple memory cards when that support arrives. Will the users be asked to decide where they want the database? Or will the Data Manager be updated to hide the physical location of the database from the programmer and silently manage it behind the scenes? (I'd personally vote for the latter, but last time I checked, I'm not on the voting committee.)

- nameP—This is the human-readable name for the database that can be up to 31 characters long, not counting the NULL terminator. It is used in other Data Manager calls that identify and locate databases on the Palm.

- creator—This is the creator ID that uniquely identifies the parent application. For the purposes of this book, I am using a test ID, but you should visit Palm Computing's Developer Zone Web site, where you can register a guaranteed unique creator ID for your application. Note that this is passed as Ulong, cast from the four-byte character representation.

- type— You can actually create several different types of databases on the Palm. For most applications, the only type you will use is data. You might be interested to know, however, that applications and resources are also stored in databases and have associated types.

  Like the creator ID, the type is actually passed as a Ulong, cast from the data definition.

- resDB—This is simply a Boolean flag that if true indicates a resource database is being created. Most calls to CreateDatabase will leave this as false.

Using Databases

Once you've created a database, the easiest way to open it is to use the DmOpenDatabaseByTypeCreator function. This function takes the same type and creator ID parameters that you used to create the database and also takes a mode parameter that indicates how you want to open the database. Mode constants can be ORed together and can be one or more of the values in Table 12.1.

TABLE 12.1   MODE CONSTANTS USED IN OPENING DATABASES

Mode Constant	Meaning
DmModeReadWrite	Opens the database for read-write access. Use this if you intend to insert, update, or delete database records.
DmModeReadOnly	Opens the database for read-only access.
DmModeLeaveOpen	Leaves the database open even after the application quits.
DmModeExclusive	Prevents other applications from opening the database while this application has it open.

The following example is standard code for determining whether a database exists by trying to open it. If the database does not exist, it is created by the application:

```
s_dbRef = DmOpenDatabaseByTypeCreator ( 'data',
                                         'GBBK',
                                         dmModeReadWrite);

if ( 0 == s_dbRef )
{
   UInt        cardNo;
   // P5. card containing the application database
   LocalID     dbID;
   // P5. handle for application database
   UInt        dbAttrs;
   // P5. database attributes

      // Not there - create it now
   Err err = DmCreateDatabase ( 0,
                       "Glenn Database",
                       'GBBK',
                       'data',
                       false);

   ErrFatalDisplayIf ( err, "Could not create new database.");

   // Let's try again...
      s_dbRef = DmOpenDatabaseByTypeCreator ( 'data',
                                              'GBBK',
                                              dmModeReadWrite);
}
```

The OpenDatabase call returns a DMOpenRef. This is a magic handle that must be used in most subsequent function calls against the database. In particular, when you are ready to close the database, call DmCloseDatabase, passing the DMOpenRef.

Browsing Palm Databases with DBBrowse

You can obtain information on the currently installed databases by walking the database list and calling `DmDatabaseInfo` on each database found.

You can walk the database list in one of two ways: getting the number of databases with `DmNumDatabases` and iterating from 0 to the count or using the `GetFirst/GetNext`-like mechanism in `DmGetNextDatabaseByTypeCreator`. I prefer the latter because it does not force me to propagate the assumption that the memory card number is 0. The card number for the current database is returned to me by the function itself.

The key pieces of information returned by `DmGetNextDatabaseByTypeCreator` are the memory card number and the local database ID of the found database. This ID simply serves to uniquely identify the location of the database on the related memory card number and should be treated as a "magic value."

You can pass the memory card number and local database ID to `DmDatabaseInfo`. In exchange, the Data Manager will give you all sorts of interesting information about the database in question, including the name, the creation data, the version, and so on. You can obtain additional information by calling `DmDatabaseSize`, which returns the number of records and the size of the database in bytes.

Listing 12.1 contains the relevant source code for the sample database browser application DBBrowse. DBBrowse provides for demonstration purposes a minimal message-box–based user interface for walking the databases on your Palm database. For each database, DBBrowse displays the database name, the number of records, and the size of the database in bytes. Figure 12.1 shows DBBrowse in action.

FIGURE 12.1

Walking the Palm database list.

LISTING 12.1   THE MAIN FORMCODE FOR DBBROWSE

```
/*
   MainFormButtonHandler:
   Handle a command sent to the main form.
   Parms:   formP    - form handling event.
            eventP   - event to be handled.
   Return:  true  - handled (successfully or not)
            false - not handled
*/
Boolean
MainFormButtonHandler (FormPtr formP, EventPtr eventP)
{
   Boolean handled = false;

   switch (eventP->data.ctlEnter.controlID)
   {
      case MainOKButton:
      {
         Err err;
         DmSearchStateType state;
         UInt uCardNo;
         LocalID dbID;

         err = DmGetNextDatabaseByTypeCreator (
                                      true, // New search
                                      &state,
                                      'data',    // All types
                                      0,    // All creators
                                      true, // Only latest version
                                      &uCardNo, // Card number
                                      &dbID );
         while ( 0 == err )
         {

            char szName[32];

            Ulong ulNumRecords;

            DmDatabaseInfo ( uCardNo,
                             dbID,
                             szName,
                             0,
                             0,
                             0,
                             0,
                             0,
                             0,
```

continues

LISTING 12.1   CONTINUED

```
                                    0,
                                    0,
                                    0,
                                    0 );

            DmDatabaseSize ( uCardNo,
                             DbID,
                             UlNumRecords,
                             0, 0);

            StrPrintF ( szMessage, "%s %d", szName, ulNumRecords );

            PalmMessageBox ( MessageBoxAlert, szName );


            err = DmGetNextDatabaseByTypeCreator (
                                      false, // Not a new search
                                      &state,
                                      0,     // All types
                                      0,     // All creators
                                      true, // Only latest version
                                      &uCardNo, // Card number
                                      &dbID );
        }

        handled = true;
        break;
    }
    default:
    {
        handled = false;
        break;
    }
  }
  return handled;
}
```

Summary

In this chapter, I introduced the Palm data storage model and showed you how to create, open, and close databases. In addition, you did some spelunking through the Palm's list of databases and learned just what is taking up all that space on your Palm device.

The next few chapters continue to explore the Data Manager in depth.

CHAPTER 13

Palm Databases: Record Management

In the preceding chapter, I introduced the Palm data storage model and walked you through how to use the Data Manager SDK functions to create, open, and close databases. In addition, I briefly covered what a record in a Palm database is.

This chapter presents a closer look at how to deal with the most important component of a Palm database: the records themselves. Specifically, I cover

- How records are associated with databases
- What record management functionality is available in the Palm Data Manager
- How to query and iterate through the records in a database
- How to create, edit, and delete a record

I close out the chapter with a simple database application that illustrates some of these concepts in action.

How Are Databases and Records Connected?

As you saw in Chapter 12, "Understanding Databases," a database is essentially a special block of memory that serves as a "header" record. The actual records in the database are allowed to exist as individual chunks strewn throughout the Palm device's nonvolatile memory storage. There is no need for individual records to be located contiguously, or even remotely near the database header or other records in the same database, as long as they are on the same memory card. (Recall that the Palm device today supports only one card anyway.) How is this possible? How can records be located quickly and efficiently using such a scheme?

The answer is that the database header tracks everything about the database, including not only the number of records, but also a list of all the records themselves. Think of the database header as the troop leader for the database.

The list of records in the database header does not contain the records themselves. Rather, each entry in the record list is a special eight-byte block, which contains the local ID of the record, some attribute bits that track the record's state, a category ID (more on categories in Chapter 15, "Categories"), and a special unique ID for the record.

Lest you get confused, let's differentiate between a record's local ID and its unique ID. The local ID, which I briefly described in the preceding chapter, is used to locate the handle of a record anywhere on a specific memory card. The Palm documentation states that all records for a database must reside on the same memory card as the database header.

The record's unique ID, on the other hand, is used to establish uniqueness within the database itself and is unrelated to the memory used to store the record. In addition, the unique ID is used during desktop synchronization to track records on both sides of the sync process. The Palm documentation states that this unique ID will remain the same no matter how many times a record is updated. Therefore, if you want to refer to another database record within your record (for example, if you have a note associated with a record), you might want to store the unique ID as the "foreign key."

As it turns out, the database header, with the help of its list of record entries, has all the information it needs to locate and get the memory handle for any record in the database. The records themselves contain only the data portion of the record; all control information is embedded in the database header.

Using the Data Manager with Records

The Data Manager hides much of the detail I just described beneath a set of functions that allow you to query, edit, create, delete, and even sort database records.

A key thing to understand is that all these operations are performed "in place." By this, I mean that when you edit a record, you are physically modifying the record as it exists on the device. No temporary copies are made. The same goes for queries; there is no such thing as a result set. The query functions take you from record to record on the physical device. This is why the Palm documentation, as well as many of the other resources on programming the Palm, often lump together the concept of databases and memory management. When you manipulate and iterate through database records, you are dealing directly with memory chunks.

My personal view on this way of looking at databases as memory is that although it is instructional to understand the implementation of databases on the Palm device, it is not a great idea conceptually to assume that when you edit a database record you are directly editing memory. The Data Manager is there for a reason, and one of those reasons is to provide a meaningful representation of databases on a device with limited capacity and storage. My own experience with other platforms and with layers of abstraction tells me that allowing assumptions such as "database record equals memory chunk" to creep into your thinking (and ultimately your program design) might cause you trouble down the road when it just isn't true anymore.

The rest of this chapter covers how to accomplish specific tasks using Data Manager. Keep in mind that the Data Manager encompasses a rather large expanse of functionality, more than I can (or need) to cover here.

Querying Database Records

If you have a database in your hand, odds are that you will want to look at what's inside it. With the Data Manager, the key to opening the door to your records is the DmOpenRef returned from DmOpenDatabase. With a DmOpenRef handle in your possession, there are several ways to get at the records in a database:

- DmFindRecordByID—Given a unique record ID (not a local ID), this returns the index of the matching record.

- DmGetRecord—Given an index to a record, this returns the handle to the record's contents. It also effectively "locks" the record, preventing another call to DmGetRecord on the same record until DmReleaseRecord is called and the record is released. This locking mechanism is enabled by setting an attribute in the database header's record entry called the "busy bit."

- DmQueryRecord—Similar to DmGetRecord in that given an index to a record, it returns the record's handle. The difference is that the record is not "locked" after the call, and calling this function will always return successfully even if another piece of code has locked the record with DmGetRecord. A record handle returned from DmQueryRecord cannot be used to write to the record—you need to use DmGetRecord instead. Finally, because the database header is not updated, this is the fastest way to get a record handle.

- DmQueryNextInCategory—Assuming you are iterating through all the records belonging to a specific category, this function returns the handle to the next record after the passed-in record index. I cover categories in depth in Chapter 15.

- DmSeekRecordInCategory—A more powerful version of DmQueryNextInCategory, this function allows you to search forward or backward within a category and also allows you to jump records from the current record in either direction.

Manipulating Database Records

Data Manager provides many functions that allow you to create, modify, or delete records in a database.

Creating a Record

You create records by calling DmNewRecord. DmNewRecord accepts an index within the database where you want the record placed and a record size. If you specify an index that is greater than the last record in the database, the record is appended to the end.

Modifying a Record

The modification functions require a pointer to a record. With a handle to a record, you obtain the pointer by using MemHandleLock. (In my humble opinion, mixing the database and memory routines is a flaw in the Data Manager APIs.) Other than to lock and unlock the record handle, you should never use the memory manager functions to write to a database record. Many hard-to-find problems can be traced to incorrectly intermixing calls to the memory manager and database APIs, so it is important to remember that they are not interchangeable.

The following functions should be used when modifying a database record:

- DmWrite writes a set of bytes into a record at a specific offset. This is akin to a MemCopy operation and can be used to update the entire record or a portion of it (a field, for example).

- DmSet writes a specific value into a contiguous set of bytes in a record, starting at a byte offset within the record. For instance, if you want to clear a string field of length 6 at offset 10 within a record, so that it contained all null characters, you call DmSet (pRecord, 10, 6, '\0');.

- DmStrCopy is similar to DmWrite but assumes you are copying a string value into a field and accounts for null termination.

Deleting a Record

`DmDeleteRecord` deletes the record from the database, which according to the documentation frees the record itself and sets the special delete bit in the database header's associated record entry. On the next synchronization, the record is then deleted from the device.

Getting Record Information

`DmRecordInfo` is primarily used for obtaining a record's unique ID.

Fish List: A Record Management Sample Application

My son, Nicholas, loves fish: squid, octopuses, sharks, and eels. He knows all their names and can tell you all you ever wanted to know about how they eat, swim, and live in the ocean. Although I can keep up with the more well-known species he throws at me, I'm often stumped when he tries to explain the difference between a gulper eel and a lion fish or between a devil ray and a manta ray.

Partly as a tribute to Nicholas's vast undersea knowledge, and partly as a way for him to teach me more about the creatures living in the deep dark sea, I created a simple application that keeps the names of the fish I want to remember in a special fish database. The user interface for the fish database allows me to see the names of all the fish I've entered so far and lets me add new fish via a simple pop-up AddFish form. Figure 13.1 shows the Fish List in the background with the AddFish form in the foreground.

FIGURE 13.1

Adding a new denizen of the deep to your database.

Although my Fish List application appears simple, there are enough database operations that I decided to isolate the database-manipulation functionality from the main form's user-interface operation. Although this book does not primarily discuss good program design, this separation is a good practice to follow and provides a clean separation between your application's user interface and the underlying data model.

The new module is reco_db.cpp, and Listing 13.1 contains the main database interface functions.

LISTING 13.1 THE SOURCE CODE FOR THE FISHLIST'S RECORD MANAGEMENT INTERFACE

```
/*
   RECO_DB.CPP

   Records application db functions

   Copyright (c) 1999 Bachmann Software and Services, LLC
   Author: Glenn Bachmann
*/

// System headers
#include <Pilot.h>
#include <SysEvtMgr.h>

// Application-specific headers
#include "record.h"
#include "reco_res.h"

#define RECORD_DB_TYPE   ('Data')
#define RECORD_DB_NAME   ("FishDB")

static DmOpenRef       s_dbFish;
static Handle        s_hRec;
static CharPtr       s_pText;
static UInt             s_recordNum = 0;

/*
   FishGetCount:
   Returns the count of records in the fish database
   Parms: none
   Returns: count

*/
UInt
FishGetCount ( void )
{
   UInt uFishCount = 0;
```

```
      if ( s_dbFish )
      {
         uFishCount = DmNumRecords ( s_dbFish );
      }
      return uFishCount;
}

/*
   FishNew:
   Creates a new Fish record
   Parms: none
   Returns: true if record created
*/
Boolean
FishNew ( void )
{
    VoidHand hFish;
    Err         err;
    Char        zero = 0;
    UInt      uIndex = 0;

    // Create a new record in the Fish database
    hFish = DmNewRecord ( s_dbFish, &uIndex, FISH_LENGTH);

    if ( hFish )
    {
        Ptr        p;

        // Get a pointer to the mem block associated with the new record
        p = (Ptr)MemHandleLock (hFish);

        // Init the record by writing a zero
        err = DmWrite ( p, 0, &zero, 1 );

        // Unlock the block of the new record.
        MemPtrUnlock ( p );

        // Remember the index of the current record.
        s_recordNum = 0;

      return true;
    }
    else
    {
      return false;
    }
}

/*
   FishGetFish:
```

continues

LISTING 13.1 CONTINUED

```
   Gets a handle to a Fish record at index uIndex
   Parms: uIndex = 0 based index of record in db
   Returns: NULL or a valid record handle
*/
Handle
FishGetFish ( UInt uIndex )
{
    Err             err;

    s_recordNum = 0;

    err = DmSeekRecordInCategory ( s_dbFish,
                                   &s_recordNum,    // Start at 0
                                   uIndex,
                                   dmSeekForward,   // Seek forward
                                   dmAllCategories);  // All categories

    // Get the record
     s_hRec = (Handle)DmGetRecord ( s_dbFish, s_recordNum );
    if ( s_hRec )
    {
       // Lock it down and get a ptr
        s_pText = (CharPtr)MemHandleLock ( s_hRec );
    }

    return s_hRec;
}


/*
   FishReleaseFish:
   Releases the currently edited fish back to the database
   Parms: none
   Returns: none
*/
void
FishReleaseFish ( void )
{
    // Unlock the record
    if ( s_hRec )
    {
        MemHandleUnlock ( s_hRec );
    }

     // Release the record, not dirty.
     DmReleaseRecord ( s_dbFish, s_recordNum, false);
```

```
      // Reset the current record number
      s_recordNum = 0;

      return;
  }


  /*
      FishGetName:
      Gets the ptr to the fish name field. Because the fish record is
      simply one field, just returns the whole record
      Parms: none
      Returns: ptr to name
  */

  CharPtr
  FishGetName ( void )
  {
      return s_pText;
  }

  /*
      FishSetName:
      Sets the name of the currently edited fish record
      Parms: pName = ptr to new name
      Returns: none
  */
  void
  FishSetName ( CharPtr pName )
  {
      // Lock down the block containing the record
      if ( s_hRec )
      {
          Ptr          p;

          p = (Ptr)MemHandleLock ( s_hRec );

          // Write the name value. Add one to strlen to make sure it's
          // null termed
          Err err = DmWrite ( p, 0, pName, StrLen ( pName ) + 1 );

          MemPtrUnlock ( p );
      }

      return;
  }
  /*
      FishOpen:
```

13

PALM DATABASES:
RECORD
MANAGEMENT

continues

LISTING 13.1   CONTINUED

```
    Opens the Fish database, retaining a ref number to the db for further
    operations
    Parms: none
    Returns: none
*/

void
FishOpen ( void )
{
    // Open the db
    s_dbFish = DmOpenDatabaseByTypeCreator ( RECORD_DB_TYPE,
                                             RECORD_FILE_CREATOR,
                                             dmModeReadWrite);

    if ( 0 == s_dbFish )
    {
        UInt        cardNo;
        // P5. card containing the application database
        LocalID     dbID;
        // P5. handle for application database
        UInt        dbAttrs;
        // P5. database attributes

        // Not there - create it now
        Err err = DmCreateDatabase ( 0,
                        RECORD_DB_NAME,
                        RECORD_FILE_CREATOR,
                        RECORD_DB_TYPE,
                        false);

        // Handle unexpected err
        ErrFatalDisplayIf ( err, "Could not create new database.");

        // Let's try to open it again...
        s_dbFish = DmOpenDatabaseByTypeCreator ( RECORD_DB_TYPE,
                                                 RECORD_FILE_CREATOR,
                                                 dmModeReadWrite);

    }

    return;
}

/*
    FishClose:
    Closes the fish db
```

```
    Parms: none
    Returns: none
*/

void
FishClose ( void )
{
   if ( s_dbFish )
   {
      DmCloseDatabase ( s_dbFish );
      s_dbFish = 0;
   }
   return;
}
```

The design goal for the new database source-code module was to remove the need for the main form user-interface code to fiddle with DmOpenRefs, hide idiosyncrasies of the database functions, and enforce a single way for the application to interface with the fish database. The FishDB API considerably simplifies the code for the main form.

Speaking of the main form, Listing 13.2 shows how it presents the list of fish in the database and the AddFish pop-up form. You'll note that because I separated the database operations, the code is not really all that different from the Shopping List application developed in Chapter 8, "Giving the User a Choice: Lists and Pop-Up Triggers."

LISTING 13.2   THE SOURCE FOR FISHLIST'S MAIN FORM

```
/*
   RECO_MAI.CPP
   Main form handling functions.
   Copyright (c) Bachmann Software and Services, 1999
   Author: Glenn Bachmann
*/

// System headers
#include <Pilot.h>
#include <SysEvtMgr.h>

// Application-specific headers
#include "record.h"
#include "reco_res.h"

static void    MainFormInit (FormPtr formP);
```

continues

LISTING 13.2   CONTINUED

```c
static Boolean MainFormButtonHandler (FormPtr formP, EventPtr eventP);
static Boolean MainFormMenuHandler (FormPtr formP, EventPtr eventP);

// Local helper functions
void MainListFill (FormPtr pForm);
void MainListDrawFunction (UInt itemNum, RectanglePtr bounds,
➥CharPtr *pUnused);

Boolean AddFish ( void );
Boolean AddFish_EventHandler (EventPtr pEvent);

/*
    MainFormEventHandler:
    Parms:  pEvent   - event to be handled.
    Return: true  - handled (successfully or not)
            false - not handled
*/
Boolean
MainFormEventHandler (EventPtr eventP)
{
    Boolean  handled = false;

    switch (eventP->eType)
    {
      case menuEvent:
      {
          FormPtr formP = FrmGetActiveForm ();
          handled = MainFormMenuHandler (formP, eventP);
          break;
      }


      case ctlSelectEvent:
      {
          // A control button was tapped and released
          FormPtr formP = FrmGetActiveForm ();
          handled = MainFormButtonHandler (formP, eventP);
          break;
      }

      case frmOpenEvent:
      {
          // Main form is opening

          FormPtr formP = FrmGetActiveForm ();

          MainFormInit (formP);

          FrmDrawForm (formP);
```

```
            handled = true;
            break;
        }

        default:
        {
            break;
        }
    }
    return handled;
}

/*
   MainFormInit:
   Initialize the main form.
   Parms:   formP - pointer to main form.
   Return:  none
*/
void
MainFormInit (FormPtr pForm)
{
    // Set the controls to an initial state

    // Walk through fish records and fill list
    MainListFill ( pForm );

    // Set the drawing function for the main list
    Word wIDMainList = FrmGetObjectIndex (pForm, MainFishList );
    ListPtr pCtlMainList = (ListPtr) FrmGetObjectPtr (pForm, wIDMainList);
    LstSetDrawFunction ( pCtlMainList, MainListDrawFunction );
}

/*
   MainFormMenuHandler:
   Handle a command sent to the main form.
   Parms:   formP     - form handling event.
            command   - command to be handled.
   Return:  true  - handled (successfully or not)
            false - not handled
*/
Boolean
MainFormMenuHandler (FormPtr /*formP*/, EventPtr eventP)
{
    Boolean handled = false;

    switch (eventP->data.menu.itemID)
    {
        default:
        {
```

continues

LISTING 13.2   CONTINUED

```c
            handled = false;
            break;
        }
    }
    return handled;
}

/*
   MainFormButtonHandler:
   Handle a command sent to the main form.
   Parms:    formP    - form handling event.
             eventP   - event to be handled.
   Return:   true  - handled (successfully or not)
             false - not handled
*/

Boolean
MainFormButtonHandler (FormPtr pForm, EventPtr eventP)
{
    Boolean handled = false;

    switch (eventP->data.ctlEnter.controlID)
    {
        case MainNewButton:
        {
            if ( AddFish () )
            {
                MainListFill ( pForm );
            }

            handled = true;
            break;
        }

        default:
        {
            handled = false;
            break;
        }
    }
    return handled;
}

/*
   MainListFill:
   Fills the fish list
   Parms: pForm - pointer to main form
   Returns: none
*/
```

```
void
MainListFill (FormPtr pForm)
{
    // Get a ptr to the fish list
    Word wIDFishList = FrmGetObjectIndex (pForm, MainFishList );
    ListPtr pCtlFishList = (ListPtr) FrmGetObjectPtr (pForm, wIDFishList);

    // Get the count of available main list items
    int iFishCount = FishGetCount ();

    // Fill the main list
    LstSetListChoices ( pCtlFishList, NULL, iFishCount );

    // Redraw the list
    LstDrawList (pCtlFishList);

    return;
}

/*
    MainListDrawFunction:
    Draws a single item in the main list
    Parms: itemNum = 0 based index of item to draw
           bound = ptr to rectangle providing drawing bounds
           pUnused = ptr to char string for item to draw. In this app, we
           never give the actual item data to the list, so we ignore
           this parm
    Returns: none
*/
void
MainListDrawFunction (UInt itemNum, RectanglePtr bounds,
➥CharPtr *pUnused)
{
    FormPtr pForm = FrmGetActiveForm ();

    CharPtr        pText;
    Handle      hFish = NULL;

    // Find the record at this index
    FishGetFish ( itemNum );

    // Get the fish name
    pText = FishGetName ();

    // Draw it
    if ( pText )
    {
```

continues

LISTING 13.2   CONTINUED

```
        WinDrawChars ( pText, StrLen (pText), bounds->topLeft.x, bounds->
        ➥ topLeft.y);
    }

    // Release it
    FishReleaseFish ();
    return;
}


/*
    AddFish:
    Invokes the Add Fish pop-up form
    Parms:    none
    Return:   none
*/
Boolean AddFish ( void )
{
    // Initialize the form
    FormPtr  pForm = FrmInitForm (AddFishForm);

    // Create a new fish record
     if ( FishNew () )
     {
        // Edit it!
        VoidHand hRecord = FishGetFish ( 0 );

        // Create a mem buffer for the new fish name
        VoidHand hText = MemHandleNew ( FISH_LENGTH );
        CharPtr pText = (CharPtr)MemHandleLock (hText);

        // Default the name of the fish
        StrCopy ( pText, "<new fish>" );
         MemPtrUnlock ( pText );


        Word wIDField = FrmGetObjectIndex ( pForm, AddFishNameField );
        FieldPtr pField = (FieldPtr) FrmGetObjectPtr ( pForm, wIDField);

        // Copy the text into the edit field
          FldSetTextHandle ( pField, (Handle)hText);

        // Display the dialog
        if ( FrmDoDialog (pForm) )
        {
```

```
        // Get the name from the dialog
        hText = FldGetTextHandle (pField);
        CharPtr pText = (CharPtr)MemHandleLock (hText);

        // Set it in the record
        FishSetName ( pText );

         MemPtrUnlock ( pText );
    }

    // Un-edit the fish record, saving changes
    FishReleaseFish ();

    // Destroy the form
    FrmDeleteForm (pForm);

    return true;
  }
  return false;
}
```

Summary

With the ability to create and manage both records and databases, you are well on your way to being able to add database support to your Palm application. You might find, as I did, that after the first couple of attempts, much of the code required for database support becomes fairly boilerplate and can be folded away in a common layer of utility functions that you can use from project to project.

The remainder of the database-oriented chapters examines more advanced database capabilities such as categories, tables, and application preferences.

13

PALM DATABASES:
RECORD
MANAGEMENT

CHAPTER 14

Tables

Presenting large amounts of data is one of the hardest user-interface design problems to solve on a device with a limited display area. Inevitably, your application has more data than can be displayed at one time. The most likely circumstance under which this problem will occur for Palm applications is when you allow the user to browse your application's database records.

You might wonder why tables were not included among the coverage of the other user-interface objects such as buttons and lists. I concluded that although technically not bound to the concept of databases, the most common use of the Palm SDK's table user-interface object is presenting a browser view of an application's database records. I felt justified in covering tables in the context of the discussion of Palm databases.

In this chapter, I cover

- What a table is and what it is used for
- What functionality is supported and not supported in a table
- When to use a table and when to use a list
- How to add support for tables in your program
- Handling scroll bars

I conclude this chapter by presenting an example of a table in action.

What Is a Table?

A table object in many ways visually resembles a grid or spreadsheet interface on many other platforms. It displays rows and columns of data and even lets you directly edit or manipulate cells (more on this later). It appears to be well-suited for tabular data.

Figure 14.1 shows the main view of the Expense application, which employs a table to display your expense records, laid out with columns for date, type, and amount.

Table Functionality

This section gets into more detail about what functionality a table supports.

A table supports the display of a group of cells, organized as rows and columns of data. Each column can represent one of several supported data types: check box, date, time, label, pop-up trigger, numeric, text, text with a note, and narrow text. (Technically, cells in the same column of a table can even have a different data type, but in practice, all cells of a column are set to the same type.)

Some data types can be edited and manipulated directly in their cells. Cells containing check boxes, pop-up triggers, and the various text types allow you to use graffiti to directly select and manipulate their contents.

In addition to the predefined data types, you can use a custom data type to render other kinds of data: custom drawing, bitmaps, and so on.

Although most examples of tables appear to have scroll bars included, in fact scroll bars are a separate type of user-interface element: They have to be added separately. Even more significant, it is up to you as the programmer to coordinate scroll events with the appearance of your table.

Tables "support" vertical scrolling (although you'll see this is not automatic). Tables do not have any support for horizontal scrolling. You cannot scroll columns left and right.

Also, note that there is no user-controlled column-manipulation support; columns cannot be moved or resized using the pen.

When to Use Tables Instead of Lists

On the surface, it would appear that tables are not much more than lists with support for columns. If columns aren't critical to your display needs, why not use a list, especially because (as you'll see) tables are much more complicated to program?

The Palm user-interface guidelines state that you should use lists for making a selection from a set of choices. Following these guidelines contributes to consistency both in your own application and across all applications, resulting in a better experience for the user.

There's another reason, however. Because tables are only aware of the number of rows that they can display at one time, they are much more suited to browsing large numbers of data records. In this sense, they are a kind of "virtual list," like a window that hovers over your data, only showing you what is directly under the window. Lists, on the other hand, must be told how many items they will hold. Technically, you could tell a list it has 2,000 items and rely on the draw function callback to inform you which items must be drawn when. The issue is less black and white when you have, say, 20-odd items to display, and you don't expect significantly more items to be added.

As a rule of thumb, follow the Palm guidelines: Use lists for the presentation of small numbers of items, and use tables for situations where the number of items can grow large and is expected to be variable (as is the case with databases).

Adding Tables to Your Program

Adding a table to your program involves roughly the same steps as adding a list. You add the table to a form using Constructor and then add code as necessary to set up the table and use it in your program. Overall, my experience is that programming with tables is a complicated affair, and the topic of tables is not one of the subjects that the SDK documentation is particularly helpful with. Creating the table resource in Constructor is the easy part, so let's start there.

For such a complex object, adding a table resource to a form in Constructor is actually pretty easy. Simply drag it on to your form, and set the attributes in the Layout Properties pane. The only attributes of note are Editable, Rows, and the Column Widths:

- Editable—This attribute is not described in the Palm documentation for the table resource but is later described under the table objects section. If set, it allows the user to edit the table's contents, assuming that you've programmed the table to permit the user to manipulate its cells.

- Rows—This is the number of rows that you want to be visible in the table. Note that Constructor will adjust the height of the rows to squeeze them all into the height of the table you have specified. Set the number of rows to 50 or 2, and you'll see what I mean. For normal tables, I use a row height of 11 pixels as a guide. A table with a height of 121 pixels that fills most of the display but leaves space for buttons at the bottom of a form works out to 11 rows.

- Column Widths—Here's where you define how many columns you want in your table and how wide they should be. To add a column, highlight the Column Width label in the Layout Properties pane and choose Edit, New Column Width. Widths are specified in pixels. Add as many columns as you will need and do your best to guess how wide each column should be. Unfortunately, Constructor is not aware of the data types that will be used, nor the fonts, nor the width of the data, so it cannot offer more help in this area. Note that you must define all your columns here because there is no way to add them programmatically later.

As a programmer, you have a lot of responsibilities to handle when adding a table to a form. In the following sections, I break the somewhat daunting overall task into manageable chunks. Along the way, I explain why each task is necessary.

Table Initialization

When your form initializes, your job is to set up your table's row and column definitions so that they work correctly later on when it's time to draw them.

It's important to understand before you go any further that the number of rows a table contains has absolutely nothing to do with how many rows of data your program has. This is somewhat counter-intuitive. It is your job to track how far up or down the user has scrolled so that you can draw the correct rows of data into the fixed rows of the table.

During initialization, you need to set the data type associated with each cell for each row in the table. In practice, it's hard to imagine a situation where cells in the same column have different data types, so the following code is fairly standard:

```
Word wRows = TblGetNumberOfRows (pTable);
for (i = 0; i < wRows; i++)
{
   TblSetItemStyle (pTable, i, colno, datatype);
   // Set other columns as well...
   ...
}
```

The column number is a zero-based value and increases for each column, left to right. Rather than embed these numbers everywhere, what I usually do is use #defines to assign "names" to my columns such as COL_LASTNAME and COL_FIRSTNAME. Then, I use the column names rather than the numeric values, making my code much more readable and maintainable.

In addition to setting the data type, you need to mark each column as usable because the default is false. Columns not marked as usable are invisible. You set this attribute by calling the TblSetColumnUsable function.

Like columns, rows also are marked either usable or unusable, with unusable rows being invisible (meaning they are not drawn). At this point in table initialization, you have not yet associated table rows with the data, so the safest thing to do is to set each row to be unusable using the TblSetRowUsable function. A good example of when you set a row to be unusable is if you have a table with 11 rows but only 10 rows of data. You set the 11th row to unusable.

The last task in setting up your table is to set any custom-handling functions for your columns. For columns of type customTableItem, you need to set a draw function using TblSetCustomDrawProcedure for the column. This function is a callback and is similar to what you saw in Chapter 8, "Giving the User a Choice: Lists and Pop-Up Triggers." It is called whenever a cell in that column needs to be drawn, passing you the row and column being referenced.

For columns using any of the text data types, which represent editable columns, you need to define a "load" procedure and a "save" procedure. Because cells in these columns essentially are field objects (see Chapter 7, "Labels and Fields"), it is your responsibility to allocate a memory handle for each cell and associate it with the cell when the user goes to edit the data. You do this via TblSetCustomLoadProcedure, which gets called

14

TABLES

when a cell is going to be drawn or is about to be edited. You also get the opportunity to capture changes when the user leaves the cell. For this, you call TblSetCustomSaveProcedure, setting a callback function that will give you the handle to the cell's contents.

Probably the best advice regarding how to handle direct editing of text fields and load and save procedures is to carefully examine how the built-in applications do it. They use a couple of different techniques. For example, the Expense application has an editable Amount field. However, it sets the column's style to custom and actually allocates a new field object on the fly when that area of the table is tapped.

The To Do application, however, uses the text style along with custom load and save procedures. In the load procedure, the actual record handle is retrieved and set as the text cell's memory handle, so in effect, the table's text field is synchronized with the database record field.

Table View Management

Because the table is an "n" row viewport into your data rows, you will have to track yourself the current data row as well as the top-most visible item from your data.

Suppose you have an 11-row table, but you have 22 rows in your database. When you first load your table, you want rows 1 through 11 of your table to correspond with your database rows 1 through 11. If the user scrolls down (I explain scrolling later) by one row, you need to redisplay the table such that it shows rows 2 through 12. This is most easily done by tracking the top visible row along with the current selected row. Any time your table's viewport on the database changes (the user adds or deletes a record or the user scrolls up or down), you re-evaluate which 11 items need to be displayed.

This sounds like a mess, but the following code pretty much takes care of things:

```
Word wIDTable = FrmGetObjectIndex (pForm, MainTableTable );
TablePtr pTable = (TablePtr) FrmGetObjectPtr (pForm, wIDTable);

// Get the number of rows defined in Constructor for the table.
// This is the number that will be visible
Word wRows = TblGetNumberOfRows (pTable);

// This all sets up what the top visible record
// should be
UInt uRecordNum = 0;

// Is there a current record?
if ( s_wCurrentRecord != -1)
{
```

```
      if ( s_wTopVisibleRecord > s_wCurrentRecord )
      {
         // The current record is before the first visible record
         // Force the current record to be the first visible record
         s_wTopVisibleRecord = s_wCurrentRecord;
      }
      else
      {
         // This tries to seek from the top visible record to the
         // last visible record.
         uRecordNum = DmSeekRecordInCategory (pDB,
s_wTopVisibleRecord,
                                    wRows - 1,
                                    dmSeekForward,
                                    dmAllCategories  );

         if ( uRecordNum < s_wCurrentRecord)
         {
            // The last visible record in the table is less than the
            // current record (so the current record is after the visible
            // portion of the table). We need to reset the top
            // visible record such that it is the current record.
            // This is a "scroll down"
            s_wTopVisibleRecord = s_wCurrentRecord;
         }
      }
   }

   // Now adjust to make sure that we have a full number of records even
   // if it's the last screen. If there's less than a screen full left,
   // we have to push TopVisible backwards until there is a full screen
   // left
   uRecordNum = FishGetPrevRecordNum ( dmMaxRecordIndex, wRows - 1);

   s_wTopVisibleRecord = min (s_wTopVisibleRecord, uRecordNum);
```

What this code does is use a couple of static variables s_wCurrentRecord and s_wTopVisibleRecord to set the topmost visible record in the table. It makes two checks to see if it needs to adjust the visible range of records so that the current record will display. First, if the current record is "above" the last visible row of the table, s_wTopVisibleRecord is set to be the current record. Otherwise, you seek forward 11 rows from the record that is currently the topmost visible to check whether the last existing record in the range encompasses the current record. If it doesn't, again you set s_wTopVisibleRecord to be the current record. Finally, because it's nice to always show a screen full of records where possible, if you are at the end of the list of records, you set s_wTopVisible to be the last record minus the number of rows.

14

TABLES

Table Data Mapping

Once you know what range of records will be visible in the table, you need to either set the data for each cell so that the table can draw it or provide a way for the table to get at that data when it is needed.

The first time you get ready to display, and every time after that the values of the records or the range of visible records change, you will walk through the displayable database records and "link" them to the correct rows in the table. How you do this depends on the type of data you have associated with the cell.

For label, date, check box, and numeric cells, you can make the association by directly setting the value for the cell. Use TblSetItemInt or TblSetItemPtr to set the cell's value based on the matching database record's field.

For text cells, use TblSetLoadDataProcedure to associate a function that will be called when the text is drawn or edited. This function passes back a handle to the proper text value. The table takes care of rendering the text.

For custom cells, use TblSetCustomDrawProcedure to associate a callback function that will be called when the cell is about to be drawn. This function is completely responsible for rendering the contents of the cell, much the same way as the draw procedure for lists was.

There's an added step for custom cells: At draw time, you are only passed a row and column to be drawn. You need to figure out which database record is associated with the row. Luckily, you can use the TblSetItemInt function to associate a two-byte value with each row. Although you can use this for anything, you typically will use this to store a record number or index into the database.

The following code illustrates how you would walk through the rows of the table and verify that a database record exists to match each row. In the example, I've elected to set the two columns as custom types. Thus, I set a record number to be associated with the row:

```
UInt uRecordNum = s_wTopVisibleRecord;

// Load records into the table, starting at top visible
// Get the record number of the top visible record
uRecordNum = s_wTopVisibleRecord;

for (i = 0; i < wRows; i++, uRecordNum++)
{
    // Is there a record at this index?
    if (DmQueryRecord ( pDB, uRecordNum ))
    {
```

```
        // Yes there is.
        // Remember the associated record number for this row
        TblSetItemInt (pTable, i, COL_FISH_NAME, uRecordNum);
        TblSetItemInt (pTable, i, COL_FISH_DESC, uRecordNum);
        TblSetRowUsable (pTable, i, true);
    }
    else
    {
        // If we are out of records, mark row as unusable
        TblSetRowUsable (pTable, i, false);
    }
    // Force a row redraw
    TblMarkRowInvalid (pTable, i );
}
```

What data types should you associate with your columns and cells? The answer mostly depends on whether you will be providing direct editing of text within the table itself. If so, you will most likely want to use one of the text data types and rely on the TblSetLoadDataProcedure and TblSetSaveDataProcedure callbacks to set and save the contents of the cell. Even so, there is a lot of other handling you need to put in to trap when the user switches to a different row, pops up another form, and so on.

If you can get away without supporting direct cell editing, your life is much easier. In that case, you can use a combination of directly setting values for numbers, dates, and labels or keep everything consistent, set all cells to custom, and draw them yourself.

Table Drawing

For custom type cells, your draw procedure will be called each time the table needs to draw the cell. You are given a pointer to the table object, the row and column being drawn, and a bounding rectangle to draw in.

Handling the call is fairly straightforward:

```
void
MainListDrawFunction (VoidPtr pTable, Word row, Word column,
➥ RectanglePtr bounds)
{
    FormPtr pForm = FrmGetActiveForm ();

    CharPtr        pText;
    Handle      hRecord = NULL;
    UInt recordNum = 0;

    // Get the record num we are drawing
    recordNum = TblGetItemInt ((TableType *)pTable,
                               row,
                               column );
```

14

TABLES

```
// Find the record at this index
hRecord = DmQueryRecord ( pDB, recordNum );

if ( COL_LASTNAME == column)
{
    // Get the last name from the record
    pText = ....
}
else
{
    // Get another field from the record
    pText = ....
}

// Draw it
  if ( pText )
  {
      WinDrawChars ( pText, StrLen (pText), bounds->topLeft.x,
      ➡ bounds->topLeft.y);
  }
return;
}
```

Given the row's associated record number, it becomes a simple task to obtain the appropriate field from the record and draw it within the bounds supplied.

Given how much work we've seen so far that needs to go into supporting tables, it's hard to believe there can be more, but there is one final thing to handle: scrolling.

You might have been dismayed when I noted at the beginning of the chapter that scrolling support was not part of the table object. Now that you understand the programming model for the table, it is clear that the table has no concept of how many data "rows" are associated with it and thus would not know how to correctly maintain the scroll positions. (I should point out that there are plenty of examples of data-bound grid controls and widgets that solve this problem, but you have to work with what you have.)

You have two options to add scroll handling to your table, using a scroll bar object or adding a set of up-arrow/down-arrow repeat buttons. The built-in applications use repeat buttons on their main table forms, so that's what I do. Note that before you dive into the next section, you might want to refresh your understanding of how to create the repeating arrow buttons by reviewing Chapter 6, "Button Controls."

As you did in Chapter 6, go back into Constructor and define two repeat buttons and place them near the bottom right of your table.

Remember that repeat buttons generate `ctlRepeatEvent` events. You'll need to trap those and update the `w_sTopVisible` variable appropriately. In addition, the Palm unit has physical scroll buttons. These generate special `keyDownEvent` events and should also update the `s_wTopVisible` variable. Here's some code that illustrates the handling necessary:

```
case ctlRepeatEvent:
    if (event->data.ctlRepeat.controlID == MainScrollUpRepeating)
    {
            // Scroll up
        DmSeekRecordInCategory ( pDB, &s_wTopVisible, 1,
        ➥dmSeekBackward, dmAllCategories);
            // Force a reload of records to the table
            .......
    }
    else if (event->data.ctlRepeat.controlID ==
    ➥MainScrollDnRepeating)
    {
            // Scroll down
        DmSeekRecordInCategory ( pDB, &s_wTopVisible, 1,
        ➥ dmSeekForward, dmAllCategories);
            // Force a reload of records to the table
            .......
    }
    break;
case keyDownEvent:
    if (event->data.keyDown.chr == pageUpChr)
    {
            // Scroll up
        DmSeekRecordInCategory ( pDB, &s_wTopVisible, 1,
        ➥ dmSeekBackward, dmAllCategories);
            // Force a reload of records to the table
            .......
        handled = true;
    }
    else if (event->data.keyDown.chr == pageDownChr)
    {
            // Scroll down
        DmSeekRecordInCategory ( pDB, &s_wTopVisible, 1,
        ➥ dmSeekForward, dmAllCategories);
            // Force a reload of records to the table
            .......
        handled = true;
    }
    break;
```

14

TABLES

Putting It All Together: FishTable

To illustrate all the programming steps you've made in this chapter, I put together an update to the FishList program that replaces the list object with a table object. The fish database now has both a name and a description field, so I use two custom draw columns in the table. (For examples of how to employ the other data types in a table, I encourage you to explore the source code for the built-in applications.)

Figure 14.2 shows the main form for the new FishTable program, and Listing 14.1 contains the code.

FIGURE 14.2

The table-driven fish database application.

LISTING 14.1   SOURCE CODE FOR THE MAIN FORM AND THE FISH DATABASE LAYER

```
/*
   TBLS_MAI.CPP
   Main form handling functions.
   Copyright (c) Bachmann Software and Services, 1999
   Author: Glenn Bachmann
*/

// System headers
#include <Pilot.h>
#include <SysEvtMgr.h>

// Application-specific headers
#include "tables.h"
#include "tbls_res.h"

static void    MainFormInit (FormPtr formP);
static Boolean MainFormButtonHandler (FormPtr formP, EventPtr eventP);
static Boolean MainFormMenuHandler (FormPtr formP, EventPtr eventP);

// Local helper functions
void MainListFill (FormPtr pForm);
```

```
void MainListDrawFunction (VoidPtr pTable, Word row, Word column,
➥RectanglePtr bounds);
void MainListCalcTopVisible (FormPtr pForm);

Boolean AddFish ( void );
Boolean AddFish_EventHandler (EventPtr pEvent);

// Current record in the table
static Word s_wCurrentRecord;
static Word s_wTopVisibleRecord;

#define COL_FISH_NAME     0
#define COL_FISH_DESC     1

/*
   MainFormEventHandler:
   Parms:    pEvent   - event to be handled.
   Return:   true  - handled (successfully or not)
             false - not handled
*/
Boolean
MainFormEventHandler (EventPtr pEvent)
{
   Boolean   handled = false;

   switch (pEvent->eType)
   {
      case menuEvent:
      {
         FormPtr pForm = FrmGetActiveForm ();
         handled = MainFormMenuHandler (pForm, pEvent);
         break;
      }


      case ctlSelectEvent:
      {
         // A control button was tapped and released
         FormPtr pForm = FrmGetActiveForm ();
         handled = MainFormButtonHandler (pForm, pEvent);
         break;
      }

      case tblSelectEvent:
      {
         // Set the current record based on user selection

         s_wCurrentRecord = TblGetItemInt ((TableType *)pEvent->
         ➥data.tblSelect.pTable,
                                    pEvent->data.tblSelect.row,
                                    pEvent->data.tblSelect.column );
```

continues

14

TABLES

Listing **14.1** CONTINUED

```
            break;
        }

        // Physical scroll buttons
        case keyDownEvent:
        {
            if (pEvent->data.keyDown.chr == pageUpChr)
                {
              FormPtr pForm = FrmGetActiveForm ();
                 s_wTopVisibleRecord = FishGetPrevRecordNum
                   ➥( s_wTopVisibleRecord, 1 );
              MainListFill ( pForm );
              FrmDrawForm ( pForm );
                 handled = true;
                }
            else if (pEvent->data.keyDown.chr == pageDownChr)
              {
              FormPtr pForm = FrmGetActiveForm ();
                 s_wTopVisibleRecord = FishGetNextRecordNum
                   ➥( s_wTopVisibleRecord, 1 );
              MainListFill ( pForm );
              FrmDrawForm ( pForm );
                 handled = true;
            }
            break;
        }

        case frmOpenEvent:
        {
            // Main form is opening

            FormPtr pForm = FrmGetActiveForm ();

            MainFormInit (pForm);

            FrmDrawForm (pForm);

            handled = true;
            break;
        }

        default:
        {
            break;
        }
    }
```

```
      return handled;
}

/*
   MainFormInit:
   Initialize the main form.
   Parms:   pForm - pointer to main form.
   Return:  none
*/
void
MainFormInit (FormPtr pForm)
{
   // Set the controls to an initial state
   s_wCurrentRecord = -1;

   // Walk through fish records and fill list
   MainListFill ( pForm );
}

/*
   MainFormMenuHandler:
   Handle a command sent to the main form.
   Parms:   pForm     - form handling event.
            command   - command to be handled.
   Return:  true   - handled (successfully or not)
            false  - not handled
*/
Boolean
MainFormMenuHandler (FormPtr /*pForm*/, EventPtr eventP)
{
   Boolean handled = false;

   switch (eventP->data.menu.itemID)
   {
      default:
      {
         handled = false;
         break;
      }
   }
   return handled;
}

/*
   MainFormButtonHandler:
   Handle a command sent to the main form.
   Parms:   pForm     - form handling event.
            eventP    - event to be handled.
```

14

TABLES

continues

LISTING 14.1   CONTINUED

```
     Return:  true  - handled (successfully or not)
              false - not handled
*/

Boolean
MainFormButtonHandler (FormPtr pForm, EventPtr eventP)
{
    Boolean handled = false;

    switch (eventP->data.ctlEnter.controlID)
    {
      case MainNewButton:
      {
        if ( AddFish () )
        {
           MainListFill ( pForm );
           FrmDrawForm ( pForm );
        }

        handled = true;
        break;
      }

       case MainScrollUpRepeating:
       {
           s_wTopVisibleRecord = FishGetPrevRecordNum
           ⮑( s_wTopVisibleRecord, 1 );
         MainListFill ( pForm );
         FrmDrawForm ( pForm );
         break;
       }
       case MainScrollDownRepeating:
       {
           s_wTopVisibleRecord = FishGetNextRecordNum
           ⮑( s_wTopVisibleRecord, 1 );
         MainListFill ( pForm );
         FrmDrawForm ( pForm );
         break;
       }


       default:
       {
         handled = false;
         break;
       }
    }
```

```
      return handled;
}

/*
   MainListFill:
   Fills the fish list
   Parms: pForm - pointer to main form
   Returns: none
*/
void
MainListFill (FormPtr pForm)
{
   // Get a ptr to the fish table
   Word wIDFishTable = FrmGetObjectIndex (pForm, MainFishTable );
   TablePtr pTable = (TablePtr) FrmGetObjectPtr (pForm, wIDFishTable);

   // Init the table

   // Get the number of rows defined in Constructor for the table
   // This is the number that will be visible
   Word wRows = TblGetNumberOfRows (pTable);
   Word i;

   for (i = 0; i < wRows; i++ )
   {
      // Set the cells to have custom drawing
      TblSetItemStyle  (pTable, i, COL_FISH_NAME, customTableItem );
      TblSetItemStyle  (pTable, i, COL_FISH_DESC, customTableItem );

      // Set the row to be unusable to start
      TblSetRowUsable (pTable, i, false);
   }

   // Set the columns to be usable
   TblSetColumnUsable  (pTable, COL_FISH_NAME, true );
   TblSetColumnUsable  (pTable, COL_FISH_DESC, true );

   // Set our draw procedure callback for each column
   TblSetCustomDrawProcedure (pTable, COL_FISH_NAME,
   ➥MainListDrawFunction );
   TblSetCustomDrawProcedure (pTable, COL_FISH_DESC,
   ➥MainListDrawFunction );

   // Reset the top visible row based on size of table and current record
   MainListCalcTopVisible (pForm);

   UInt uRecordNum = 0;

   // Load records into the table, starting at top visible
```

continues

LISTING 14.1   CONTINUED

```c
// Get the record number of the top visible record
uRecordNum = s_wTopVisibleRecord;

for (i = 0; i < wRows; i++, uRecordNum++)
{
    UInt uNextRecordNum = 0;

    if (FishQueryFish ( uRecordNum ))
    {
        // Remember the associated record number for this row
        TblSetItemInt (pTable, i, COL_FISH_NAME, uRecordNum);
        TblSetItemInt (pTable, i, COL_FISH_DESC, uRecordNum);
        TblSetRowUsable (pTable, i, true);
    }
    else
    {
        // If we are out of records, mark row as unusable
        TblSetRowUsable (pTable, i, false);
    }
    // Force a row redraw
    TblMarkRowInvalid (pTable, i );
}

return;
}

/*
    MainListCalcTopVisible:
    Sets the top visible item in the table
    Parms: none
    Returns: none
*/
void
MainListCalcTopVisible (FormPtr pForm)
{
    // Get a ptr to the fish table
    Word wIDFishTable = FrmGetObjectIndex (pForm, MainFishTable );
    TablePtr pFishTable = (TablePtr) FrmGetObjectPtr (pForm, wIDFishTable);

    // Get the number of rows defined in Constructor for the table
    // This is the number that will be visible
    Word wRows = TblGetNumberOfRows (pFishTable);

    // This all sets up what the top visible record
    // should be
    UInt uRecordNum = 0;

    if ( s_wCurrentRecord != -1)
    {
```

```
        if ( s_wTopVisibleRecord > s_wCurrentRecord )
        {
            // The current record is before the first visible record
            // "Scroll up"
            s_wTopVisibleRecord = s_wCurrentRecord;
        }
        else
        {
            // This tries to seek from the top visible record to the
            // last visible record.
            uRecordNum = FishGetNextRecordNum ( s_wTopVisibleRecord,
                                                wRows - 1 );

            if ( uRecordNum < s_wCurrentRecord)
            {
                // The last visible record in the table is less than the
                // current record (so the current record is after the visible
                // portion of the table). We need to reset the top
                // visible record such that it is the current record.
                // This is a "scroll down"
                s_wTopVisibleRecord = s_wCurrentRecord;
            }
        }
    }

    // Now adjust to make sure that we have a full number of records even
    // if it's the last screen. If there's less than a screenful left,
    // we have to push TopVisible backwards until there is a screenful
    // of records
    uRecordNum = FishGetPrevRecordNum ( dmMaxRecordIndex, wRows - 1);

    s_wTopVisibleRecord = min (s_wTopVisibleRecord, uRecordNum);
    return;
}

/*
    MainListDrawFunction:
    Draws a single cell in the main table
    Parms: pTable = table ptr
           row = row of item
           column = cell
           bounds = bounding rectangle for cell
    Returns: none
*/
void
```

continues

LISTING 14.1   CONTINUED

```
MainListDrawFunction (VoidPtr pTable, Word row, Word column,
➥RectanglePtr bounds)
{
   FormPtr pForm = FrmGetActiveForm ();

    CharPtr        pText;
    Handle       hFish = NULL;
   UInt recordNum = 0;

   // Get the record num we are drawing
   recordNum = TblGetItemInt ((TableType *)pTable,
                                 row,
                                 column );

   // Find the record at this index
   FishGetFish ( recordNum );

   if ( COL_FISH_NAME == column)
   {
      // Get the fish name
      pText = FishGetName ();
   }
   else
   {
      // Get the fish desc
      pText = FishGetDesc ();
   }

   // Draw it
    if ( pText )
   {
       WinDrawChars ( pText, StrLen (pText), bounds->topLeft.x, bounds->
       ➥topLeft.y);
   }

   // Release it
   FishReleaseFish ();
   return;
}


/*
   AddFish:
   Invokes the Add Fish popup form
   Parms:    none
   Return:   none
*/
```

```
Boolean AddFish ( void )
{
   // Initialize the form
   FormPtr  pForm = FrmInitForm (AddFishForm);

   // Create a new fish record
    if ( FishNew () )
   {
      // Edit it!
      VoidHand hRecord = FishGetFish ( 0 );

      // Create a mem buffer for the new fish name
      VoidHand hName = MemHandleNew ( FISH_NAME_LEN + 1 );
      CharPtr pName = (CharPtr)MemHandleLock (hName);
      // Default the name of the fish
      StrCopy ( pName, "<new fish>" );
       MemPtrUnlock ( pName );

      // Create a mem buffer for the new fish description
      VoidHand hDesc = MemHandleNew ( FISH_DESC_LEN + 1 );
      CharPtr pDesc = (CharPtr)MemHandleLock (hDesc);
      // Default the desc of the fish
      StrCopy ( pDesc, "" );
       MemPtrUnlock ( pDesc );

      Word wIDName = FrmGetObjectIndex ( pForm, AddFishNameField );
      FieldPtr pNameField = (FieldPtr) FrmGetObjectPtr ( pForm, wIDName);
      // Copy the text into the edit field
        FldSetTextHandle ( pNameField, (Handle)hName);

      Word wIDDesc = FrmGetObjectIndex ( pForm, AddFishDescField );
      FieldPtr pDescField = (FieldPtr) FrmGetObjectPtr ( pForm, wIDDesc);
      // Copy the text into the edit field
        FldSetTextHandle ( pDescField, (Handle)hDesc);

      // Display the dialog
      if ( FrmDoDialog (pForm) )
      {
         // Get the name from the dialog
         hName = FldGetTextHandle (pNameField);
         CharPtr pName = (CharPtr)MemHandleLock (hName);
         hDesc = FldGetTextHandle (pDescField);
         CharPtr pDesc = (CharPtr)MemHandleLock (hDesc);

         // Set it in the record
         FishSetName ( pName );
         FishSetDesc ( pDesc );

          MemPtrUnlock ( pName);
```

14

TABLES

continues

LISTING 14.1   CONTINUED

```
            MemPtrUnlock ( pDesc);
    }

    // Un-edit the fish record, saving changes
    FishReleaseFish ();

    // Destroy the form
    FrmDeleteForm (pForm);

    return true;
    }
    return false;
}

/*
    TBLS_DB.CPP

    Records application db functions

    Copyright (c) 1999 Bachmann Software and Services, LLC
    Author: Glenn Bachmann
*/

// System headers
#include <Pilot.h>
#include <SysEvtMgr.h>

// Application-specific headers
#include "tables.h"
#include "tbls_res.h"

#define TABLES_DB_TYPE   ('Data')
#define TABLES_DB_NAME   ("FishDB")


typedef struct
{
    char szName[FISH_NAME_LEN + 1];
    char szDesc[FISH_DESC_LEN + 1];
} FishRecord;

static DmOpenRef        s_dbFish;
static Handle       s_hRec;
static FishRecord * s_pFish;
static UInt             s_recordNum = 0;

/*
    FishGetCount:
    Returns the count of records in the fish database
```

```
   Parms: none
   Returns: count

*/
UInt
FishGetCount ( void )
{
   UInt uFishCount = 0;
   if ( s_dbFish )
   {
      uFishCount = DmNumRecords ( s_dbFish );
   }
   return uFishCount;
}


/*
   FishNew:
   Creates a new Fish record
   Parms: none
   Returns: true if record created
*/
Boolean
FishNew ( void )
{
   VoidHand hFish;
   Err        err;
   Char        zero = 0;
   UInt      uIndex = 0;

   // Create a new record in the Fish database
   hFish = DmNewRecord ( s_dbFish, &uIndex, sizeof ( FishRecord ) );

   if ( hFish )
   {
      Ptr          p;

      // Get a pointer to the mem block associated with the new record
      p = (Ptr)MemHandleLock (hFish);

      // Init the record by writing a zero
      err = DmWrite ( p, 0, &zero, sizeof ( FishRecord ) );

      // Unlock the block of the new record.
      MemPtrUnlock ( p );

      // Release the record to the database manager.

      DmReleaseRecord ( s_dbFish, uIndex, true);
```

14

TABLES

continues

LISTING 14.1 CONTINUED

```
            // Remember the index of the current record.
            s_recordNum = 0;

        return true;
    }
    else
    {
        // Handle unexpected err
          ErrFatalDisplayIf ( err, "Could not create new record.");

        return false;
    }
}

/*
    FishGetFish:
    Gets a handle to a Fish record at index uIndex
    Parms: uIndex = 0 based index of record in db
    Returns: NULL or a valid record handle
*/
Handle
FishGetFish ( UInt uIndex )
{
    Err              err;

    s_recordNum = 0;

    if ( s_dbFish )
    {
        err = DmSeekRecordInCategory ( s_dbFish,
                            &s_recordNum,     // Start at 0
                            uIndex,
                            dmSeekForward,   // Seek forward
                            dmAllCategories);   // All categories

        // Get the record
         s_hRec = (Handle)DmGetRecord ( s_dbFish, s_recordNum );
        if ( s_hRec )
        {
           // Lock it down and get a ptr
            s_pFish = (FishRecord *)MemHandleLock ( s_hRec );
        }
    }

    return s_hRec;
}

/*
    FishReleaseFish:
```

```
    Releases the currently edited fish back to the database
    Parms: none
    Returns: none
*/
void
FishReleaseFish ( void )
{
    // Unlock the record
    if ( s_hRec )
    {
        MemHandleUnlock ( s_hRec );
    }

     // Release the record, not dirty.
     DmReleaseRecord ( s_dbFish, s_recordNum, false);

    // Reset the current record number
    s_recordNum = 0;

    return;
}


/*
    FishGetName:
    Gets the ptr to the fish name field.
    Parms: none
    Returns: ptr to name
*/

CharPtr
FishGetName ( void )
{
    return s_pFish->szName;
}

/*
    FishGetDesc:
    Gets the ptr to the fish desc field.
    Parms: none
    Returns: ptr to name
*/

CharPtr
FishGetDesc ( void )
{
    return s_pFish->szDesc;
}

/*
    FishSetName:
```

continues

LISTING 14.1 CONTINUED

```
    Sets the name of the currently edited fish record
    Parms: pName = ptr to new name
    Returns: none
*/
void
FishSetName ( CharPtr pName )
{
    // Lock down the block containing the record
    if ( s_hRec )
    {
        Ptr            p;

        p = (Ptr)MemHandleLock ( s_hRec );

        // Write the name value. Add one to strlen to make sure it's
        // null termed
        Err err = DmWrite ( p, 0, pName, StrLen ( pName ) + 1 );

        MemPtrUnlock ( p );
    }

    return;
}

/*
    FishSetDesc:
    Sets the desc of the currently edited fish record
    Parms: pDesc = ptr to new desc
    Returns: none
*/
void
FishSetDesc ( CharPtr pDesc )
{
    // Lock down the block containing the record
    if ( s_hRec )
    {
        Ptr            p;

        p = (Ptr)MemHandleLock ( s_hRec );

        UInt offset = FISH_NAME_LEN + 1;

        // Write the name value. Add one to strlen to make sure it's
        // null termed
        Err err = DmWrite ( p, offset, pDesc, StrLen ( pDesc ) + 1 );

        MemPtrUnlock ( p );
    }
```

```
      return;
}

/*
   FishOpen:
   Opens the Fish database, retaining a ref number to the db for further
   operations
   Parms: none
   Returns: none
*/

void
FishOpen ( void )
{
   // Open the db
    s_dbFish = DmOpenDatabaseByTypeCreator ( TABLES_DB_TYPE,
                                   TABLES_FILE_CREATOR,
                                   dmModeReadWrite);

    if ( 0 == s_dbFish )
    {
      // Not there - create it now
        Err err = DmCreateDatabase ( 0,
                            TABLES_DB_NAME,
                            TABLES_FILE_CREATOR,
                            TABLES_DB_TYPE,
                            false);

      // Handle unexpected err
        ErrFatalDisplayIf ( err, "Could not create new database.");

        // Let's try to open it again...
       s_dbFish = DmOpenDatabaseByTypeCreator ( TABLES_DB_TYPE,
                                     TABLES_FILE_CREATOR,
                                     dmModeReadWrite);

      // Handle unexpected err
      if ( 0 == s_dbFish )
      {
          ErrFatalDisplayIf ( true, "Could not open new database.");
      }
    }

   return;
}

/*
   FishClose:
   Closes the fish db
```

14

TABLES

continues

LISTING 14.1 CONTINUED

```
   Parms: none
   Returns: none
*/

void
FishClose ( void )
{
   if ( s_dbFish )
   {
      // if the database is open, close it
       DmCloseDatabase ( s_dbFish );
      // reset the database handle to null
      s_dbFish = 0;
   }
   return;
}

/*
   FishGetNextRecordNum:
   Obtains the record number for a record that is a designated number
   of database rows past the starting record
   Parms: uRecordNumStart = the index of the starting record
          uRowsToSkip = the number of rows to jump past to get to the
          desired record
   Returns: the record number of the desired record
*/

UInt
FishGetNextRecordNum ( UInt uRecordNumStart, Word wRowsToSkip )
{
   UInt uRecordNumNext = uRecordNumStart;

   if ( s_dbFish )
   {
      Err err = DmSeekRecordInCategory ( s_dbFish,
                                         &uRecordNumNext,
                                         wRowsToSkip,
                                         dmSeekForward,
                                         dmAllCategories);

   }
   return uRecordNumNext;
}

/*
   FishGetPrevRecordNum:
   Obtains the record number for a record that is a designated number
   of database rows before the starting record
   Parms: uRecordNumStart = the index of the starting record
```

```
                  uRowsToSkip = the number of rows to jump back to get to the
                  desired record
        Returns: the record number of the desired record
*/

UInt
FishGetPrevRecordNum ( UInt uRecordNumStart, Word wRowsToSkip )
{
    UInt uRecordNumPrev = uRecordNumStart;

    if ( s_dbFish )
    {
        DmSeekRecordInCategory ( s_dbFish,
                                 &uRecordNumPrev,
                                 wRowsToSkip,
                                 dmSeekBackward,
                                 dmAllCategories);
    }
    return uRecordNumPrev;
}

/*
    FishQueryFish:
    Returns the record handle for the record matching the passed in
    record number
    Parms: uRecordNum = record number of desired record
    Returns:handle to record
*/

VoidHand
FishQueryFish ( UInt uRecordNum )
{
    UInt uRecordNumTemp = uRecordNum;

    VoidHand hRecord = DmQueryNextInCategory ( s_dbFish,
                                               &uRecordNumTemp,
                                               dmAllCategories );
    return hRecord;
}
```

14

TABLES

Summary

Tables are by far the most complex user-interface element in terms of programming effort. If you need to manage the display and manipulation of databases such that your users can easily browse and edit their data, tables are the right choice. I hope this chapter has given you enough background and sample code to help you add table support to your application with minimum frustration.

CHAPTER 15

Categories

The Palm OS has built-in support for a concept called a record "category." If you've worked with a Palm device at all, you'll no doubt agree that the ability to use categories for organizing personal information is quite useful.

Unfortunately, categories are a rather complicated subject (perhaps unnecessarily so) for programmers to deal with. Implementing category support in an application requires making nontrivial changes in three areas of your code: database creation, record management, and user interface.

In this chapter, I

- Explain what categories are and how they are used in built-in Palm applications
- Review category support in Palm SDK
- Enumerate the programming tasks involved in adding category support to your application

At the end of the chapter, I rework the Fish List program from Chapter 13, "Palm Databases: Record Management," to add category support.

What Is a Category?

On the Palm, each database record contains a dedicated storage area to hold an application-defined category. To be precise, the record entry in the database header contains a category field. This field is present in the record entry no matter how you create your database, and regardless of whether you support categories in your application.

Categories are application-specific. At first glance, it may appear that the built-in applications might all share the same categories, but that is not the case. Each Palm application is free to define any category names that it (or its users) deem appropriate. Unless the underlying databases are shared, multiple applications will not have access to each other's categories. This at times can be annoying to users of the built-in applications, and you could argue it would be nice to not define the same categories to be used in the address book, to-do list, date book, and so on.

Each Palm application can define up to 16 categories for its own use. These categories can be completely reserved for the user to define, or they can be partially or even completely defined and fixed by the application developer.

Finally, categories are "flat"; they cannot be nested or defined in a hierarchical manner. Depending on your application, this may or may not be a significant functional restriction for your users.

Figures 15.1 through 15.3 capture what the user interface for category support looks like in the Address Book application.

FIGURE 15.1

The main address book view with the categories dropped down.

FIGURE 15.2

Setting the category for an address book record.

FIGURE 15.3

*The standard Edit
Categories form.*

Palm SDK Support for Categories

As I hinted in this chapter's introduction, category support in the Palm SDK falls into several different areas of functionality:

> Database initialization of categories
>
> Database functions that use categories
>
> Standard category user interfaces
>
> `CategorySelect`

If that's not enough for you, you need to perform some steps in Constructor in order to properly initialize categories in your application.

The next section examines each of these areas in more detail.

How to Add Category Support to Your Application

Next, we walk through these areas of support and understand the development steps required for each area.

Preparing Your Database for Categories

The preparation is certainly the most complicated step, so it's good to discuss it first. The first requirement for providing category support in your application is to create a special `AppInfo` record and set the local ID for the record in your database header when the database is created.

15

CATEGORIES

An `AppInfo` block has the following structure:

```
Typedef struct
{
    Uint renamedCategories;
    Char categoryLabels[dmRecNumCategories][dmCategoryLength];
    Byte categoryUniqueIDs[dmRecNumCategories];
    Byte lastUniqueID;
    Byte reserved1;
    Byte reserved2;
} MyAppInfo;
```

Although you must define such a structure in your application, and you must allocate a database record of this size, you actually do not need to be concerned with the internal structure of the record. Assuming you do all the right things in the right order, Palm takes care of the `AppInfo` structure.

The magic sequence for adding an `AppInfo` record to your database follows:

1. Launch Constructor and load your application's resources.

2. Find App Info String Lists, and create a new string list resource.

3. Double-click the resource to edit it.

4. In the App Info String List window, repeatedly add new string list entries until there are 16 in total, including the Unfiled entry.

5. Type values for as many of the categories you want to predefine for your users.

After you've saved your Constructor session, you are ready to add the code to initialize your database:

1. Use `DmOpenDatabaseInfo` to obtain the memory card number and local ID associated with your open database.

2. Call `DmDatabaseInfo` to obtain the current `AppInfo` ID, if any.

3. If `AppInfo` was not previously defined, use `DmNewHandle` to allocate a new database handle large enough to hold the `AppInfo` structure.

4. Obtain the local ID associated with the newly created database handle by using the `MemHandleToLocalID` utility function.

5. Stuff the `AppInfo` handle's local ID into the `AppInfoID` database header attribute by calling `DmSetDatabaseInfo`.

6. Initialize the `AppInfo` structure by using `DmSet` to zero out all members.

7. Call `CategoryInitialize`, passing in the `AppInfo` block and the resource ID of your App Info String List resource you created in Constructor.

All of this code should be wrapped up in a function that gets called in tandem with the creation of your database.

Whew! The good news is that this is the kind of routine you can write once, call once from your code, and never worry about it again. The bad news is that if you get it wrong, your database and category support will not work correctly.

Adding Category Awareness to Your Database Calls

Basically, categories affect the way you perform database operations in two ways. The first is that you can use category-aware database query and seek functions. In particular, `DmNumRecordsInCategory` will give you the number of records that fall into a given category. `DmSeekRecordInCategory` will limit its record seeking to a specific category.

The second thing to know is that you are responsible for initializing and modifying a record's category based upon user selection. For this, you use `DmSetRecordInfo` to pass a `UInt` into which the desired category is ORed.

Supporting Categories in Your User Interface

The final area you need to handle in supporting categories is your user interface. It is a good idea to follow the visual examples set by the built-in applications. The main forms of those applications all allow filtering of the main record lists via a categories drop-down list in the upper-right corner of the display. (For complete instructions on how to define a drop-down list using pop-up triggers, see Chapter 8, "Giving the User a Choice: Lists and Pop-Up Triggers.")

In addition, each application offers the user the ability to assign a record to a category as part of the record-editing user interface. The application also supports the ability for the user to define or modify the category list for the application.

Aside from the tediousness of defining the user interface in Constructor, all of this user-interface functionality is actually fairly simple to program. Palm Computing has graciously provided a handy function called `CategorySelect`. Here's how you use it: When the pop-up trigger associated with either your main list view or your record edit form is fired, you pass the IDs of the associated pop-up trigger, list, and other parameters. `CategorySelect` takes it from there, automatically filling the drop-down list with the available categories and even guiding the user through the Edit Categories process. If it turns out the user selected a category, the ID of the selected category is returned to you. That's all there is to it.

Fish List Revisited: What Kind of Fish Is That?

To illustrate the changes needed in an application to support categories, I modified the Fish List program introduced in Chapter 13, so for each fish you can store the type of fish you are entering. The users are free to categorize their entries any way they want: Small, Medium, or Large, Crustaceans, Mollusks, and Mammals, whatever. Fish List supports the standard look and feel of the built-in applications' category user interfaces. Figure 15.4 shows how FishList lets the user choose which category of fish to display in the main form, while Figure 15.5 shows the user interface for setting the category for a selected fish.

FIGURE 15.4

Choosing a category to filter fish by type.

FIGURE 15.5

Setting the category for a manta ray.

Listings 15.1 and 15.2 represent the new Fish List implementation. Listing 15.1 is cate_db.cpp, which contains the most changes for categories, including a FishInitAppInfo function that takes care of the messy AppInfo initialization task.

LISTING 15.1   DATABASE-RELATED CODE FOR FISHLIST, WITH CATEGORY SUPPORT

```
/*
   CATE_DB.CPP

   Categories application db functions

   Copyright (c) 1999 Bachmann Software and Services, LLC
   Author: Glenn Bachmann
*/

// System headers
#include <Pilot.h>
#include <SysEvtMgr.h>

// Application-specific headers
#include "category.h"
#include "cate_res.h"

#define CATEGORY_DB_TYPE  ('Data')
#define CATEGORY_DB_NAME  ("FishDB")

static Word              s_wCurrentCategory = dmAllCategories;
static char              s_szCategoryName[dmCategoryLength];
static DmOpenRef      s_dbFish;
static Handle       s_hRec;
static CharPtr      s_pText;
static UInt              s_recordNum = 0;

static Err    FishInitAppInfo (DmOpenRef pDB);

/*
   FishGetCount:
   Returns the count of records in the fish database
   Parms: none
   Returns: count

*/

UInt
FishGetCount ( void )
{
   UInt uFishCount = 0;
   if ( s_dbFish )
   {
      uFishCount = DmNumRecordsInCategory ( s_dbFish,
      ➥s_wCurrentCategory );
   }
```

continues

15

CATEGORIES

LISTING 15.1   CONTINUED

```c
    return uFishCount;
}

/*
   FishNew:
   Creates a new Fish record
   Parms: none
   Returns: true if record created
*/

Boolean
FishNew ( void )
{
    Ptr         p;
    VoidHand hFish;
    UInt        uIndex = 0;
    Err         err;
    Char        zero = 0;
    UInt        attr;

    // Create a new record in the Fish database
    hFish = DmNewRecord ( s_dbFish, &uIndex, FISH_LENGTH );

    if (hFish)
    {
        // Get a pointer to the mem block associated with the new record
        p = (Ptr)MemHandleLock (hFish);

        // Init the record by writing a zero
        err = DmWrite ( p, 0, &zero, 1 );

        // Unlock the block of the new record.
        MemPtrUnlock ( p );

        // Obtain the record's attribute info, and set it to reflect the
        // currently selected category
        DmRecordInfo ( s_dbFish, uIndex, &attr, NULL, NULL);

        attr &= ~dmRecAttrCategoryMask;        // Remove all category bits

        if ( s_wCurrentCategory == dmAllCategories)
        {
            attr |= dmUnfiledCategory;
        }
        else
        {
```

```
            attr |= s_wCurrentCategory;
        }

        DmSetRecordInfo ( s_dbFish, uIndex, &attr, NULL);


        // Release the record to the database manager.
        DmReleaseRecord ( s_dbFish, uIndex, true);

        // Remember the index of the current record.
        s_recordNum = 0;
      return true;
    }
    else
    {
      return false;
    }

}

/*
   FishGetFish:
   Gets a handle to a Fish record at index uIndex
   Parms: uIndex = 0 based index of record in db
   Returns: NULL or a valid record handle
*/

Handle
FishGetFish ( UInt uIndex )
{
    Err             err;

    s_recordNum = 0;

    if ( s_dbFish )
    {
       err = DmSeekRecordInCategory ( s_dbFish,
                                    &s_recordNum,
                                    uIndex,
                                    dmSeekForward,
                                    s_wCurrentCategory);

       // Get the record
        s_hRec = (Handle)DmGetRecord ( s_dbFish, s_recordNum );
       if ( s_hRec )
       {
          // Lock it down and get a ptr
```

continues

LISTING 15.1   CONTINUED

```c
            s_pText = (CharPtr)MemHandleLock ( s_hRec );
        }

    }

    return s_hRec;
}

/*
   FishReleaseFish:
   Releases the currently edited fish back to the database
   Parms: none
   Returns: none
*/

void
FishReleaseFish ( void )
{
    if ( s_hRec )
    {
        MemHandleUnlock ( s_hRec );
    }

     // Release the record, not dirty.
     DmReleaseRecord ( s_dbFish, s_recordNum, false);

    s_recordNum = 0;

    return;
}

/*
   FishUpdate:
   Commits changes to the category information back to the record
   Parms: none
   Returns: none
*/

void
FishUpdate ( void )
{
    UInt        attr;

    DmRecordInfo (s_dbFish, s_recordNum, &attr, NULL, NULL);
    attr &= ~dmRecAttrCategoryMask;

    if ( s_wCurrentCategory == dmAllCategories)
    {
```

```
            attr |= dmUnfiledCategory;
        }
        else
        {
            attr |= s_wCurrentCategory;
        }

    // Update the attributes
    DmSetRecordInfo ( s_dbFish, s_recordNum, &attr, NULL);
    return;
}

/*
    FishSelectType:
    Performs Category Selection in order to choose the fish type
    If the category is changed, updates the current category
    Parms: pForm = parent form
           pTypeID = out param for new type
           wTriggerID = id of popup trigger control
           wListID = id of listbox
    Returns: true if selection made
*/

Boolean
FishSelectType ( FormPtr pForm, Word *pTypeID, Word wTriggerID,
➡Word wListID )
{
    Boolean bChanged = false;

    Word category;
    Boolean bEdited;

    // Process the category pop-up list
    // Save the current one in a temp
    category = s_wCurrentCategory;

    bEdited = CategorySelect ( s_dbFish,
                                    pForm,
                                    wTriggerID,
                                        wListID,
                                    true,
                                    &category,
                                    s_szCategoryName,
                                    1,
                                    0);

    if (bEdited || (category != s_wCurrentCategory))
    {
```

continues

15

CATEGORIES

LISTING 15.1 CONTINUED

```
        // Category is new - save it and refill the fish list!
          s_wCurrentCategory = category;

        *pTypeID = category;
        return true;
    }
    return false;
}

/*
   FishGetCurrentType:
   Obtains the name of the currently selected category/fish type
   Parms: pType= buffer to receive name of type
   Returns: none
*/

void
FishGetCurrentType ( CharPtr pType )
{
    CategoryGetName ( s_dbFish,
                      s_wCurrentCategory,
                      s_szCategoryName);

    StrCopy ( pType, s_szCategoryName );
    return;
}

/*
   FishGetName:
   Gets the ptr to the fish name field. Because the fish record is
   simply one field, just returns the whole record
   Parms: none
   Returns: ptr to name
*/

CharPtr
FishGetName ( void )
{
    return s_pText;
}

/*
   FishSetName:
   Sets the name of the currently edited fish record
   Parms: pName = ptr to new name
```

```
    Returns: none
*/

void
FishSetName ( CharPtr pName )
{
    // Lock down the block containing the record
    if ( s_hRec )
    {
        Ptr         p;

        p = (Ptr)MemHandleLock ( s_hRec );

        // Write the name value. Add one to strlen to make sure it's
        // null termed
        Err err = DmWrite ( p, 0, pName, StrLen ( pName ) + 1 );

        MemPtrUnlock ( p );
    }

    return;
}

/*
    FishOpen:
    Opens the Fish database, retaining a ref number to the db for further
    operations
    Parms: none
    Returns: none
*/

void
FishOpen ( void )
{
    // Open the db
    s_dbFish = DmOpenDatabaseByTypeCreator ( CATEGORY_DB_TYPE,
                                             CATEGORY_FILE_CREATOR,
                                             dmModeReadWrite);

    if ( 0 == s_dbFish )
    {
        UInt        cardNo;
        LocalID     dbID;
        UInt        dbAttrs;

        // Not there - create it now
        Err err = DmCreateDatabase ( 0,
                                     CATEGORY_DB_NAME,
                                     CATEGORY_FILE_CREATOR,
```

continues

LISTING 15.1   CONTINUED

```
                                CATEGORY_DB_TYPE,
                                false);

        // Handle unexpected err
          ErrFatalDisplayIf ( err, "Could not create new database.");

          // Let's try to open it again...
          s_dbFish = DmOpenDatabaseByTypeCreator ( CATEGORY_DB_TYPE,
                                        CATEGORY_FILE_CREATOR,
                                        dmModeReadWrite);

          // Store category info in the application's information block.
          FishInitAppInfo(s_dbFish);
    }

    // Get the name of the current category from the app info block.
    if ( s_dbFish )
    {
        CategoryGetName ( s_dbFish, s_wCurrentCategory, s_szCategoryName);
    }
    return;
}

/*
    FishClose:
    Closes the fish db
    Parms: none
    Returns: none
*/

void
FishClose ( void )
{
    if ( s_dbFish )
    {
        DmCloseDatabase ( s_dbFish );
    }
    return;
}

/*
    FishInitAppInfo:
    Initializes the App Info portion of the database header and sets
    the category area
```

```
    Parms: pDB = ptr to fish db
    Returns: 0 = success

*/

Err
FishInitAppInfo (DmOpenRef pDB)
{
    UInt cardNo;
    VoidHand handle;
    LocalID dbID;
    LocalID appInfoID;
    FishAppInfo * pAppInfo;
    FishAppInfo * pNull = 0;

    if ( DmOpenDatabaseInfo ( pDB, &dbID, NULL, NULL, &cardNo, NULL ))
    {
        return dmErrInvalidParam;
    }
    if ( DmDatabaseInfo ( cardNo, dbID,
                          NULL,
                          NULL,
                          NULL,
                          NULL,
                          NULL,
                          NULL,
                          NULL,
                          &appInfoID,
                          NULL,
                          NULL,
                          NULL ))
    {
        return dmErrInvalidParam;
    }

    if ( NULL == appInfoID )
    {
        handle = DmNewHandle ( pDB, sizeof (FishAppInfo) );
        if ( NULL == handle )
        {
            return dmErrMemError;
        }

        appInfoID = MemHandleToLocalID ( handle );
        DmSetDatabaseInfo ( cardNo, dbID,
                            NULL,
                            NULL,
```

15

CATEGORIES

continues

LISTING 15.1 CONTINUED

```
                              NULL,
                              NULL,
                              NULL,
                              NULL,
                              NULL,
                              &appInfoID,
                              NULL,
                              NULL,
                              NULL );

     pAppInfo = (FishAppInfo *)MemLocalIDToLockedPtr ( appInfoID,
     ➥cardNo );

     DmSet ( pAppInfo, 0, sizeof ( FishAppInfo ), 0 );

     CategoryInitialize ( (AppInfoPtr)pAppInfo, FishTypesAppInfoStr );

     MemPtrUnlock ( pAppInfo );

  }
  return 0;
}
```

Listing 15.2 shows a few (but not many) modifications to the main form-handling code in cate_mai.cpp.

LISTING 15.2 THE NEW MAIN FORM CODE FOR FISHLIST

```
/*
   CATE_MAI.CPP
   Main form handling functions.
   Copyright (c) Bachmann Software and Services, 1999
   Author: Glenn Bachmann
*/

// System headers
#include <Pilot.h>
#include <SysEvtMgr.h>

// Application-specific headers
#include "category.h"
#include "cate_res.h"

static void    MainFormInit (FormPtr formP);
static Boolean MainFormButtonHandler (FormPtr formP, EventPtr eventP);
static Boolean MainFormMenuHandler (FormPtr formP, EventPtr eventP);

// Local helper functions
void MainListFill (FormPtr pForm);
```

```
void MainListDrawFunction (UInt itemNum, RectanglePtr bounds,
➥CharPtr *pUnused);
Boolean AddFish ( void );
Boolean AddFish_EventHandler (EventPtr pEvent);

/*
    MainFormEventHandler:
    Parms:   pEvent   - event to be handled.
    Return:  true  - handled (successfully or not)
             false - not handled
*/
Boolean
MainFormEventHandler (EventPtr eventP)
{
    Boolean   handled = false;

    switch (eventP->eType)
    {
        case menuEvent:
        {
            FormPtr formP = FrmGetActiveForm ();
            handled = MainFormMenuHandler (formP, eventP);
            break;
        }


        case ctlSelectEvent:
        {
            // A control button was tapped and released
            FormPtr formP = FrmGetActiveForm ();
            handled = MainFormButtonHandler (formP, eventP);
            break;
        }

        case frmOpenEvent:
        {
            // Main form is opening

            FormPtr formP = FrmGetActiveForm ();

            MainFormInit (formP);

            FrmDrawForm (formP);

            handled = true;
            break;
        }

        default:
        {
```

15

CATEGORIES

continues

LISTING 15.2 CONTINUED

```
            break;
        }
    }
    return handled;
}

/*
   MainFormInit:
   Initialize the main form.
   Parms:   formP - pointer to main form.
   Return:  none
*/
void
MainFormInit (FormPtr pForm)
{
    char szType [dmCategoryLength];

    // Set the controls to an initial state
    // Here we set the name of the currently selected category
    FishGetCurrentType ( szType );

    Word wID = FrmGetObjectIndex (pForm, MainTypePopTrigger );
    ControlPtr p = (ControlPtr) FrmGetObjectPtr (pForm, wID);

     CategorySetTriggerLabel ( p, szType );

    MainListFill ( pForm );

    // Set the drawing function for the main list
    Word wIDMainList = FrmGetObjectIndex (pForm, MainFishList );
    ListPtr pCtlMainList = (ListPtr) FrmGetObjectPtr (pForm, wIDMainList);
    LstSetDrawFunction ( pCtlMainList, MainListDrawFunction );
}

/*
   MainFormMenuHandler:
   Handle a command sent to the main form.
   Parms:   formP     - form handling event.
            command   - command to be handled.
   Return:  true  - handled (successfully or not)
            false - not handled
*/
Boolean
MainFormMenuHandler (FormPtr /*formP*/, EventPtr eventP)
{
    Boolean handled = false;

    switch (eventP->data.menu.itemID)
    {
```

```
      default:
      {
         handled = false;
         break;
      }
   }
   return handled;
}

/*
   MainFormButtonHandler:
   Handle a command sent to the main form.
   Parms:   formP    - form handling event.
            eventP   - event to be handled.
   Return:  true  - handled (successfully or not)
            false - not handled
*/

Boolean
MainFormButtonHandler (FormPtr pForm, EventPtr eventP)
{
   Boolean handled = false;

   switch (eventP->data.ctlEnter.controlID)
   {
      case MainNewButton:
      {
         if ( AddFish () )
         {
            MainListFill ( pForm );
         }

         handled = true;
         break;
      }

      case MainTypePopTrigger:
      {
         FormPtr pForm;
         UInt wType;

          pForm = FrmGetActiveForm ();

         if ( FishSelectType ( pForm, &wType, MainTypePopTrigger,
         ➥MainTypeList ) )
         {
             MainListFill ( pForm );
         }
```

continues

15

CATEGORIES

LISTING 15.2   CONTINUED

```
            handled = true;
            break;
        }
        default:
        {
            handled = false;
            break;
        }
    }
    return handled;
}

/*
    MainListFill:
    Fills the fish list based upon the currently selected category
    Parms: pForm - pointer to main form
    Returns: none
*/
void
MainListFill (FormPtr pForm)
{
    // Get a ptr to the fish list
    Word wIDFishList = FrmGetObjectIndex (pForm, MainFishList );
    ListPtr pCtlFishList = (ListPtr) FrmGetObjectPtr (pForm, wIDFishList);

    // Get the count of available main list items from the selected aisle
    int iFishCount = FishGetCount ();

    // Fill the main list based on the combo selection
    LstSetListChoices ( pCtlFishList, NULL, iFishCount );

    // Redraw the list
    LstDrawList (pCtlFishList);

    return;
}

/*
    MainListDrawFunction:
    Draws a single item in the main list
    Parms: itemNum = 0 based index of item to draw
           bound = ptr to rectangle providing drawing bounds
           pUnused = ptr to char string for item to draw. In this app, we
           never give the actual item data to the list, so we ignore
           this parm
    Returns: none
*/
void
MainListDrawFunction (UInt itemNum, RectanglePtr bounds,
➡CharPtr *pUnused)
```

```
{
    FormPtr pForm = FrmGetActiveForm ();

    CharPtr        pText;
    Handle     hFish = NULL;

    // Find the record in the category
    FishGetFish ( itemNum );

    pText = FishGetName ();

    if ( pText )
    {
        WinDrawChars ( pText, StrLen (pText), bounds->topLeft.x,
        ➥bounds->topLeft.y);
    }

    FishReleaseFish ();
    return;
}


/*
    AddFish:
    Parms:   none
    Return:  none
*/
Boolean AddFish ( void )
{
    // Initialize the form
    FormPtr  pForm = FrmInitForm (AddFishForm);

    if ( FishNew () )
    {
        // Edit it!
        VoidHand hRecord = FishGetFish ( 0 );
        VoidHand hText = MemHandleNew ( FISH_LENGTH );
        CharPtr pText = (CharPtr)MemHandleLock (hText);

        StrCopy ( pText, "<new fish>" );

        MemPtrUnlock ( pText );


        Word wIDField = FrmGetObjectIndex ( pForm, AddFishNameField );
        FieldPtr pField = (FieldPtr) FrmGetObjectPtr ( pForm, wIDField);

        // Copy the text into the edit field
        FldSetTextHandle ( pField, (Handle)hText);

        // Set the current trigger label
        char szType [dmCategoryLength];
```

continues

LISTING 15.2   CONTINUED

```
        FishGetCurrentType ( szType );
        Word wID = FrmGetObjectIndex (pForm, AddFishTypePopTrigger );
        ControlPtr p = (ControlPtr) FrmGetObjectPtr (pForm, wID);
         CategorySetTriggerLabel ( p, szType );

         // We set an event handler for the form
         FrmSetEventHandler (pForm, AddFish_EventHandler );

        // Display the dialog
        if ( FrmDoDialog (pForm) )
        {
           hText = FldGetTextHandle (pField);
           CharPtr pText = (CharPtr)MemHandleLock (hText);

           FishSetName ( pText );

            MemPtrUnlock ( pText );
        }

        FishReleaseFish ();

        // Destroy the form
        FrmDeleteForm (pForm);

        return true;
    }
    return false;
}


/*
   AddFish_EventHandler:
    Handles form events for form
   Parms:    pEvent = ptr to event handler
   Return:   TRUE if we handled the event
*/

Boolean AddFish_EventHandler (EventPtr pEvent)
{
    Boolean   bHandled = false;
    static UInt s_wNewType;

    switch (pEvent->eType)
    {
       case ctlSelectEvent:
         {
           // A control button was pressed and released.
            switch (pEvent->data.ctlSelect.controlID)
             {
```

```
        case AddFishOKButton:
        {
        // Save the fish!
        FishUpdate ();

            // Remove the details form and display the edit form.
            bHandled = false;
            break;
        }

        case AddFishCancelButton:
        {
            // The cancel button was pressed, just go back to
            // the edit form.
            bHandled = false;
            break;
        }

        case AddFishTypePopTrigger:
        {
        // User wants to pick a fish type
        FormPtr pForm = FrmGetActiveForm ();
        FishSelectType ( pForm, &s_wNewType,
        ➥AddFishTypePopTrigger, AddFishTypeList );
        bHandled = true;
        break;
        }
        }
    }
    }
    return bHandled;
}
```

Summary

I found that adding category support to my applications was more time-consuming and error-prone than adding database support in the first place. I hope this chapter will save you time in developing your own application's category support. Depending on your application and your users, the inclusion of good, standard category support can make quite a difference in the usability of your program.

CHAPTER 16

Saving Program State: Application Preferences

The Palm OS today does not support the execution of multiple applications simultaneously. It might come as a bit of a surprise to developers who come to the Palm from other platforms that their applications actually shut down if their users need to switch to another Palm application such as Address Book. Simply tapping the Applications icon is enough to close your application.

If you do nothing else, every time a user taps on your application to launch it, she will be greeted with your main screen, regardless of how her last session with your program ended. It is as if she were starting over every time; in fact, from the perspective of your application, she has.

This chapter explains the problems associated with loss of program state and introduces the application preferences facility as a way to effectively deal with those problems.

The Problem with Application Switching

Losing state causes some obvious (and not-so-obvious) problems with many applications. For example, it might not be acceptable to lose the current application state. Let's say the user is composing a long email, and he suddenly needs to look at his calendar. Poof! His email is lost.

Another example is the problem of how to maintain user preferences and configuration settings. The user could get quite annoyed if he preferred "sort by company" in the address book, yet the Address Book application always reverted to "sort by name" when it started.

On Windows or other multitasking platforms, this sort of inconvenience is not a problem because applications retain state as they are activated and deactivated on the desktop and there are system facilities available, such as profile-initialization files and the Registry, to easily store configuration settings and user preferences in a standard manner.

On the Palm, with no "file system" per se, what tools are available to the developer to address this problem? The answer lies in the Palm SDK's system (or application) preference functions.

What Are Application Preferences?

Application preferences allow you to save the state of your application from one execution to the next. They are maintained in a special Palm database called "Preferences," (you can see this database using DBBrowse from Chapter 12, "Understanding Databases") which is dedicated to managing the preferences for all applications, as well as the user's system preferences such as date and time format.

You don't have to do anything to create your application's special entry in the Preferences database: It is automatically maintained by the Palm OS.

When Should I Use Application Preferences?

Application preferences are best employed for storing your program's state and configuration settings. For example, you have good candidates for preferences if you want to have your program initialize to one of three possible initial main views or if you have sort or other data-view–oriented settings.

Using preferences for things such as partially completed records or most recently accessed data is less desirable. The problem lies in the link to data elsewhere on the Palm that might be either changed or deleted by another process.

Using the Palm SDK Functions to Handle Application Preferences

Application preferences essentially have two functions: `PrefGetAppPreferences` and `PrefSetAppPreferences`.

`PrefSetAppPreferences` stores an application-defined block of memory into the application's preferences database entry. In this sense, this process is much like using `DmWrite` to save a block of memory to a record, with the application being responsible for interpreting the record structure properly. Here's an example:

```
// Define the structure of our application preferences
// block

typedef struct
{
    UInt ViewID;
    UInt CurrentSort;
}AppPreferences;
...
static AppPreferences s_Prefs;
static Sword s_wVersion = 2;
// In your NormalLaunch handler in your main event loop
...
Sword wSize = sizeof (AppPreferences);
// Load the app's preferences
PrefGetAppPreferences ( 'TEST',
            TEST_PREFS_MAIN,
s_wVersion,
            (VoidPtr)&s_Prefs,
            &wSize,
            TRUE);
...
// Do your main event loop
...
// App is closing, store preferences
PrefSetAppPreferences ( 'TEST',
TEST_PREFS_MAIN,
s_wVersion,
            (VoidPtr)&s_Prefs,
            sizeof (AppPreferences),
            TRUE);
```

For this fictional example, we have defined our own structure that contains two application preferences: a view ID (corresponding to one of several possible form views) and a current sort, which stores the user's preferred sort order. The general logic flow is all driven from your `PilotMain` code in your `sysAppLaunchCmdNormalLaunch` handler.

When your application is first launched, before you do anything else you should read your application's preferences from the system into local storage where they can be read from the various parts of your program. You do this by calling `PrefGetAppPreferences`. To correctly identify the proper preferences, you provide the creator ID, the ID of the preference set (you are allowed to create multiple sets of preferences for your application, so you need to identify which one you are interested in), and your application's version number. The version number is insurance against changes in the block size or layout for the application's preferences over time. If you increment the version number for an associated change in the preferences structure, Palm will create a new preferences block tied to that unique version number.

Note that `PrefGetAppPreferences` has a `prefsSize` parameter that is both an in and an out parameter. You need to tell `PrefGetAppPreferences` the size of the preferences block you are passing in, but the function also passes back the actual size of the block to you if it succeeds in locating a block. You should check the return value, and even if the function call succeeds, make sure that the returned block size is what you expect.

Once you've loaded your application's preferences, you should copy them to some place where they will be accessible (ideally not directly) by other program modules in your application.

After preferences are loaded, you proceed to enter your application's main event loop as normal. When the event loop exits, indicating application termination, you should save the current settings of the application to the preferences database. This process simply involves the inverse of the `PrefGetAppPreferences` call.

System Preferences

In addition to application preferences, predefined system preferences control some of the operation and appearance of the OS itself. These are defined in the SDK header file preferences.h in the enumerated type `SystemPreferencesChoice`. Some of the supported preferences are fairly useful, depending on your application's needs: date and time format, daylight savings, starting day of the week, and so on. Others are either undocumented or somewhat obscure in purpose (`RonamaticChar` and `AllowEasterEggs`).

System preferences are set individually using `PrefSetPreferences`, passing it the `SystemPreferencesChoice` you want to modify. There is a function to get all the preferences at once in a `SystemPreferences` structure, but it's hard to imagine why you would need so many of them. Note that all preferences are stored as word-size values.

Conversely, you can retrieve an individual preference by calling `PrefGetPreferences`, which returns the associated word value.

Summary

Palm has made it fairly easy for application developers to maintain state across program executions by encapsulating a special common storage location behind well-defined SDK functions. You should carefully evaluate your application and determine how you can use application preferences to simplify your users' experiences.

Memory Management

PART
IV

IN THIS PART

CHAPTER 17

Palm OS Memory Management

It seems as though every programming book that describes how to develop applications for a given operating system contains the obligatory chapter on memory management. These books include pages of discussion revolving around concepts such as heaps, free stores, and stack pointers, as well as one or two impressive-looking diagrams that map out how the operating system divides memory.

I usually plow through such chapters, as if I should feel guilty if I don't commit the internals of the operating system to memory. Inevitably, I read this material and then forget it over time. On those rare occasions when I have a programming task in front of me that requires I be intimate with the actual memory architecture, I generally consult the operating system vendor's documentation anyway.

As I explained in my coverage of the Palm OS database storage model, this book is intended to provide practical knowledge and examples of how to intelligently use the Palm SDK to create applications. Today, much better resources than this book provide a detailed treatment of the Palm OS memory management model, and I'm confident that books and articles that come after this one will also cover the topic with much greater depth and skill than I ever could.

This chapter therefore will (very briefly) give you a sense of the memory architecture of the Palm OS. You will actually use this knowledge primarily as background for the memory allocation limitations your application will face as it runs on the Palm. After the architectural overview, I will get into the practical matters that all programmers face every day about how to acquire, use, and release memory.

Overview of the Palm OS Memory Manager

The memory for a Palm device lives on a memory card. Although the Palm documentation states that the Palm can theoretically support up to 256 cards, no shipping Palm devices as yet contain more than one card (card 0).

Each card contains either one or two groupings of memory called stores. Today's single card contains two stores, one for ROM (read-only memory) and one for RAM (random-access memory). The ROM store contains the Palm OS itself, the default built-in applications (such as Address Book), and the default databases associated with the built-in apps.

RAM is where most of the action occurs for programmers and users. It contains applications other than the built-in ones, system preferences, dynamic memory required by running applications, and user data (stored in databases).

Size Matters

The good news is that the Palm has a theoretical physical address space of 4GB. Exciting, right? Can't wait to use all that memory? Forget it. First, recall that most Palm devices in the field today have either 1MB or 2MB of memory. (The recently available IIIx devices have 4MB.) You say, "It's not 4GB, but 2MB still sounds like a lot of memory." Well, let me tell you about dynamic RAM and storage RAM.

The architects of the Palm OS made a design decision to favor small, fast applications and large storage space. That design resulted in the division of the RAM store into two areas: dynamic RAM and storage RAM. Dynamic RAM contains the memory heap available to applications as dynamically allocatable working space. Any memory in the RAM store that is not dedicated to dynamic RAM is designated for storage RAM. Storage RAM is primarily devoted to databases.

Now, you might be starting to worry (and rightly so). "Just how much of my precious 2MB is available to my application for its dynamic memory needs?" you wonder. The answer is not pretty no matter how you slice it, but things are slightly better with version 3.0 of the OS. Ready? The dynamic heap on Palm OS version 2.0 is only 64KB, of which approximately 12KB is likely to be available to your application for dynamic allocations.

Let me help you up. Take your time, have a glass of water, and let your heartbeat get back down to normal. Things aren't so bad with version 3.0. On Palm OS 3.0, the dynamic heap is 96KB in size, with approximately 36KB available to your application.

The implication of this architecture on your application's design is significant. In some ways, it requires a complete rethinking of how you develop software. Even if you could guarantee that all your users are running OS 3.0, 36KB is hardly any memory whatsoever to play with. We've all been spoiled by Moore's law, with superfast PCs containing 128MB of RAM now common. I've certainly written my share of large applications that expect and need megabytes of memory available to them.

It helps to think back to earlier days of PC computing, when DOS applications were designed with low memory conditions assumed. Many of the same rules apply:

- Memory is limited.
- Allocate only as much memory as you need.
- Free memory as soon as you are done with it.
- Carefully consider the bare minimum information that you need to load into memory from permanent storage.
- Do not attempt to load arrays of user data into dynamic memory. Rather, read and write data "in place."
- Processor- or memory-intensive modules that cannot be eliminated or redesigned should be offloaded to external systems.

Do not despair. With the right mindset and a healthy respect for the Palm device, you can develop highly functional and useful applications that look great and run fast on the Palm. You just need to shed the notion that you can port that multimegabyte desktop application lock, stock, and barrel onto the Palm.

The Persistence of Memory

When the device is powered off or goes to sleep, the Palm's memory contents are retained by the system batteries. If the batteries are removed, the contents are still retained for approximately one minute.

If the device experiences a "soft" reset, the dynamic heap, including the running application and all its allocations, is rebuilt. During a "hard" reset, the storage heap (including all stored user data) is also reset, resulting in the device reverting to its default configuration.

As with many operating systems, the Palm OS will clean up after your program exits, freeing all allocations still unfreed by your application. Naturally, you should not rely on this safety net, and you should diligently work to remove any memory leaks in your application.

Allocating and Using Memory

On the Palm, dynamic memory allocations are called chunks and are limited to slightly less than 64KB for each allocation.

Memory allocations result in either a memory handle or a memory pointer being returned to you by the memory manager. Handles and pointers are the source of some confusion, so let's define them.

A memory handle is a reference to a moveable block of memory. This handle must be locked in order to yield a pointer that is usable by your code.

A memory pointer is a pointer to a nonmoveable memory chunk. A pointer can be allocated either directly by the programmer, or it can be returned as the result of locking a moveable memory handle. It is important to remember that a pointer that results from a handle lock is only valid while that handle is locked. If a handle is subsequently unlocked and then relocked, there is no guarantee that the same pointer value will be returned.

When should you use a handle, and when should you use a pointer? Remember that a pointer returned from locking a handle is virtually the same in terms of its usability as a pointer that was directly allocated. But there is one important difference: A handle can be moved by the operating system as it sees fit in response to further memory allocations. Allocating your memory as moveable handles gives the operating system much more flexibility in how it manages memory, and thus, it has a much better chance of being able to allocate more memory for your application.

With this in mind, for short-lived, small allocations, it is fine to directly allocate memory pointers. For longer-lived or larger allocations that might seriously create a sandbar in the dynamic heap, it is advisable to allocate a memory handle and only lock it down to a pointer as needed.

Memory Allocation Functions

The majority of memory manager functions that are applicable to most application needs can be grouped into handle-based functions and pointer-based functions.

One important point to make: Never use these functions to manipulate memory associated with database records, and never use database functions to manipulate memory blocks allocated by the memory manager functions. They address two different kinds of heaps, and you are asking for trouble by mixing the two.

Handle Functions

You use MemHandleNew to allocate a block of moveable memory, returning a handle. It is similar in usage to the old runtime library malloc, except for the handle part. When you want to actually use the memory, you need to lock it down and obtain a pointer. You do this by calling MemHandleLock. Locks should be brief in nature: After you are done using the memory, you should use MemHandleUnlock to return the block to a moveable state. Finally, when you no longer need the memory at all, MemHandleFree returns it to the operating system.

You can obtain the size of a memory block using a handle by calling MemHandleSize. You can resize memory blocks by calling MemHandleResize, with the caveat that you can only be successful in resizing a block if it is unlocked.

Pointer Functions

Pointer functions are essentially parallel to the handle-based functions, with the exception that they don't need to be locked and unlocked. MemPtrNew allocates a new, nonmoveable block of memory and returns a pointer to the caller, ready for use. Use MemPtrFree to free the pointer. Pointers can also be resized, but be aware that because the underlying block is nonmoveable, the resize can only be successful if the extra space is available directly after the block's location in the heap.

Memory Manipulation

Memory manipulation functions are few in the Palm SDK. You can use MemSet and MemMove to manipulate the contents of blocks of memory, and MemCmp allows you to do a byte comparison of two blocks of memory. There is no MemCopy function.

Summary

The memory architecture of the Palm presents restrictions and challenges to the application designer, requiring a shift in mindset by the developer to accommodate the needs of the platform. Well-designed applications will work with the Palm OS design and not fight it. Those who produce such applications will be rewarded with happy users, who can make a large number of diverse applications work on their devices simultaneously.

17

PALM OS
MEMORY
MANAGEMENT

CHAPTER 18

Large Applications

Even though the Palm documentation, the style guidelines and recommendations, and various resources and discussion groups on the Internet repeat the mantra "keep it simple, keep it small," you might at some point find yourself in the unenviable position of developing a Palm application that has grown too large. You might enter the design phase for a new Palm program and wonder how much functionality can (and should) be incorporated into the application.

A Palm program can be considered "too large" for a couple of different reasons, and proving that your program is too large is often difficult: You might see hard evidence such as an inability to build your program in CodeWarrior, or the symptoms might be more subtle, surfacing only sporadically as mysterious, hard-to-replicate system crashes.

This chapter sheds some light on the problems experienced by large Palm programs and offers advice on ways to remedy those problems. Specifically, I

- Define the limitations on size
- Present guidelines for reducing stack and memory usage
- Explain how to create multiple-segment projects
- Explore options for partitioning your application

How Large Is Too Large?

A Palm application can "get large" in several ways:

- Excessive dynamic memory allocation.
- Exceeding available stack space.
- The size of the application exceeds 64KB.
- One part of the application is making a call to another part that is more than 32KB away.

I can't think of a really "good" time for a developer to be in any one of these situations, but I assume that because you are reading this chapter, it is possible that you fall into one of these categories. Let's review them one at a time.

Excessive Dynamic Memory Allocation

If you read the previous chapter on Palm memory architecture, you might recall that I scared you out of your wits by proclaiming that on the Palm III, your application will have approximately 36KB of dynamic RAM at its disposal during program execution. Compared with the vast amounts of memory available to applications on desktop operating systems, this seemed positively puny and maybe just a wee bit unfair. No matter—you must find a way to make your program live within these limits and use restraint in how much dynamic memory is required at any one time.

If built-in applications such as the Address Book can manage thousands of records, so can your program. Several strategies can alleviate the problems associated with limited heap space:

- Allocate handles rather than pointers for your memory. Palm OS can move handle-based memory around to avoid heap fragmentation, but pointers are locked down in memory and reduce the ability for the heap manager to locate free space.
- Do not load a lot of data into memory from database storage. Instead, read and write database records in place.
- Keep out a sharp eye for potential memory leaks.
- Do not hang on to memory chunks longer than necessary: Return them to the free store as soon as possible.
- Religiously check memory allocation calls for the possibility of failure and design a strategy for handling out-of-memory situations.

Exceeding Available Stack Space

Unless you fiddle with the Palm OS header definitions, your Palm program will be limited to approximately 2KB of stack space. The stack cannot grow larger than this during your program's execution. If your program pushes more than 2KB on the stack at any one time, you have "blown your stack," with consequences ranging anywhere from system crashes to data loss to sporadic bizarre program behavior.

In developing any reasonably complex application, it is easy to quickly use up stack space with automatic variables such as large character arrays for receiving entered form data or displaying messages to the user. Declarations such as `char szMessage[200];` might look innocent enough in a single function, but consider that the function in question might be called by another function having similar automatic variable declarations and so on. It doesn't take much of this to quickly approach the stack limit. As is the case with the other types of problems described in this chapter, it is no fun to scour your program code the day before a product release, looking for ways to reduce your stack usage.

Some strategies for avoiding stack problems follow:

- Allocate small, temporary dynamic memory chunks rather than place character arrays on the stack.
- If necessary, prefer global variables over large local variables.
- Do not use recursion!
- Keep an eye on careless overuse of the larger data types such as floating-point numbers.
- Use recent versions of POSE that support stack-checking diagnostics.

18

LARGE
APPLICATIONS

An Application Size Greater Than 64KB

In the previous chapter, I mentioned that memory chunks are limited to 64KB in size. Applications that consist of a single code resource (also known as a code segment) also live under this restriction because they are stored as a single chunk on the device.

CAUTION

When an application under development starts exhibiting some random, odd behavior, check whether it has exceeded the 64KB limit.

Is there a way around the 64KB limit for application size? In CodeWarrior, the answer is multiple-segment applications. Recent versions of CodeWarrior allow you to create a multiple-segment project in the IDE, in which each segment by itself can be up to 64KB in size. To create a multiple segment application, perform the following steps in CodeWarrior:

1. At the top of your project window, click the Segments tab.

2. Under the Project menu, choose Create New Segment, and give the segment a name.

Repeat the last step as many times as you want to logically break up your application into segments smaller than 64KB. You can add to or move files among segments by dragging them with the mouse. The only rule is that your first segment should contain the runtime Pilot library (typically MSL RuntimePilot (2i).lib) as well as the source file that contains your `PilotMain` and any other code that `PilotMain` directly calls when it receives a normal launch code. (This is another reason why I broke out `PilotMain` and event loop handling into a separate source file back in Chapter 2, "Anatomy of a Palm Application.")

Making Calls to Functions More Than 32KB Away

As your application nears 64KB in size, and even more so after you create multiple segments to build a program greater than 64KB, you might begin experiencing the linker error "16-bit reference out of range"—if you are lucky. If you are not so lucky, the linker will try to link your application anyway, and you will get a program that sporadically goes bonkers.

The reason for this error is that Palm OS uses 16-bit signed values to represent function call jumps, imposing a hard limit of 32KB as the maximum distance between a piece of code and the destination function it is trying to call. Although you might be able to squeak by if you are lucky and move your source files around in the project to create a link order in which calls are not greater than 32KB, ultimately this is time-consuming and exceedingly error-prone. CodeWarrior again comes to the rescue with the "Code Model" project setting. To edit this setting, go to your project's settings in CodeWarrior, and click the 68K Processor category in the left pane. The top-most setting is Code Model, and you have a choice between small, smart, and large.

The small code model is the default and results in the 32KB limit just described because all calls are 16-bit. Because of the small jump size, code compiled in this model is most efficient in terms of function-call processing.

The large code model forces the compiler to simulate "far jumps" by creating code that can jump by a 64-bit value. Although this neatly solves the far jump problem, there is a penalty in performance by making the processor do extra work with each function call. Depending on how desperate you are to solve the 32KB problem, you might or might not care about this performance loss.

The smart code model attempts to create the best of both the small and large models: Calls made within the same source file are assumed to be less than 32KB and thus use 16-bit jumps. Calls made across source files are assumed to be greater than 32KB and thus use 64-bit calls.

How you organize your source files in the Project window, especially in a multiple-segment project, can drastically affect how much the 32KB limit comes into play. If you can group logically related files together so most calls are made within the same segment, you will probably not experience as many problems as you would with a project with random distribution of source files across the project tree. I happen to really like organizing my projects into subcomponents, so this arrangement works well for me.

Other Options for Alleviating Size Problems

In some cases, size problems highlight architectural issues that are best addressed at design time. If you can plan for the logical partitioning of your application into components that have a clear, well-defined purpose, you will give yourself the best chance of avoiding (or at least preparing for) the possibility of large application problems.

Some options to consider as you are partitioning your application follow:

- How much of the application truly needs to be on the Palm?

    As I pointed out earlier, complex user interfaces requiring heavy data entry are not well suited for the Palm—nor are processor-intensive algorithms and number-crunching routines. If your application has any of these characteristics, you might want to consider moving some of the functionality off the Palm and onto either the desktop or a remote server application (assuming Internet connectivity is an option). It is unrealistic to assume a large application that formerly ran on fast workstations with 128MB of RAM will be suitable for a direct port to the Palm.

- Break off one or more components into shared libraries.

  Shared libraries, which are covered in Chapter 19, "Shared Libraries: Extending the Palm OS," are somewhat akin to dynamic link libraries (DLLs) under Windows. Unfortunately, shared libraries are tagged with a bit of black-magic mystique in that not too many developers understand how to create them (or so the number of available shared library components would have you believe). Part of this is no doubt due to the relatively sparse documentation on the subject.

  This is a shame because they offer a way to package a set of program services in a .PRC and make them available to one application or even many applications at the same time. Some examples of shared libraries are the Palm OS built-in Serial Manager and the IR Library.

Summary

With the Palm's rise in popularity, the temptation to move more functionality onto the Palm platform will only grow as time goes on. The natural progression in such matters will virtually guarantee a corresponding rise in the number of large applications created for the Palm.

Large applications are not in and of themselves a bad thing, if properly planned. Developers can use the information in this chapter to keep an eye out for the signs that their program has exceeded one or more of the size limitations and apply the appropriate remedies.

Advanced Topics

PART

V

IN THIS PART

CHAPTER 19

Shared Libraries: Extending the Palm OS

"Assembly of Japanese bicycle requires great peace of mind."

Robert Pirsig, *Zen and the Art of Motorcycle Maintenance*

Encapsulating Functionality: Shared Libraries

Packaging your code into shared libraries provides many benefits. Libraries provide a mechanism for reusing your code among two or more applications, thereby reducing development time. Multiple applications can use the same library, reducing both the installed and in-memory footprint. The lifetime of a shared library is not strictly tied to that of its clients, so its state can be maintained across applications. Architecturally, shared libraries reduce coupling between modules; reduced coupling results in more stable and maintainable code.

In these early days of the Palm Computing Platform, shared libraries are still on the wild frontier. There is limited support from the CodeWarrior tools: a handful of articles and white papers, and one example on the Palm Web site. But shared libraries are not nearly as complicated as they seem.

In this chapter you'll learn about

- The Palm shared library model
- The components of a shared library
- How to use Palm development tools to create shared libraries
- The development effort required for successfully creating a shared library

The Palm Shared Library Model

A shared library is a Palm database whose type is 'libr', which can be loaded and used by client applications. Shared libraries can be used by one or more clients. These clients might be applications or other shared libraries. The Palm OS comes with several shared libraries pre-loaded into ROM: SerialMgr and IrMgr are examples.

From the client side, the use of a shared library is straightforward. First the client retrieves the reference number for the shared library. This can be obtained either from SysLibLoad or SysLibFind by passing a pointer to an integer, which will receive the reference number upon success. If the library is being referenced for the first time, SysLibLoad then loads the library. If the library is already loaded, SysLibLoad returns an error, in which case SysLibFind returns the reference number of the loaded library. SerialMgr and IrMgr are used by the OS, so they are always loaded.

After the client obtains a reference number, it calls the shared library's functions, starting with the Open function. Under the Palm OS, inter-module function calls are resolved by a trap identifier rather than an address; and the system uses the library reference number to multiplex calls into shared libraries. All shared library functions must take this reference number as their first parameter.

When the client is finished with the shared library, the client might need to remove it from memory using SysLibRemove. It is recommended that the library should return success (zero) if it can be unloaded, or an error (a non-zero value) if it still has active clients.

Traps and the Palm SDK

If you examine any Palm OS header file, you'll notice that every function is followed by a SYS_TRAP macro. The meaning of the SYS_TRAP macro will be discussed in depth later; for now it is sufficient to understand that every Palm OS SDK function is mapped by the compiler into the appropriate trap invocation. It is the job of the shared library developer to provide the appropriate mapping from function call to system trap and back to function call.

The SDK trap identifiers are unique throughout the operating system. Shared library function trap identifiers are unique only within the library. The header System\SysTraps.h lists the trap identifier for every SDK function. These are defined as an enumeration beginning with sysTrapBase (0xA000). This header also defines sysLibTrapBase (0xA800), which is the starting value for a shared library's trap identifiers. There are six predefined identifiers: sysLibTrapName, sysLibTrapOpen, sysLibTrapClose, sysLibTrapSleep, sysLibTrapWake, and sysLibTrapCustom. The specific uses of each of these will be described later. For now, what is important is that your custom function trap identifiers must start with sysLibTrapCustom and increment by one.

What Palm OS Provides

The system provides the three services for shared libraries: the system trap dispatcher, the system library table, and the library reference number.

The system trap dispatcher dispatches calls by library reference number to the appropriate library. When a client invokes a function by trap identifier, it generates an exception. The trap dispatcher handles this exception by putting the address of the appropriate function onto the stack. When the exception returns, program execution is transferred to this address.

For each shared library open in the system, there is a corresponding entry in the system library table. This entry holds both the library's dispatch table and the memory allocated by the library for its global memory. These items are discussed in more detail in the next section.

The library reference number is assigned by the system when the library is loaded for the first time. The client retrieves this number either from SysLibLoad, which loads the library, or SysLibFind, if the library is already loaded. This reference number must be the first parameter to every shared library call; the system trap dispatcher uses it to locate the correct library.

What the Shared Library Must Provide

The shared library provides an installation entry point and the library's dispatch table. It also implements domain-specific functionality.

The installation entry point is named __Startup__, and it must be the first function in the library's link order. It returns 0 for success or a negative error code. SysLibLoad returns the error code to the client application. The system passes the library's entry in the system library table as a parameter to this function; the library sets the dispatch table.

The library dispatch table contains a list of all routines in the library. This is a lookup table used by the system trap dispatcher, and it is described in great detail in the following sections.

Implementing a Shared Library

Three components are in a shared library: the API declaration, the API implementation, and the dispatch table. The API declarations specify how clients use the shared library. The API implementation provides this functionality. The dispatch table maps the declarations to the implementation via the system trap mechanism.

The API Declaration

The shared library publishes a header file describing the API to clients. Function declarations specify how the client invokes the API, including parameter information and return types. Trap identifiers allow the system to invoke the function using the trap mechanism on which the Palm OS relies. Result codes provide an expected set of errors for which the client should check. Domain-specific structures and constants provide additional information required by the custom portion of the API.

Function Declarations

Every shared library must publish four standard functions:

- Open—The client must call this function first. It allows the shared library to initialize any resources it needs. No other API functions can be called prior to this function.

- Close—The client calls this function last. It allows the shared library to release any resources it is holding. When this function is called, the library is in an invalid state; it must be reopened before it can be used.

- Sleep—The operating system calls this function before the device enters sleep mode. It allows system-level libraries to shut down hardware components to conserve power.

- Wake—The operating system calls this function when the device returns sleep mode. It allows system-level libraries to re-enable any hardware components that were shut down when the device entered sleep mode.

The shared library also publishes domain-specific functions. As a rule, these functions must be invoked after Open and before Close, to make sure that the library has valid resources. The one exception is a function that retrieves the API version of the library, which might be invoked before Open to ensure compatibility.

Function Trap Identifiers

If you examine the Palm OS SDK headers, you'll notice that every function declaration includes the SYS_TRAP macro:

```
Err SerOpen(UInt refNum, UInt port, ULong baud)
              SYS_TRAP(sysLibTrapOpen);
```

For the CodeWarrior compiler, this declaration expands to a Metrowerks extension called *opcode inline* syntax.

```
Err SerOpen(UInt refNum, UInt port, ULong baud)
= {m68kTrapInstr + sysDispatchTrapNum, trapNum}
```

opcode inline syntax allows you to specify the 68k opcodes for the function's implementation. When you call an opcode inline function, the compiler replaces the function calls with the specified opcodes. This feature supports calls through the 68k processor's A-Trap mechanism; it generates the exception that is handled by the Palm OS's system trap dispatcher.

Invoking a call to a shared library function is a two-step process. First, for client code, the function declaration expands into a call to the "A-Trap" mechanism. This mechanism uses the library's reference number to identify the appropriate entry in the system library table; the library's reference number must be the first parameter to any shared library function. Then, using the trap identifier as an offset into the entry's dispatch table, the appropriate library function is called.

If this all seems like an awful lot of work, just remember that the compiler takes care of it; your job is to declare the trap ID enumeration, and make sure that you use the right trap for each function declaration.

The system defines traps for the required Open, Close, Sleep, and Wake functions. You define the rest, starting with sysLibTrapCustom, and incrementing sequentially.

Errors

The public API also contains the errors that the functions might return. These are based on the appErrorClass, which is defined in SystemMgr.h. The library functions should not return any results that are not either a success or one of the API-defined errors.

Structures and Constants

In addition to the functional API, there might be structures or constants defined by the library. For example, a printing library might publish a font structure and constants for bold, italic, or underline.

API Implementation

The functions described in the public header are implemented in a standard C file. In this module, the SYS_TRAP macro is disabled so that the function declarations evaluate to standard C declarations.

Open

The Open function is responsible for allocating memory for this information and storing it in the system library table entry for the shared library. After this is done, it performs any domain-specific initialization.

Close

The Close function is responsible for releasing memory allocated for the library's globals and removing this value from the system library table entry. Any domain-specific cleanup should be done prior to releasing this memory. By convention, this function returns 0 if the library should be removed, or an error code indicating that the library is still in use by other clients.

Sleep and Wake

The Sleep function handles notification from the system that the system is about to shut down. This notification allows system-level libraries to shut down hardware components in order to conserve power.

The Wake function handles notification from the system that the system is about to wake up again. This notification allows system-level libraries to re-enable hardware components that were shut down when the system went to sleep.

Because these functions are invoked by system interrupts, they might only use interrupt-safe system services, and must not take a long time.

Custom Functions

Domain-specific API functions depend on the global data allocated in the Open function, and so should only be invoked between the Open and Close functions. These functions follow a standard pattern. First, they retrieve the library's global data. Then they perform the domain-specific task they provide. Finally, they release the global data.

There are exceptions to this rule. For example, many libraries provide a function to retrieve the API version of the library. Because this function does not rely on any global information, it might be called before the Open or after the Close function. Indeed, it probably should be called prior to Open to ensure compatibility between the client and the library.

Dispatch Table Implementation

The dispatch table implementation is provided by two functions: Install and DispatchTable. The system invokes the Install function as part of SysLibLoad; this function invokes the DispatchTable function, which returns the address of the dispatch table. This address is stored in the library's entry in the system library table. DispatchTable is coded in Assembler and includes the declaration of the dispatch table, in addition to the code that returns its address.

The first section of the dispatch table is an array of offsets from the beginning of the dispatch table. The first offset points to the library name. This string is stored at the very end of the table. The remaining offsets point to entries in the next section, which is an array of jump instructions. The second offset points to a jump to the Open function; the third, a jump to the Close function, and so on. The library name is stored as a null-terminated string at the end of the jump table.

Let's say, for example, that you had a shared library named FooLibrary, with only one function—Foo. The dispatch table would look like Table 19.1.

TABLE 19.1   THE DISPATCH TABLE FOR THE FOOLIBRARY SHARED LIBRARY

Section	Address	Contents	Comments
Offsets	0	20	Address of name string
	2	12	Offset to Open jump
	4	14	Offset to Close jump
	6	16	Offset to Sleep jump
	8	18	Offset to Wake jump
	10	20	Offset to Foo jump
Jumps	12	JMP Open	Jump to Open
	14	JMP Close	Jump to Close
	16	JMP Sleep	Jump to Sleep
	18	JMP Wake	Jump to Wake
	20	JMP	Jump to Foo
Lib Name	22	FooLibrary	Library name

19

SHARED
LIBRARIES:
PALM OS

The system executes library traps using this table. Using the trap identifier as an index into the first section of the dispatch table, it retrieves the offset to the jump instruction corresponding to the trap. The system moves to this offset in the dispatch table and executes the next instruction. This instruction is a jump to the appropriate shared library function.

FIGURE 19.1

A conceptual model of a dispatch table.

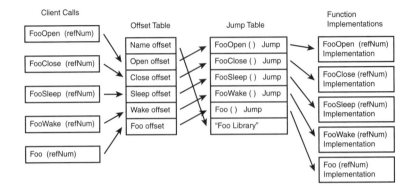

Conceptually, this is no different from the implementation of virtual tables under C++. The client invokes a function that is mapped to an offset in a function table. Using this offset, the compiler retrieves the address of the function to execute. The main difference is that in C++ the compiler takes care of all this plumbing transparently; with shared libraries, we must do it ourselves.

More Rules of the Road

Just in case shared libraries weren't daunting enough, there are some rules and caveats of which you should be aware.

Do Not Use Static and Global Values

Shared libraries are stored on the device as resource databases. The memory occupied by the library is, therefore, on the storage heap. By default, this memory is protected; it can only be written to with the appropriate DataMgr function. A downstream effect of this is that all global or static values are, effectively, read-only.

You could use static or global variables in your shared library. But if you do, you need to allocate a writeable data segment for them, and initialize this data segment by hand. When you enter a library function, you need to set the A4 register to point to this data segment. When you exit the function, you need to set it back to its original value. You also need to do this "A4 magic" before calling certain SDK functions, like MemHandleNew. In general, it's best not to use them at all.

Install Linkage

A shared library's Install function is actually a macro for the library entry point, `__Startup__`. The system expects this function to be the first entry point into the library. This function must therefore be first in the linkage order. I put it in its own module, and list that module first in the Segments panel of the project.

Library Resources

Palm application resources are opened with the application at all times. If you want to show a form, or raise an alert, it is a straightforward task. Resources associated with a shared library are not left opened with the library; the library must specifically load its resource database. Consequently, it must unload the database as well.

Debugging

Bugs are a fact of life in software development. As a result, so are debuggers. Unfortunately, the CodeWarrior debugger does not currently support tracing into shared library code. This support is rumored to be coming in an upcoming release. Until this support is available, you must embed code in your library to display errors, variable values, and so on. You can use alerts, error messages, or the emulator logging facility. On some projects, I have created a debug message console on the Palm device. A more detailed discussion of debugging without a visual debugger is beyond the scope of this chapter.

Example—ShrLib—A Simple Shared Library

My example allows the client application to get and set a text string. In addition to the standard Open, Close, Sleep, and Wake, I will provide functions to determine the library's API version and to get and set the text string.

The Project File—ShrLib.mcp

You can use the project file and directory structure as a basis for your shared library development. There is no stationery for these projects, so I started with the Palm OS C application stationery and modified it, as shown in Table 19.2.

19

SHARED
LIBRARIES:
PALM OS

TABLE 19.2 TARGET SETTINGS MODIFIED FROM THE PALM OS C APPLICATION STATIONERY

Panel	Setting	Value
Target Settings	Target Name	`ShrLib`
Access Paths	Always Search User Paths	`Checked`
68k Target	Project Type	`PalmOS Code Resource`
	File Name	`ShrLib.tmp`
	ResType	`libr`
PilotRez	Mac Resource Files	`ShrLib.tmp`
	Creator	`SHRL`
	Type	`libr`

Note that the 68k Target—File Name setting must match the Pilot Rez—Mac Resource Files setting. Also, the shared library's creator ID must be registered with Palm to avoid conflicts with other applications or libraries.

The Public Header—ShrLib.h

The header, ShrLib.h, includes the declarations for the library used by client applications. Our library publishes seven functions. Four of these are the standard functions every library must publish: ShrOpen, ShrClose, ShrSleep, and ShrWake. Additionally, we publish one function to determine the library's version, ShrAPIVersion. The last two functions, ShrGetText and ShrSetText, are custom functions that allow client applications to retrieve and modify the shared library's text string.

Trap Handling

The first thing you'll notice in this file is the definition of the SHRLIB_TRAP macro:

```
#ifdef BUILDING_LIBRARY
#define SHRLIB_TRAP(trapNum)
#else
#define SHRLIB_TRAP(trapNum) SYS_TRAP(trapNum)
#endif
```

The SHRLIB_TRAP macro is used in declaring the API functions. If the BUILDING_SHRLIB macro is defined, this macro does nothing and the functions are declared as normal C function calls. Otherwise, BUILDING_SHRLIB expands to the SDK SYS_TRAP macro, and the functions are declared using the Palm OS trap mechanism. The only place where the

BUILDING_SHRLIB macro should be defined is in the implementation of the API functions; source files that want to invoke these functions should do so by the trap mechanism.

Library Identifiers

Clients identify a shared library in two ways. To load the library, the client needs creator and library type identifiers:

```
#define shrCreatorID 'SHRL'
#define shrTypeID    'libr'
```

These values are passed to SysLibLoad, and must match the respective project settings. Creator must match the PilotRez—Creator. Type must match both 68k Target—ResType and PilotRez—Type.

To find a library that has already been loaded, the client needs the library's name:

```
#define shrName      "Shared Library"
```

The client passes the library name to SysLibFind, which compares it to the names of the currently loaded libraries. This constant is also used internally in the dispatch table.

Error Declarations

I define three errors:

```
#define shrErrAlreadyOpen   (appErrorClass ¦ 1)
#define shrErrParam         (appErrorClass ¦ 2)
#define shrErrMemory        (appErrorClass ¦ 3)
```

shrErrAlreadyOpen is returned if the client attempts to open a library that is already opened. My library does not support multiple clients.

shrErrParam is returned when at least one of the function parameters is invalid. An example of this would be if a NULL pointer were passed as an out-param.

shrErrMemory is returned when the allocation of memory or another resource fails.

Function Trap Identifiers

For each of the three custom functions published by my library, I define the corresponding trap identifier:

```
typedef enum {
    shrTrapAPIVersion = sysLibTrapCustom,
    shrTrapGetText,
    shrTrapSetText
} ShrTrapNumberEnum;
```

19

SHARED
LIBRARIES:
PALM OS

These are declared as an enumeration to ensure sequential values. Notice that the trap enumeration begins with the SDK constant sysLibTrapCustom.

Function Declarations

I provide function declarations for both standard and custom functions. I include declarations for Sleep and Wake for completeness; they are only ever called by the operating system and must conform to a standard declaration:

```
// Standard Library Functions:
extern Err ShrOpen(UInt refNum)
            SHRLIB_TRAP(sysLibTrapOpen);

extern Err ShrClose(UInt refNum)
            SHRLIB_TRAP(sysLibTrapClose);

extern Err ShrSleep(UInt refNum)
            SHRLIB_TRAP(sysLibTrapSleep);

extern Err ShrWake(UInt refNum)
            SHRLIB_TRAP(sysLibTrapWake);

// Get our library API version
extern Err ShrAPIVersion(UInt refNum, DWordPtr dwVerP)
            SHRLIB_TRAP(shrTrapAPIVersion);

// Retrieve the text stored by the library.
extern Err ShrGetText(UInt refNum, CharPtr string, UInt size)
            SHRLIB_TRAP(shrTrapGetText);

// Set the text stored by the library.
extern Err ShrSetText(UInt refNum, CharPtr string)
            SHRLIB_TRAP(shrTrapSetText);
```

All functions must take the library reference number as their first parameter. `ShrSleep` and `ShrWake` are invoked only by the operating system, so they must take only the reference number parameter. The trap mechanism returns an integer, so all library functions should do so as well.

These declarations are wrapped with macros that check if the header is being included in a C++ source file. If so, these functions are declared as extern 'C'. This prevents function name mangling by the C++ compiler.

API Implementation—ShrLib.c

Now that you've declared your API to the public, it's time to implement it. You do this in ShrLib.c. Before you implement these functions, though, there are some supporting declarations you need to make.

Library Globals

As a rule, global or static variables are prohibited in a shared library. There are techniques to get around this prohibition, but they are best avoided. Instead, values that must persist between function calls are stored in a structure:

```
#define shrMaxText   (99)

struct ShrGlobalsType {
   UInt  refNum;
   Char  text [shrMaxText+1];
   };
```

This structure is stored in the system library table entry associated with the loaded library. The `refNum` attribute is used to store the shared library's reference number; this is the number returned to the client by SysLibLoad or SysLibFind.

The text attribute is used to store the string managed by this shared library. In your shared library, you would replace this attribute with domain-specific attributes.

ShrOpen

ShrOpen allocates the globals structure and associates it with the library in the system library table. First you retrieve a pointer to the system library table entry for the library:

```
// Retrieve the system library table entry.
   SysLibTblEntryPtr libEntryP = NULL;
   libEntryP = SysLibTblEntry(refNum);
```

Next you check the entry's `globalsP` attribute. If this attribute is not NULL, the library is already in use by another client and the function returns shrErrAlreadyOpen:

```
// Make sure the globals have not been initialized.
   if (NULL != libEntryP->globalsP)
   {
      // Globals already initialized.
      // Library is open for another client.
      return shrErrAlreadyOpen;
   }
```

Otherwise, the function allocates a block of memory to hold the globals structure. Set the owner of this memory to 0 (the system) using MemHandleSetOwner. This allows the library to maintain state between applications; if you didn't, the memory would be freed when the calling application exited. Even though your library will only support a single client application, the client application might start and stop as the user switches to other applications.

```
VoidHand globalsH = NULL;

// Allocate enough memory to hold data.
// Note: We allocate a memory handle rather than a
//       (locked) pointer so that the memory manager
//       can move the block around. Remember, this
//       library may be around for a long time.
globalsH = MemHandleNew (sizeof (ShrGlobalsType));

// Set owner of global data memory block to "system"
// (zero).
// Note: If the application were to remain the owner
//       of the memory, the memory would be freed
//       when the application exited.  For the library
//       to maintain state between applications, this
//       must not happen.  Any other allocated memory
//       blocks should likewise be adopted by the system.
MemHandleSetOwner(globalsH, 0);
```

When the memory is allocated, store its handle in the library's system table entry. Use movable memory to minimize dynamic heap fragmentation, so you have to cast the handle to a pointer, as expected by the entry.

```
// Save the handle of our library globals in the
// system library table entry so we can later
// retrieve it using SysLibTblEntry().
// Note: lib entry structure expects a void pointer,
//       so we must cast our handle accordingly.
libEntryP->globalsP = (void*) globalsH;
```

Finally, initialize the values of structure. Lock the handle, set the reference number and text attributes, and then unlock the handle again.

```
ShrGlobalsType* globalsP = NULL;

// Lock the memory and cast it to a ShrGlobalsType pointer.
globalsP = (ShrGlobalsPtr)MemHandleLock(globalsH);

// Begin library-specific open functionality.

// Initialize global data's reference number.
globalsP->refNum = refNum;

// Initialize global data's text buffer.
StrCopy (globalsP->text,
         "Shared Library Example Text");
```

```
// End library-specific open functionality.

// Unlock globals.
MemHandleUnlock (globalsH);
```

To optimize system performance, the memory should be locked only when needed, and unlocked as soon as possible. This allows the memory manager to move the block around as necessary.

ShrClose

Closing the library is fairly straightforward. You retrieve the global data handle and perform any domain-specific close functionality (in this case, there is none). Then you free the global data memory and set the library entry's globalsP attribute to NULL.

```
// Retrieve library system table entry.
   SysLibTblEntryPtr libEntryP = SysLibTblEntry(refNum);

   // Retrieve the handle of our library globals from the
   // system table entry.
   VoidHand globalsH = (VoidHand)(libEntryP->globalsP);

   // Begin library-specific close functionality.

   // End library-specific close functionality.

   // Clear library system table entry's global data.
   libEntryP->globalsP = NULL;

   // Free global data memory.
   MemHandleFree(globalsH);
```

ShrSleep and ShrWake

The implementations of ShrSleep and ShrWake are trivial; they simply return success; you have no hardware to disable or enable.

ShrAPIVersion

ShrAPIVersion returns the version number for the library. This version number is calculated according to the scheme defined in SystemMgr.h.

Version numbers are formatted as 0xMMmfsbb, where:

MM	Major Version of library
m	Minor Version of library
f	Bug fix flag
s	Stage of version (see stages, following)
bbb	Build number (for non-releases)

19

Stages of development are defined as:

0	Development build
1	Alpha build
2	Beta build
3	Release build

Examples of this scheme are:

v1.2 Dev build 12	0x0120000 0C
v1.1 Alpha 2	0x011001002
v1.1 Beta 3	0x011002003
v1.0 Release	0x010003000

The Palm SDK provides a set of macros for both creating and decoding versions. The `sysMakeROMVersion` takes the major version, minor version, bug fix flag, stage and build number and creates a DWord representing the version number. The macros `sysGetROMVerMajor`, `sysGetROMVerMinor`, `sysGetROMVerFix`, `sysGetROMVerStage`, and `sysGetROMVerBuild` extract the respective values from a version number. These macros are defined in SystemMgr.h.

ShrGetText and ShrSetText

The implementations for custom functions are fairly boilerplate. The function retrieves a pointer to the library's system library table entry and locks the globals memory:

```
// Retrieve library system table entry.
SysLibTblEntryPtr libEntryP = SysLibTblEntry(refNum);

// Retrieve the handle of our library globals
// from the library system
// table entry.
VoidHand globalsH = (VoidHand)(libEntryP->globalsP);

// Lock the memory and cast it to a ShrGlobalsType.
ShrGlobalsType* globalsP =
    (ShrGlobalsType*)MemHandleLock(globalsH);
```

The functions do their thing; then unlock the globals and return.

Dispatch Table Implementation—ShrDisp.c

The dispatch table is the heart of a shared library. It provides the mapping from the library's trap identifiers to the appropriate function implementations. This is not for the faint of heart; creating the dispatch table involves a fair amount of hand-coding assembler. You might want to take a deep breath before we dive in.

Declarations

Before we explore the implementation of the dispatch table, there are a few declarations in ShrDisp.c that we should examine.

As in ShrLib.c, you define `BUILDING_SHRLIB`, which turns off the SYS_TRAP macro and yields standard C declarations of our API functions. The dispatch table requires the actual addresses of these functions to implement the trap-mapping mechanism.

You also declare a macro, `ShrInstall`, which expands to `__Startup__`. `__Startup___` is the entry point to the library, which is invoked by the system when the library is loaded.

Finally, we declare the function `ShrDispatchTable`. This is the function that implements the dispatch table and returns its address. This function has an interesting declaration:

```
static Ptr asm ShrDispatchTable(void)
```

Ptr refers to a generic pointer (it is actually a typedef of char* to maintain compatibility with the Mac). The asm qualifier means that the function itself is implemented in assembler.

ShrInstall

`ShrInstall` initializes the dispatch table in the library's system library table entry. The `ShrInstall` function takes two parameters: a reference number and a pointer to the library's system library table entry. It assigns the return value of `ShrDispatchTable` to the entry's dispatch table attribute:

```
// Install pointer to our dispatch table
entryP->dispatchTblP = (Ptr*)ShrDispatchTable();
```

This function also clears the entry's globals attribute:

```
// Initialize globals pointer to zero (we will set up
// our library globals in the library "open" call).
entryP->globalsP = 0;
```

Finally, you return 0 to indicate success. If you returned a negative error code, `SysLibLoad` would fail and return this error.

ShrDispatchTable

The `ShrDispatchTable` function itself simply loads the address of the dispatch table into the A0 register and returns. The A0 register holds function return values.

```
LEA    @Table, A0    // table ptr
RTS                  // exit with it
```

The actual dispatch table is coded into this function as well. First, declare a series of macros to simplify the hand-coding effort required.

We define the total number of traps published by the library. There are the four standard traps for Open, Close, Sleep, and Wake, and three custom traps for GetAPIVersion, GetText, and SetText:

```
#define numTraps (7)
```

We add one to the number of traps to determine the number of entries in the dispatch table. The extra entry is for the library name:

```
#define numEntries (numTraps) + 1
```

Starting with the number of entries, you can calculate the offset from the beginning of the table to the first jump. For each entry, there is a word in the dispatch table.

```
#define offsetToJumps ((numEntries) * 2)
```

The last piece of information we need is the size of the jump instructions. Because Palm OS uses short jumps, this is 4 bytes; 2 for the JMP instruction and 2 for the address in which to jump:

```
#define jumpSize (4)
```

From these macros, we can define a macro that calculates the offset to a specific jump by index:

```
#define libDispatchEntry(index) \
(offsetToJumps + ((index)*jumpSize))
```

We use this macro to define the address of the dispatch entry for each trap:

```
@Table:
        // Offset to library name
        DC.W    @Name

        // Start of standard traps
        DC.W    libDispatchEntry(0)    // Open
        DC.W    libDispatchEntry(1)    // Close
        DC.W    libDispatchEntry(2)    // Sleep
        DC.W    libDispatchEntry(3)    // Wake

        // Start of the Custom traps
        DC.W    libDispatchEntry(4)    // GetAPIVersion
        DC.W    libDispatchEntry(5)    // GetText
        DC.W    libDispatchEntry(6)    // SetText
```

Note that the index parameters passed to the macro `libDispatchEntry` are numbered consecutively, beginning with zero. This is required to make sure that they point to the correct entry in the jump table. Also note that the first entry is the address of the Name label. This label is at the end of the jump table.

The jump table is a set of jumps to the addresses of the functions published by the library:

```
// Standard library function handlers
@GotoOpen:
    JMP         ShrOpen
@GotoClose:
    JMP         ShrClose
@GotoSleep:
    JMP         ShrSleep
@GotoWake:
    JMP         ShrWake

// Custom library function handlers
@GotoAPIVersion:
    JMP         ShrAPIVersion
@GotoGetText:
    JMP         ShrGetText
@GotoSetText:
    JMP         ShrSetText
```

The final entry in the dispatch table is the library name:

```
    DC.B        shrName
```

This name identifies the library to the system, which looks for its address at the beginning of the dispatch table. Client applications can check if the library is loaded by passing the library name, defined by shrName, to SysLibFind. If the library is already loaded, the library's reference number will be returned.

It is important to note that the order of the trap values must match the order of the dispatch entries, which must match the order of the jumps in the jump table.

A Final Note on Dispatch Tables

If all this sounds horribly complex and scary, it shouldn't be. The dispatch table in this chapter can be copied and modified to suit your shared library. You don't need to know how or why it works, only that it does. There are a few things to remember, though:

- The order of the trap identifiers as declared in the public header **must** match the order of the respective functions in the jump table.
- The numTraps macro **must** be equal to the number of public functions declared.
- There **must** be one entry in the dispatch table for each public function.
- The standard functions **must** appear first in the jump table and in the correct order: Open, Close, Sleep, and Wake.

If your library is crashing, or the wrong functions are being invoked, these are the first things to check.

Summary

Shared libraries are not hard to create. Conceptually, they are simply function tables that follow specific rules. The bad news is that these rules are not necessarily intuitive. The good news is that when you've created your first library, you can use it for a template and stop worrying about these rules. The best news is that you've just created your first library.

Shared libraries are not particularly hard to implement, but they require care and patience. Used correctly, they will repay the investment with greater code reuse, increased application stability, and reduced resource requirements. You might think of them as peace of mind, encapsulated.

CHAPTER 20

Using the Communications Libraries, Part 1: Serial Manager

The Palm has achieved an incredible level of success, proving to be an indispensable personal information management tool as well as a platform for a rapidly growing raft of third-party and vertical market software.

In many application domains, however, to be a truly useful tool, the Palm platform needs to communicate with the "outside world." Storing and managing information within the device itself is extremely valuable; however, the ability to share that information is a vital component to any platform's long-term success and market viability. A key component to the Palm OS success today is its ability to communicate and achieve connectivity with other applications, platforms, devices, and networks. Perhaps the most visible expression of that connectivity is the hot-sync facility, which allows the exchange of information between the Palm and a host system.

With a platform that can both manage and transfer information, the user is empowered to change the way she performs her day-to-day tasks and become more productive and efficient. Of course, the other side to this topic is that communications can (and should be!) fun. In addition to the business activities that can be performed with the transmission of data, a new world of personal communications, messaging, gaming, and other applications is opened to this community.

I begin the discussion of communications topics with the Serial Manager, Palm's low-level API, which exposes the Palm device's built-in serial port. I conclude this chapter with a sample application that will engage a hosting PC in a "terminal" session. To get the most from this chapter, you will need an application such as Windows Terminal or HyperTerminal running on your PC or other development platform.

The Hardware

The present-day Palm device has one physical serial port that is similar to the ports found on your PC, though not entirely compatible. The Palm device uses a UART chip (Universal Asynchronous Receiver and Transmitter), which is compliant to the HPSIR/IrDA Physical Communication Protocol. (Page 5 of the tech sheet for Motorola Dragonball processor MC68328 talks about the UART's properties.) This chip differs from your PC's UART in that it does not give you access to all the signals you might be accustomed to, such as ring indicator (RI) and data terminal ready (DTR). Additionally, your PC UART typically has a 16-byte buffer for both the send and receive buffer, whereas the Palm's UART buffers each hold 8 bytes. The Palm supports serial communications at baud rates ranging from 300 to 115,200bps.

There are a number of ways to "connect" your Palm to the outside world and make use of serial communications. The Palm talks via the cradle to the PC or other device. To communicate with a parallel device (such as a laser or line printer), you can purchase (or build, if you are adventurous!) a serial-to-parallel converter cable. If you want to connect the Palm to a modem, your best bet is to pick up a Palm modem cable. This cable is specially wired to make up for some of the "missing" signals I mentioned. Depending on the device you want your Palm to communicate with, you might need a special cable created. You can visit Palm's Web site for more information on the signals available from the Palm device itself and the wiring pin-outs of the cradle.

I discuss IR communications in the next chapter, but it is important to mention now that in the Palm III device, the IR port and the serial port share the one and only UART chip. This means that you cannot operate the IR port and the serial port simultaneously. This arrangement might change with future releases of the platform, as you will learn in the next section, where I discuss the software interface to the serial port.

The Software

Many layers of software make up the entire serial communications "stack." Your application's needs and your interest in creating your own "protocols" will determine where your program will interact with the Palm's communications facilities. The lowest layer above the hardware itself is referred to as the Serial Manager. The Serial Manager provides for byte-level input and output and the ability to set port parameters such as baud rate and parity.

Beyond the Serial Manager, there are layers for modem management and a connection management protocol. Additionally, for packet-oriented communications, the Palm OS provides the Serial Link protocol. The Serial Link protocol offers an interface similar to sockets, where multiple "conversations" can occur over a single physical connection. Of course, the partner application (whatever is running on the PC or other connected device) must use the same protocol.

The best way to learn is to do, and you want to get up and running quickly with serial communications. In this chapter, we will build a Palm application to conduct a terminal session with a host PC. Before you can dive into the application, you need to learn some of the core Serial Manager APIs and concepts. I discuss the high points of the Serial Manager, giving you enough ammunition to get started as a Palm OS communications programmer. For the intricate details of the Serial Manager functions, refer to the Serial Manager documentation from Palm Computing as well as review the SerialMgr.h file shipped with the Palm OS SDK.

Serial Manager Essentials

Palm OS exposes its low-level serial port access via the Serial Manager, as I discussed earlier. To gain access to the Serial Manager, you need to load it at runtime. This is done by calling SysLibFind.

The Serial Manager is a system library, meaning it is provided by the operating system itself. Once you load the library, you have access to all the functions therein. Each application making use of the serial library needs to call SysLibFind to obtain a handle. Each subsequent Serial Manager function call will require this handle.

The following code shows how to use SysLibFind to load Serial Manager:

```
Err e;
UInt SerialRefNum;

// Load the serial library
e = SysLibFind("Serial Library",&SerialRefNum);

if (e)
{
    FrmCustomAlert(ErrorAlert,"Failed To Load Library!","","");
    return;
}
```

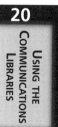

Once the Serial Manager library is loaded, you can do things such as open and close serial ports and change properties such as baud rate and handshaking.

Opening the Port

Before you use the serial port, you have to open it via SerOpen. This function takes three parameters, the handle to the Serial Manager library, the port number, and the initial baud rate desired. As I mentioned earlier, this library has support for multiple serial ports (sort of). At the moment, the device has but one, so the port value must be 0. The baud rate should be set to a standard rate in the range of 300–115,200bps. A successful return code for this function will be either 0 or serErrAlreadyOpen.

It is possible for multiple tasks to have the port open simultaneously. However, if your application expects to have full control of the serial port and the SerOpen function returns serErrAlreadyOpen, your application needs to call SerClose and not perform any further action with the serial port functions:

```
e = SerOpen(SerialRefNum,0,9600);
if (e)
{
FrmCustomAlert(ErrorAlert,"Failed To Open Port 0!","","");
return;
}

// Let's keep track of when the port is open
Connected = 1;
```

Closing the Port

Another key function, SerClose shuts down the Palm's serial port. This function should only be called if a previous call to SerOpen returned 0 or serErrAlreadyOpen. Please note that there is no "port" parameter to this function. All you pass is the handle to the library returned by SysLibFind. This function will shut all ports (one at the moment) opened by your application. It is anticipated that as the hardware progresses to include multiple serial ports, the Serial Manager API functions will be modified to let you select the desired port.

It is important to note that you should call SerClose prior to exiting your Palm OS application. This can present a challenge in Palm OS because of the way tasks are closed or terminated with limited warning. To close down the port, you might want to practice using a variable to indicate the port's status. If you are about to switch applications, as notified by the application's event loop, check that variable. If your port is open, make a call to close it prior to exiting. Failing to do so can cause problems with other applications that need to use the UART, including your own application the next time it is invoked, the IR port, and hot-sync. (You have been warned!)

```
// Close port
if (0 == Connected) return;
e = SerClose(SerialRefNum);
if (e)
{
 FrmCustomAlert(ErrorAlert,"Error during Close!","","");
}
// Keep track of our state
Connected = 0;
```

SerGetSettings and SerSetSettings

The `SerGetSettings` and `SerSetSettings` functions allow you to modify the serial port's baud rate, handshaking, and other communications properties. It is a good practice to retrieve the serial port's settings prior to changing them. You want to make a call to `SerGetSettings` first, passing in the handle to the Serial Manager library and the address of a variable of type `SerSettingsType`. Once you have this, you can make the appropriate modifications and then call `SerSetSettings` to make the changes take effect:

```
SerSettingsType sstSetup;
SerGetSettings( SerialRefNum, &sstSetup );
// Let's set the baud rate & other serial comms properties
sstSetup.baudRate = 9600;
sstSetup.flags =    serSettingsFlagBitsPerChar7 ¦
                    serSettingsFlagParityOnM ¦
                    serSettingsFlagParityEvenM ¦
                    serSettingsFlagStopBitsM ¦
                    serSettingsFlagStopBits1;
sstSetup.ctsTimeout = serSettingsFlagRTSAutoM
 ¦ serSettingsFlagCTSAutoM;

// Ask Serial Manager to update the port settings
SerSetSettings( SerialRefNum, &sstSetup );
```

SerReceiveFlush

The `SerReceiveFlush` function acts to "reset" the serial port. It discards data from Serial Manager's receive queue and clears the saved error status. It takes two parameters, the Serial Manager's library handle and an interbyte timeout (in system ticks). `SerReceiveFlush` will block until a timeout occurs while waiting on the next byte:

```
// Let's clear the port, just in case some garbage is
// sitting there
SerReceiveFlush (SerialRefNum, 100 );
```

SerReceiveCheck

The `SerReceiveCheck` function will tell the application the number of bytes waiting in the receive queue. This is an effective way of performing nonblocking I/O. The function takes the handle to the Serial Manager library and the address of an unsigned long (`UlongPtr`). Examine the value of this unsigned long argument to determine whether your application needs to service the receive queue:

```
// See if there is anything in the queue ... "peek"
e = SerReceiveCheck(SerialRefNum,&ulBytes);
if (ulBytes)
{
    // Read from queue
}
```

SerReceive

The `SerReceive` function will read from the receive queue. The parameters are the library handle, buffer for receiving data, count of bytes desired, interbyte timeout in system ticks, and the address of an `Err` variable. This function will return the number of bytes read. Examine the value of the error variable; it should be zero for a successful read. This value might be `serErrTimeOut`, which indicates that the `SerReceive` function is returning due to a timeout during the read process. The application should check the number of bytes actually read:

```
SerReceive(SerialRefNum,&szBuf[index],1,0,&e);
// Check for read error
if (e)
{
    FrmCustomAlert(ErrorAlert, "Error Reading Serial Port!","","");
    SerReceiveFlush(SerialRefNum,100);
    index = 0;
    return;
}
```

SerReceiveWait

`SerReceiveWait` will wait a given number of system ticks for the receive queue to accumulate a certain amount of data. For example, you would use this function if you needed to read in records of 20 bytes each and your application could not handle partial records. To call this function, the application must pass the Serial Manager library handle, the number of bytes to accumulate, and the number of system ticks to wait:

```
// Wait for 20 bytes to accumulate
e = SerReceiveWait(SerialRefNum, 20, 200);
if (e)
{
```

```
    // Process timeout or line error
}
else
{
    // Read in the bytes
}
```

SerSend

To send data via the serial port, use the SerSend function. This function takes the Serial Manager library handle, a pointer to the memory buffer holding the data you want to send, the count of bytes to send, and the address of an Err variable. The function returns the count of bytes actually transferred:

```
// Let's send our message!
UlBytes = SerSend(SerialRefNum, (unsigned char *) pText,
➥    StrLen(pText),&e);
if (e)
{
FrmCustomAlert(ErrorAlert, "Error Sending Message!","","");
}
```

SerSendWait

At times, an application will send a stream of bytes and then want to close down the serial port, switch to another application, and so on. It is important to wait until all your data has been sent before closing down the port with SerClose; otherwise, the trailing portion of your transmission might never reach its destination.

The arguments for SerSendWait are the Serial Manager library handle and the number of system ticks to wait. This second parameter is actually not implemented as of Palm OS version 3.0. The application programmer must use a value of -1 for the timeout parameter:

```
// Let's wait for the port to flush
e = SerSendWait(SerialRefNum,-1);
```

PalmTalk: A Palm OS Serial Terminal Application

Now that you have looked at the components of a Serial Manager application, let's build a sample application. PalmTalk allows a Palm device that is sitting in its cradle to communicate with its host PC via the PC's connected COM port.

One topic that I have not addressed is the topic of receiving data during the normal operation of the program. Open, close, and send activities are initiated by the press of a button or a menu selection, but we need to display information as it is available from the port. To achieve this, we will modify the standard application event loop to check the port for incoming data.

Normally, the `EvtGetEvent()` function's second parameter is `evWaitForever`. We have replaced this with a timeout value of 100 system ticks. The following code segment services the receive queue during each cycle. If you didn't modify the `EvtGetEvent` function's timeout parameter, the queue would be serviced only when an event such as a pen stroke or button press was processed.

The following shows how to modify the event loop to handle this:

```
void
AppEventLoop (void)
{
   EventType    event;

   do
   {
      EvtGetEvent (&event, 100);
      MainFormReadSerial();
      // Ask system to handle event.
      if (false == SysHandleEvent (&event))
      {
         // System did not handle event.

         Word         error;
         // Ask Menu to handle event.
         if (false == MenuHandleEvent (0, &event, &error))
         {
            // Menu did not handle event.
            // Ask App (that is, this) to handle event.
            if (false == AppEventHandler (&event))
            {
               // App did not handle event.
               // Send event to appropriate form.
               FrmDispatchEvent (&event);
            }
         }
      }
   }
   while (event.eType != appStopEvent);

   // Just in case we still have the port open!
   MainFormCloseSerial();
}
```

Note that at the end of this function, we make a call to close the serial port to free it for other applications.

To test this application, you need to configure your terminal emulation software for a direct connection over a COM port. The settings should be 9,600 baud, 7 data bits, and even parity with 1 stop bit. When you've built PalmTalk successfully, you should be able to get a session going between PalmTalk and HyperTerminal as shown in Figure 20.1.

FIGURE 20.1

PalmTalk speaks!

The relevant source code for PalmTalk follows in Listing 20.1, and the entire project appears on the accompanying CD-ROM.

LISTING 20.1 PALMTALK'S RELEVANT SOURCE CODE

```
/*
    PalmTalkmain.cpp
    Serial Manager Sample Program, Chapter 20
    Copyright (c) Bachmann Software and Services, 1999
    Author: W.F. Ableson
*/

#include <Pilot.h>
#include <SysEvtMgr.h>
#include <SerialMgr.h>
#include "PalmTalkmain.h"        // MainFormEventHandler ()
#include "PalmTalk_res.h"


static void    MainFormInit (FormPtr formP);
static Boolean MainFormButtonHandler (FormPtr formP, EventPtr eventP);
static Boolean MainFormMenuHandler (FormPtr formP, EventPtr eventP);
void    MainFormOpenSerial (FormPtr formP);
```

continues

LISTING 20.1   CONTINUED

```
void    MainFormWriteSerial (FormPtr formP);
static void    MainFormVersion (FormPtr formP);


static UInt SerialRefNum;
static int Connected = 0;


/*
   MainFormEnableControl:
   Parms:   formP form pointer,
            object id of button to enable/disable,
            true for enable ¦ false to disable
   Return:  none
*/
static void
MainFormEnableControl(FormPtr formP, Word objectId, Boolean enabled)
{
  // Get object index from form
  Word objectIndex = FrmGetObjectIndex(formP,objectId);

  // Get ptr to control
  ControlPtr controlP = (ControlPtr) FrmGetObjectPtr
  (formP, objectIndex);

  // Set enabled
  CtlSetEnabled(controlP, enabled);

  if (enabled)
  {
    CtlShowControl (controlP);
  }
  else
  {
    CtlHideControl (controlP);
  }
}



/*
   MainFormEventHandler:
   Parms:   pEvent   - event to be handled.
   Return:  true  - handled (successfully or not)
            false - not handled
*/
Boolean
```

```
MainFormEventHandler (EventPtr eventP)
{
    Boolean  handled = false;

    switch (eventP->eType)
    {
        case menuEvent:
        {
            FormPtr formP = FrmGetActiveForm ();
            handled = MainFormMenuHandler (formP, eventP);
            break;
        }

        case ctlSelectEvent:
        {
        // A control button was pressed.
            FormPtr formP = FrmGetActiveForm ();
            handled = MainFormButtonHandler (formP, eventP);
            break;
        }

        case frmOpenEvent:
        {
            FormPtr formP = FrmGetActiveForm ();
            MainFormInit (formP);
            FrmDrawForm (formP);
            handled = true;
            break;
        }

        default:
        {
            break;
        }
    }
    return handled;
}

/*
    MainFormInit:
    Initialize the main form.
    Parms:   formP - pointer to main form.
    Return:  none
*/
void
MainFormInit (FormPtr /*formP*/)
{
}

/*
```

continues

LISTING 20.1   CONTINUED

```
    MainFormButtonHandler:
    Handle a command sent to the main form.
    Parms:   formP    - form handling event.
             command  - command to be handled.
    Return:  true  - handled (successfully or not)
             false - not handled
*/
Boolean
MainFormMenuHandler (FormPtr formP, EventPtr eventP)
{
    Boolean handled = false;
/*
    switch (eventP->data.menu.itemID)
    {

    }
*/
    return handled;
}

/*
    MainFormButtonHandler:
    Handle a command sent to the main form.
    Parms:   formP    - form handling event.
             eventP   - event to be handled.
    Return:  true  - handled (successfully or not)
             false - not handled
*/
Boolean
MainFormButtonHandler (FormPtr formP, EventPtr eventP)
{
    Boolean handled = false;

    switch (eventP->data.ctlEnter.controlID)
    {
        case MainBtnOpenButton:   // User selected Open Serial button.
        {
            MainFormOpenSerial (formP);
            handled = true;
            break;
        }

        case MainBtnSendButton:   // User selected Write Serial button.
        {
            MainFormWriteSerial (formP);
            handled = true;
```

```
            break;
        }

        case MainBtnCloseButton:    // User selected Close Serial button.
        {
            MainFormCloseSerial();
            // Modify user interface
            MainFormEnableControl(formP,MainBtnCloseButton,false);
            MainFormEnableControl(formP,MainBtnSendButton,false);
            MainFormEnableControl(formP,MainBtnOpenButton,true);

            handled = true;
            break;
        }


    }
    return handled;
}


/*
    MainFormOpenSerial:
    Handle the main form's OpenSerial command.
    Parms:   formP    - form handling event.
    Return:  none
*/
void
MainFormOpenSerial (FormPtr formP)
{
    Err e;
    SerSettingsType sstSetup;


    // Load the serial library
    e = SysLibFind("Serial Library",&SerialRefNum);
    if (e)
    {
        FrmCustomAlert(ErrorAlert,"Failed To Load Library!","","");
        return;
    }

    // Now, let's open the port itself.  We will request an initial
    // baud rate of 9600.
    e = SerOpen(SerialRefNum,0,9600);
    if (e)
    {
```

continues

LISTING 20.1   CONTINUED

```
          FrmCustomAlert(ErrorAlert,"Failed To Open Port 0!","","");
          return;
     }

     // Let's keep track of when the port is open
     Connected = 1;

     // Before we can set the parameters on the port, it is a good
     // practice to retrieve them first.
     SerGetSettings( SerialRefNum, &sstSetup );

     // Let's set the baud rate and other serial comms properties
     sstSetup.baudRate = 9600;
     sstSetup.flags =      serSettingsFlagBitsPerChar7 |
                           serSettingsFlagParityOnM |
                           serSettingsFlagParityEvenM |
                           serSettingsFlagStopBitsM |
                           serSettingsFlagStopBits1;
     sstSetup.ctsTimeout = serSettingsFlagRTSAutoM |
     ➥serSettingsFlagCTSAutoM;

     // Ask Serial Manager to update the port settings
     SerSetSettings( SerialRefNum, &sstSetup );

     // Let's clear the port, just in case some garbage is sitting there
     SerReceiveFlush (SerialRefNum, 100 );

     // Change the state of some buttons on our main form
     MainFormEnableControl(formP,MainBtnCloseButton,true);
     MainFormEnableControl(formP,MainBtnSendButton,true);
     MainFormEnableControl(formP,MainBtnOpenButton,false);
}


/*
   MainFormWriteSerial:
   Handle the main form's WriteSerial command.
   Parms:   formP    - form handling event.
   Return:  none
*/
void
MainFormWriteSerial (FormPtr formP)
{
   unsigned short usRegister;
   int i;
   Err e;
   Word wIDField;
   FieldPtr pCtlField;
```

```
    Handle hText;
    CharPtr pText;


    // Check connected .. just in case
    if (Connected == 0) return;

    // Get message from our field
    wIDField = FrmGetObjectIndex(formP,MainMessageField);
    pCtlField = (FieldPtr) FrmGetObjectPtr(formP,wIDField);
    hText = FldGetTextHandle (pCtlField);
    pText = (CharPtr) MemHandleLock(hText);

    // Let's send our message!
    SerSend(SerialRefNum,(unsigned char *) pText,StrLen(pText),&e);
    if (e)
    {
        FrmCustomAlert(ErrorAlert,"Error Sending Message!","","");
    }
    MemHandleUnlock(hText);
    // Let's send along a newline, so we can use PalmTalk on two devices
    // connected together with a null modem cable!
    SerSend(SerialRefNum,(unsigned char *) "\n",1,&e);
    if (e)
    {
        FrmCustomAlert(ErrorAlert,"Error Sending Message!","","");
    }


}


/*
    MainFormReadSerial:
    Handle the main form's ReadSerial command.
    Parms:   none
    Return:  none
*/
void
MainFormReadSerial ()
{
    static unsigned char szBuf[1024];
    static int index = 0;
    Err e;
    ULong ulBytes;


    if (Connected == 0) return;
```

continues

LISTING **20.1**   CONTINUED

```
// See if there is anything in the queue ... "peek"
e = SerReceiveCheck(SerialRefNum,&ulBytes);

// Ensure there were no errors
if (e)
{
   FrmCustomAlert(ErrorAlert, "Error Checking Serial Port!","","");
   return;
}

// Is there something waiting for us ?
if (ulBytes)
{
  // Let's retrieve the info!

  // First, make sure the amount to read is not too large
  if ((ulBytes + index) > sizeof(szBuf))
  {
     ulBytes = sizeof(szBuf) - index - 1;
  }

  // Retrieve one byte at a time, looking for our
  // end of message indicator
  while (ulBytes)
  {
     SerReceive(SerialRefNum,&szBuf[index],1,0,&e);
     // Check for read error
     if (e)
     {
        FrmCustomAlert(ErrorAlert, "Error Reading Serial Port!","","");
        SerReceiveFlush(SerialRefNum,100);
        index = 0;
        return;
     }
     switch (szBuf[index])
     {
        case 0x0a:
          szBuf[index] = 0x00;
          // We have our newline indicator .. that will mark the end
          // of this "message" so let's display it!
          FrmCustomAlert(MessageAlert,(CharPtr) szBuf,"","");
          index = 0;
          break;
        default:
          index++;
          break;
     }
```

```
        ulBytes--;
      } // while
   }

}

/*
   MainFormCloseSerial:
   Handle the main form's CloseSerial command.
   Parms:   none
   Return:  none
*/
void
MainFormCloseSerial()
{
   Err e;

   // Close port
   e = SerClose(SerialRefNum);
   if (e)
   {
      FrmCustomAlert(ErrorAlert,"Error during Close!","","");
   }

   // Keep track of our state
   Connected = 0;

}
```

Summary

In this chapter, you learned how to make your first use of one of the Palm's means of communicating with the world around it. You should now be able to develop applications that used Serial Manager to communicate with other devices, host PCs, and even modems. In the next chapters, you will continue exploring the Palm's communication capabilities, covering the Palm III's infrared port, and even taking a first peek at the brand new Palm VII wireless device.

CHAPTER 21

Using the Communications Libraries, Part 2: Infrared

In the preceding chapter, you learned how serial communications can further improve productivity by providing the opportunity to print and share all the useful information. Unfortunately, to make it all work, you have to carry along a multitude of cables, wires, adapters, and power supplies. We live in an increasingly wireless world and to maximize the usefulness of our Palm devices (and to send us off the scale in the "cool" department), we need to "beam." That's right, Star Trek meets Silicon Valley! With infrared communications at our command, we become truly portable (if not the most advanced gadgeteer in the office, which is of course a prize in itself).

There are a few types of infrared (IR) communications available to the Palm user. The specific needs and resources available for a particular application will dictate the approach you take for IR communications on the Palm, although everyone's first desire to have a deluxe universal remote control is not one of the options. To those of you looking only for this summit of TV enjoyment, I implore you to read on! There are many worthy applications available to the Palm: For instance, take a quick look at your digital cell phone. Many new phones are equipped with built-in IR capability. (Just don't send us the phone bill!)

I continue the discussion of communications topics with the Infrared Library, Palm OS's implementation of the IrDA standard. IrDA (the Infrared Data Association, http://www.irda.org) is the standards organization setting the direction of infrared communications for devices and appliances. Major manufacturers and software houses are members of IrDA today, and this effort will continue to grow in the years ahead. Learning to program to the IrDA specification will put you in the fast lane for Palm OS development. Where else would you want to be? I conclude this chapter by looking at the included sample application, IrDemo. IrDemo provides a framework for writing head-to-head, Palm-to-Palm games (err, I mean applications).

The Standard

The IrDA specifications call for two types of infrared communications, namely SIR (Standard IR) and FIR (Fast IR). SIR effectively provides serial communications replacing the copper wires in your modem cable with light waves in the infrared spectrum. The transmission speeds of SIR match those of traditional serial communications in the 300–115,000 bps range. Fast IR is capable of delivering substantially higher transmission speeds. FIR is being used on some platforms to implement local area networking connectivity because it is capable of throughput of up to 4 Mbits per second. To put this in perspective, your normal Ethernet network is capable of either 10 or 100 Mbits per second.

Like many communications specifications, the IrDA standard defines many protocol layers that form the IR stack. Each layer offers distinct services upon which additional services are built. At the bottom of the stack is SIR/FIR, which is strictly hardware, involving an IR device that emits light waves and a controller. The controller takes the form of a UART or other chip (for FIR). Riding atop the physical layer is the Infrared Link Access Protocol (IrLAP). This layer provides the actual data path for IrDA communications. There is one IrLAP "connection" per IR device. The Infrared Link Management Protocol (IrLMP) handles one or more sessions over the single IrLAP connection. Higher levels of the stack include TinyTP, IrCOMM, IrLAN, IrLPT, and OBEX. Additional layers coming into play include protocols for IR keyboards. This is a 10,000-foot view of the stack. You are encouraged to visit the IrDA's Web site for more detailed information.

Not all the IrDA standards are implemented by Palm OS. However, because the required layers are supported in the IR Library, you can roll your own implementations of the missing layers. The Palm's Exchange Manager implements OBEX, but you will need to develop the code to interact with other devices such as a printer using either IrCOMM or IrLPT. The sample program demonstrates my own IrDemo implementation.

Palm OS IR Capabilities

The first Palm OS release to support infrared communications was Palm OS 3.0. Therefore, IR applications require the 3.0 SDK. The addition in Palm OS 3.0 of primary concern is irlib.h (and the IR Library itself, of course). irlib.h lays out all the data types needed for IR programming.

The Palm device's single UART chip provides services for both serial and infrared communications. As I touched upon briefly in Chapter 20, "Using the Communications Libraries, Part 1: Serial Manager," it is important to reiterate that the Palm III device's sole UART controls both serial and IR communications. This means that you cannot operate the IR port and the serial port simultaneously. The mutual exclusivity between IR and serial communications also has implications for the debugging environment. In short, you cannot use the Metrowerks debugging environment to trace IR calls. In addition, POSE does not currently emulate IR functionality. Included in the IrDemo application is an example of debugging on the Palm, using a home-grown `printf` function.

IR Library Essentials

Before I jump right into the IR Library's API, it is important to have a brief discussion on the architecture of an IR application.

When your Palm application wants to communicate with another device, such as another Palm device, a printer, or cell phone, the first task is to "discover" the other device. This is essentially the IR device looking around for other devices to talk to. Once this process is complete, the application will have the address of the remote device and can initiate a connection. Once you have a low-level connection (IrLAP) to the other device, you need to look up the service you want to communicate with. The Information Access Service (IAS) provides a database of information for the services available for a particular device. When you have received the attribute information from IAS, the application can establish a session with the appropriate service. Let's look at a real-world analogy.

Suppose you need an electrician. You open the Yellow Pages and look under Electricians. This is akin to the IR device performing discovery. It is looking for devices that "speak IR."

Now that you are on the correct page, you review each of the advertisements, selecting the most appealing electrician service and recording the phone number. In the same way, a discovery process on the Palm might find many devices but needs to select one with which to communicate. This will yield an address to use in the connection process.

Okay, so you call the electrician's office and ask for someone with the expertise to install a refrigerator. On the Palm, you initiate an IAS query looking for, say, IrLPT for printing services.

The receptionist replies, "Dial extension 123." The IAS query responds with the LSAP selector where IrLPT is found.

You call extension 123 and speak with the electrician who can help you install the refrigerator. The Palm IR application connects to the IrLPT service and can now print!

The IR Library relies upon two callback functions for event notification. I must provide both of the callback functions in the application because there is no default event handler provided by Palm OS. The first callback function, named `IrHandler` in IrDemo, shoulders the majority of the workload in the application. `IrHandler` receives all notifications for `IrStack`-related events, such as IrLAP connect and disconnect, IrLMP session requests and confirmation, data receipt, discovery completion, and so on. This function is installed during the `IrBind` function call. The other callback function I have named `IASHandler`. `IASHandler` receives notification when IAS queries have completed.

Because callback events can occur at any time in the Palm application, it is important to avoid the use of alerts or other potentially time-consuming functions. In an effort to provide detailed information during the execution and avoid these problems, IrDemo uses a simple `printf` function for displaying information. The messages appear in a "window" showing five lines toward the bottom of the Palm's display area.

Without further delay, let's work our way through the IR functions and build our application!

Implementing Infrared Connectivity in a Palm Application

Because it is a shared library (see Chapter 19, "Shared Libraries: Extending the Palm OS"), to use the IR Library, you must first load it with the following code:

```
Err e;              // For error result
UInt refNum;        // 'Handle' to library

e = SysLibFind( irLibName, &refNum );
```

(Note: `irLibName` is defined in irlib.h.)

After this call, e should be 0 or an error otherwise.

Using the Communications Libraries, Part 2: Infrared

CHAPTER 21

303

21

COMMUNICATIONS
LIBRARIES:
INFRARED

Once the library is loaded, you must open it for the application's use:

```
e = IrOpen( refNum, irOpenOptSpeed9600 );
```

irOpenOptSpeed9600 is defined in irlib.h along with other constants indicating the initial speed for the port. This is similar to the way in which the Serial Manager works, as described in Chapter 20.

Again, this call should return 0 or an error otherwise.

Once the IrOpen call has been made successfully by an application, it must call IrClose prior to application termination. Due to the way in which Palm applications terminate when the task is switched, it is important to detect the application switching to clean up properly.

Now that the library is opened by the application, you need to initialize it with a function named IrBind. Binding will associate an IrConnect structure, defined in the application along with a callback function that the IR Library uses to notify you of completion of certain IR-related events:

```
e = IrBind( refNum, &irCon, IrHandler );
```

See irlib.h for a description of the irCon parameter. It is actually a structure of type IrConnect.

IrBind must return 0 or an error otherwise.

Now that you have bound an IrConnect structure and the IrHandler, you go on to advising the IrStack who you are. This is done with the IrSetDeviceInfo function. The return value of this function is not the generic Palm OS error type, Err, but rather the type IrStatus. See irlib.h for a description of this type and the possible values it can hold:

```
IrStatus irStat;
static Byte OurDeviceInfo[] = {IR_HINT_PDA, IR_CHAR_ASCII,
➥ 'P','A','L','M','D','E','M','O'};

if (IrSetDeviceInfo( refNum, OurDeviceInfo ,OurDeviceInfoLen ) !=
                        IR_STATUS_SUCCESS)
{
    IrUnbind( refNum, &IrCon );
    IrClose( refNum );
    printf("IrSetDeviceInfo Failed!" );
    return;
}
```

`OurDeviceInfo` is a byte array that cannot exceed the size defined in irlib.h of `IR_MAX_DEVICE_INFO`. This array contains hint bytes. The hint bytes are bit masks to indicate the type of device in this application. If there is more than one hint byte to be used, you can use `IR_HINT_EXT`, which indicates that the device info contains an additional byte of hint information. Here is an example:

```
// Device info for standard irComm device
static Byte irCommDeviceInfo[] = {
    IR_HINT_PRINTER|IR_HINT_EXT, IR_HINT_IRCOMM, IR_CHAR_ASCII,
    'I','r','C','O','M','M'};
```

This function should result in `IR_STATUS_SUCCESS`.

At this point, you have successfully loaded and opened the IR Library. You have bound it for use and told the `IrStack` who you are. If you want to advertise a service for other devices to connect to, you use the IAS database. This is a generic database. Each IrDA-compliant device maintains this repository to hold information regarding which services the device offers. This is similar to the way TCP service maps names to ports (such as `FTP -> 21` or `WWW -> 80`):

```
static Byte OurDeviceName[] = { IAS_ATTRIB_USER_STRING,
  IR_CHAR_ASCII,
  8,'P','A','L','M','D','E','M','O'};
static Byte OurDeviceNameLen = sizeof(OurDeviceName);
/* "Standard" class name for our demo is IrDemo with attribute of
    IrDA:IrLMP:LsapSel
*/
static Byte irdemoQuery[] =  { 6,'I','r','D','E','M','O',
18,
'I','r','D','A',':','I','r','L','M','P',
':','L','s','a','p','S','e','l'};
const irdemoQuerySize = sizeof(irdemoQuery);
/* Result for IrDemo */
Byte irdemoResult[] = {
    0x01,                  /* Type for Integer is 1 */
    0x00,0x00,0x00,0x02    /* Assumed Lsap */
};
/* IrDemo attribute */
const IrIasAttribute irdemoAttribs = {
(BytePtr) "IrDA:IrLMP:LsapSel",18,
(BytePtr)irdemoResult, sizeof(irdemoResult)};
static IrIasObject irdemoObject ={
  (BytePtr)"IrDemo",6,1,
  (IrIasAttribute*)&irdemoAttribs};


IrIAS_SetDeviceName( refNum, OurDeviceName,OurDeviceNameLen);
IrIAS_Add( refNum, &irdemoObject);
```

Using the Communications Libraries, Part 2: Infrared
CHAPTER 21

305

21

COMMUNICATIONS
LIBRARIES:
INFRARED

To connect to another device, you must find the device's address. To obtain this, you use the function IrDiscoverReq:

```
// Initiate a discovery and IrLAP connection
while ( ++lCounter <= lTimeout)
{
   irStat = IrDiscoverReq( refNum, &IrCon );
   switch (irStat)
   {
      case IR_STATUS_MEDIA_BUSY:
         printf("Media Busy");
         continue;
      case IR_STATUS_FAILED:
         printf("Failed in Discovery");
         IrUnbind( refNum, &IrCon );
         IrClose( refNum );
   FrmCustomAlert(ErrorAlert,
"Failed to Discover.  Ending Application","","");
         MemSet(&evtExit, sizeof(EventType), 0);
         evtExit.eType = appStopEvent;
         EvtAddEventToQueue(&evtExit);
         return;
      case IR_STATUS_PENDING:
         // This is the one we want!
         // At this point we need to wait for the discovery process to
         // complete ...
         printf("Discovery Pending!!!");
         return;
   }
} // while
```

irStat can come back with one of the following values:

> IR_STATUS_MEDIA_BUSY indicates that the media is busy and you should retry the function.

> IR_STATUS_FAILED indicates an error in the stack.

> IR_STATUS_PENDING is the one you want; it indicates a successful start of the discovery process.

Because it is possible for the IrDiscoverReq function to come back busy a few times and then become pending, you wrap this call into a while loop with a timeout on the iterations. This gives the application a healthy chance of finding another device, able to withstand a couple of media busy responses without a disappointing failure in the connection process.

The completion of the discovery process is notified via the callback function registered during the IrBind call, namely IrHandler.

Once discovery has completed successfully, you will have the address for a remote device. Actually, you might have many devices in range, and you will need to sift through them all to select the one you want. You can sort through any available IR devices by examining the hint bytes and nickname that is returned by the discovery process. Once you have selected a device, you want to establish an IrLAP connection. You do this with the function IrConnectIrLap:

```
// Check for a valid device
if (pCBParms->deviceList->nItems == 0)
{
    printf("No Devices Found!");
    return;
}

// At least one device has been found, we will
// assume that the first (and probably only!) device
// found is the one we want.
g_irDevice = pCBParms->deviceList->dev[0].hDevice;
printf("Found %d.%d.%d.%d",g_irDevice.u8[0],g_irDevice.u8[1],
        g_irDevice.u8[2],g_irDevice.u8[3]);
// Let's make an IrLAP connection to this address
while ( ++lCounter <= lTimeout)
{
    irStat = IrConnectIrLap( refNum, g_irDevice );
    switch (irStat)
    {
      case IR_STATUS_MEDIA_BUSY:
        printf("IrLap Media Busy");
        continue;
      case IR_STATUS_FAILED:
        printf("Failed in IrConnectIrLap" );
        return;
      case IR_STATUS_PENDING:
        // This is the one we want!
        // At this point we need to wait for the connect process to
        // complete ...
        printf("Connect Lap Pending!!!");
        return;
    }
} // while
```

You are looking for IrLAP to return IR_STATUS_PENDING.

As in the discovery process, you wrap this IrConnectIrLap function in a while loop with a timeout to give it a chance to connect without a single IR_STATUS_MEDIA_BUSY pushing you off course.

When the IrLAP connection has been established, you next want to find out what services the remote device is offering. Here is where the IAS database comes in. You will
query the device for a specific service that you are interested in. You will actually execute two IAS queries. The first will demonstrate obtaining the device name. The device
name is a required field to be maintained in the IAS, as defined by IrDA:

```
// Initiate query for remote service we are interested in
// This first query will provide the remote device name
// as defined by the device's IAS

IrIAS_StartResult(&clientQuery);
clientQuery.result = queryResult;
clientQuery.resultBufSize = sizeof(queryResult);
clientQuery.callBack = IASHandler;
clientQuery.queryBuf = irGetQuery;
clientQuery.queryLen = irGetQuerySize;
IrIAS_Query(refNum, &clientQuery);
// Now that we have the device we want
// we need to determine how to connect to it, ie. what lsap?
IrIAS_StartResult(&clientQuery);
clientQuery.result = queryResult;
clientQuery.resultBufSize = sizeof(queryResult);
clientQuery.callBack = IASHandler;
clientQuery.queryBuf = irdemoQuery;
clientQuery.queryLen = irdemoQuerySize;
IrIAS_Query(refNum, &clientQuery);
```

The last area to look at is the IASHandler callback function. This function is invoked
when the results of an IAS query are ready. Because the IAS database stores information
in an unstructured format, each attribute must be stored with a data type identifier. When
processing the results of an IAS query, you first look at the data type, and then process
the value:

```
switch ( IrIAS_GetType(&clientQuery) )
{
   case IAS_ATTRIB_MISSING:
      printf("Attribute is Missing?!");
      break;
   case IAS_ATTRIB_INTEGER:
      printf("Get Integer Value");
      IrCon.rLsap = IrIAS_GetIntLsap(&clientQuery);
      irPack.len = 0;
      // We have the address for the service we want to connect to
      // Let's establish the LMP session

   ...
}
```

The connection process "propels" itself along via the callbacks. To review, to connect to a device via the IR Library, the steps are

1. Load the IR Library using `SysLibFind()`.

2. Open the IR port using `IrOpen()`.

3. Initialize the port using `IrBind()`.

4. Use `IrDiscoveryReq()` to obtain the device's address.

5. From the `IrHandler` callback function, when discovery finishes, you request the `IrLapConnection()` with `IrLapConnectReq()`.

6. When this completes, you query the IAS for the service you want.

7. When the IAS is complete and `IASHandler` is called, you make a request for an LMP connection with `IrConnectReq()`.

8. When this is complete (signaled, of course, by the `IrHandler` callback), you have an up-and-running connection to the other device!

IrDemo: Building a Palm OS IR Application

The IrDemo application is designed to be informative and provide you with a launching pad for your own IR projects. You should understand that it is not intended to be a production-ready application. In a number of areas, I have left comments for to-do's, such as handling the case when a connection request is unsuccessful.

All the code is on the CD-ROM. To build the application, be sure to compile with the Palm OS 3.0 SDK.

To run the application, you need two Palm devices. (If you have read this far, you might even have three Pilots!) The interface has four buttons: Start, Connect, Send, and Finish.

Place the devices head to head so the IR ports can see one another. Select Start on both devices. You should see some status information scrolling at the bottom of the display. On one (and only one) device, select the Connect button. The applications will display status information, indicating the connection activities. Note that the messages will differ on each device. At this point, you will see connection confirmation on both devices, and you can select the Send button on either device. The data will be received and displayed. When complete, select the Finish button on each device, and the application will terminate.

An interesting thing to try is to move the devices apart and note the messages that are displayed. Move the devices back together (so IR transmission can continue), and notice the display. Move the devices during the discovery process.

Summary

The IrDemo application is designed to demonstrate the fundamentals of IrDA. I hope this will help you develop your own applications, whatever they are used for. Our own Bachmann Print Manager product uses infrared connectivity to enable graphics and text printing on popular laser printers. With so many devices supporting the IrDA standard, there is certainly a world of possibilities for creating special capabilities on the Palm device.

For further reading, check out the following resources:

- Infrared Data Association (IrDA): `http://www.irda.org`
- Linux IR Project: `http://www.cs.uit.no/linux-irda/`
- Chapter 9 of the Palm OS 3.0 documentation

CHAPTER 22

The Internet in Your Hand: Introduction to the Palm VII

When Joe Sipher, the Director of Wireless Products at Palm Computing, completed his keynote speech introducing the new Palm VII handheld device at the 1998 Palm Developer Conference, he left the stage to a long, thunderous standing ovation. The audience had observed the first public demonstration of a Palm device with built-in wireless Internet access, and it knew it had witnessed the unveiling of a remarkable new product with the potential to finally create a palatable marriage of handheld mobile computing devices and wireless connectivity.

This chapter describes the newest member of the Palm Computing family of handheld devices and introduces you to the design philosophy behind the product called the Palm VII. We investigate the infrastructure that enables the device to work in concert with the Internet to create a productive and enjoyable experience for the user. Finally, because this is a book about programming, we review the SDK changes and new developer-oriented features in store for you, the Palm programmer.

(Note: The Palm VII is scheduled to be available to the public in the second half of 1999. Developer information on programming the Palm VII is becoming available at the time of this writing and is therefore subject to change. Consult the latest documentation from Palm Computing for the most up-to-date SDK information.)

What Is the Palm VII?

The Palm VII can be described most simply as a new handheld device based on the Standard Palm III model with the addition of a built-in, two-way wireless modem. The most visible sign that the VII is different from the III is the appearance of an integrated antenna that moves up and down via a hinge on the right-hand side of the unit. In all other respects, the device resembles a Palm III, from the built-in address book, to-do list, and other applications to the cradle and stylus. Figure 22.1 shows the main application view for the Palm VII. Note the new application icons!

FIGURE 22.1

The main application list (icon view) for the Palm VII.

Although the inclusion of a wireless modem with virtually no change in the successful form factor of the Palm device is in itself somewhat remarkable, hardware changes are not what has people so excited about the Palm VII.

The thing that differentiates the Palm VII from other Palm units, and other handheld computing devices in general, is the design philosophy embodied in the Palm OS that is most visibly expressed by the bundled application software. The Palm VII was not envisioned as a Palm III that is capable of browsing the Internet. Rather, the architects of the Palm VII acknowledged and studied the unique problems those before them in the mobile/wireless computing industry tried to solve. The Palm VII delivers a promising solution to those problems and creates a new platform for distributed, Internet-aware applications for the mobile professional.

To understand why the Palm VII solution is so attractive, you need to understand why it has taken so long for wireless connectivity to become viable on a handheld device.

The Problem with Wireless Internet Connectivity

Although the Internet as a pervasive technology in our daily lives is a fairly recent phenomenon, most of you access the Internet via a relatively high-speed connection. The minimum connection these days tends to use a 28.8Kbps dial-up. Although on occasion frustratingly slow, this speed still provides an Internet experience that is acceptable for the most part. Some of us achieve faster connections via ISDN and other technologies that push the speed of the ISP connection to 64Kbps or higher. Still faster, the luckiest among us connect at T-1 speeds.

With such connection speeds the norm, Web content designers make assumptions accordingly about the amount of data that can be tolerably downloaded by a user visiting their sites. As a result, today's Web pages are increasingly heavily formatted and are laden with large images, complex graphics, animations, Java applets, and more. All these fancy page elements need a big enough pipe to travel through in order to get to your Web browser before you become tired of waiting and move on to the next Web site.

What if tomorrow, someone walked up to your computer and replaced your 28.8Kbps Internet connection with a connection that was 8Kbps or less than one third as fast? When you logged on to the Internet, how pleasant would your Web-surfing experience be? How long before you logged off in frustration, tired of waiting 5, 10, or more minutes for a single page to download? Unfortunately, most wireless networks today run at speeds little faster than 8Kbps.

Of course, most Web sites are designed with another bias in mind: It is assumed that your browser display resolution will be at minimum 640×480 pixels, if not higher. What if someone replaced that big, heavy monitor with a little miniature screen with less than 25 percent as much viewable area? How many of the Internet's beautifully crafted Web pages would make any kind of sense when viewed under these conditions?

If you are now thinking that surfing today's World Wide Web under these conditions wouldn't be much fun, you are beginning to understand the problem of wireless Internet connectivity on mobile computers. Many computer users and even several prominent companies in the computer industry have persisted in a PC-centric view of mobile computing, assuming that because people worked a certain way on their 300MHz personal computer, they would insist on being able to work in the same way on a handheld device.

As it turns out, at least with the wireless technology generally available today, surfing the Web is simply not a viable application on a handheld device using a wireless connection. Although several general-purpose Web browsers have come to market for the various handheld computing platforms, and no doubt more will be developed, the truth is that few people will want to surf the Web from their cell phones or PDAs under the conditions I describe.

Finally, mobile computer users as a group are not likely to want to aimlessly spend time browsing the Web. They are on the go, looking to perform a few targeted actions with their Palms. They have a specific need for a piece of information, and they want to get at that information with a minimum of fuss. Navigating through pages of graphics and text to get at the data nugget they need is inefficient and unacceptable.

Palm Computing looked at the history of attempts to develop and deliver a handheld wireless solution, considered the problems of bandwidth and screen display, and came up with a solution. They call it "Web clipping."

Enter Web Clipping and Palm.Net

The expression "Web clipping" refers to the act of capturing only the information you need from the content available on the World Wide Web, just as you would clip a single article or advertisement from a magazine or newspaper. Palm Computing wanted to apply this concept to the Web so that a Palm unit could access useful data from the Web efficiently, in terms of the quantity of data transferred.

As implemented by Palm Computing, the Web clipping feature has a few key components.

Palm.Net

Palm.Net is a broad description for the special network housed at 3Com that acts as a "proxy server" for all communications between a Palm VII and the "real" Internet. Palm.Net provides security via encryption and also provides special compression and protocol translation both inbound and outbound to achieve the low-traffic levels required by the wireless data network.

It is important to understand that all traffic to and from the Palm VII must run through Palm.Net, which automatically re-routes requests to the proper Internet host after the appropriate compression/decompression and security checks. At least with the initial release of the Palm VII, it is not possible for the unit to use wireless connectivity to directly communicate with hosts on or outside of the Internet.

In addition to these services, Palm.Net also automatically strips bandwidth-unfriendly content from requested Web pages, including graphics, pictures, frames, Java, and scripting commands.

Content Providers

As I've noted, most Internet content is not created with the Palm's display in mind. In preparation for the rollout of the Palm VII, Palm Computing has worked with key content providers to help them design and create specially formatted content that is appropriate for display on the Palm. This content is similar to what's normally provided but is targeted at the Palm user who wants quick and convenient information without wading through extraneous data.

Palm Computing has provided a style guide that gives helpful suggestions and guidelines for designing and formatting content intended for the Palm VII user. The mantra is "less is more," meaning that users will have a better experience (not to mention a lower subscriber cost) if you strip unnecessary information from your content.

Figure 22.2 illustrates this point via a screen from the sports content provider ESPN.

FIGURE 22.2

A sports junkie's dream: catching up on the latest baseball news—live as it happens!

Palm Query Applications

To prevent unnecessary re-transmission of content, Palm Computing concluded that it was necessary to partition Web sites and applications such that the initial page was created, installed, and stored locally on the Palm device itself.

Essentially compressed HTML with special tag support, these locally stored pages are called Palm Query Applications, or PQAs for short. Although almost any type of HTML page can be turned into a PQA, the most common example of a PQA is that of a form for querying Web content.

PQAs are created via a new SDK tool, Query Application Builder, which loads an HTML file and converts it to a .PQA file. This file is then loaded into the Palm just as a .PRC file is, using the Palm Installer tool.

The next chapter actually walks you through the process of creating a PQA, installing it, and running it on the Palm VII.

Wireless Email: iMessenger

Aside from the Web clipping capability, the Palm VII also comes with a built-in wireless Internet messaging service called iMessenger. iMessenger is not a replacement for the Palm Mail application (which manages mail via hot-sync to and from the desktop host), but rather a live email system that takes advantage of the always available wireless Internet connectivity of the Palm VII to enable fast and convenient message exchange via standard Internet protocols. Figure 22.3 shows the iMessenger application in action.

FIGURE 22.3

Reading a new message received via the iMessenger application.

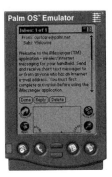

What's New for Developers

With the Palm VII comes a new version of the Palm OS, dubbed version 3.2. (Version 3.1 is shipped with the Palm IIIx and Palm V units.) Along with enabling the entire Web clipping and PQA architecture, Palm OS 3.2 exposes new APIs that let application developers take advantage of some of the Palm VII's wireless connectivity features.

Note that at the time of this writing, details on these new APIs were just being released.

PQA and Web Integration

The next chapter delves into the creation of a PQA, but there are also ways to integrate PQAs with your applications. The following new capabilities are available to your application with Palm OS 3.2:

- Launch either a local PQA or a remote URL from an application via special launch code.
- Launch a Palm application from a tag in a downloaded HTML file. (This is conceptually similar to the tags that support local execution of Java or ActiveX applications.)
- Call a specific function within a Palm application from a tag.

iMessenger Integration

The built-in wireless messaging service lets you add basic messaging to your application. You can embed a special mailto tag in your HTML that will launch the iMessenger application. Code written in C can also launch iMessenger and directly set message attributes such as the subject, to, and cc fields.

Wireless Networking

Palm OS 3.2 will expose InetLib, which allows C application developers to directly call the same OS extensions that Palm does in the Web clipping and messaging applications. Keep in mind that programming to InetLib will still not allow you to bypass the Palm.Net proxy and get directly at your own host.

Summary

This chapter introduced the Palm VII and explained some of the unique problems that drove Palm Computing to create such a unique platform for wireless mobile computing applications. Only time will tell whether the Palm VII becomes as successful in enabling wireless Internet access as the Palm II and III were in enabling mobile personal productivity. My own assessment is that ultimately, we will all become "walking nodes on the Internet," with all the Web-based services we need following us around wherever we go. If not the last word in pursuing this goal, the Palm VII is certainly a giant leap in the right direction.

Because of the wealth of new concepts to cover in introducing the Palm VII, this chapter provides only a tantalizing glimpse of what programming the new device is like. The next chapter rewards your patience by showing you how to quickly and easily create your own Palm Query Application.

CHAPTER **23**

Creating Palm Query Applications

As you saw in Chapter 22, "The Internet in Your Hand: Introduction to the Palm VII," the Palm VII is a member of the Palm family of devices that contains built-in wireless access to Internet-based content as well as messaging services. One of the most noteworthy features on the VII is the support for Palm Query Applications, which appear to the user as normal Palm applications yet provide front ends to Internet-based content and services over the wireless network.

This chapter examines Palm Query Applications (PQAs) in more detail. I provide a developer's perspective on what a PQA is, explain important issues related to designing and creating PQAs, and describe the steps involved in developing your own PQA. I finish the chapter by presenting a PQA for this book, as an example of one of the more simple uses of the Palm VII technology.

If you haven't read through the introduction to the Palm VII in Chapter 22, before you go any further, you should stop and do so because this chapter assumes that you understand the design philosophy and facilities associated with the Palm VII.

It is also important to note that the early field tests of the Palm VII are occurring as I write this with the public release of the unit still several months away. Some of the information provided here might change after publication. When in doubt, you should refer to the current Palm Computing documentation for the most accurate information.

What Is a PQA?

A PQA is not really an "application," at least not of the same type that you've been learning how to build throughout this book. A PQA is really HTML (Hypertext Markup Language), the *lingua franca* of the Internet. A PQA file is a set of HTML pages, links, and graphics stored locally on the Palm in compressed format as a special type of database. Just like any other type of database, a PQA database contains records. In the case of a PQA, each record represents an HTML page.

You know that HTML by itself is not an executable program. On other systems, you rely on a Web browser to load and display HTML stored either locally or on a host system. On the Palm, you don't do general-purpose browsing; rather, you launch special-purpose PQAs. It turns out that when you launch a PQA, the Palm OS launches a hidden program called Clipper.

Clipper can be considered the Palm's "browser," and it is Clipper's job to load, decompress, and render your PQA as HTML. In case you were wondering, you can use Clipper from your own application to load either local or remote content by passing it a URL as a launch code.

A Palm Query Application is only one half of the picture, however. The rest of the content to be supported by your PQA actually appears on your Web site. This content is returned to the Palm as "clippings." The Web server houses the remainder of the logic, returning results, or clippings, in the same manner as is done on millions of Web sites.

Effectively, your Palm application is "partitioned" into a client/server architecture. Of late, it has become fashionable to talk of thin clients, one expression of which is a browser-based application that presents a program's user interface as HTML. A PQA is not that "thin" because at least the main page for your program must be stored on the Palm itself. Through Palm's HTML extensions, it is possible for your client to be "fat" by calling into and thus relying on other code provided by you (or another vendor) in a Palm .PRC.

It is typical that a PQA consists largely of an HTML form that uses standard CGI to submit the form's contents to the Web server and receive the results as HTML. However, you are free to do anything you want with your local HTML, as long as it falls within the subset of HTML 3.2 supported by Palm. (See the Palm SDK documentation for a complete list of what HTML is supported and what is not.)

One more thing: It might appear that the quickest way to get your existing Web content onto the Palm VII is to create a simple front-end PQA that links to your existing Web site. This is a mistake. If you don't recall why this is a bad thing, re-read Chapter 22, and review the reasons why general Web browsing is not well supported on handheld wireless platforms. You will need to re-evaluate the content returned by your Web site and possibly reconsider your Web site's design.

What Works, What Doesn't

It is important to understand what works with PQAs and what either is not supported or will not work well.

Size of Content

The first thing you should know is that the entire viewable area for your content will be 153 pixels wide by 144 pixels high. You've obviously encountered this limitation throughout the book, but until now, it's been a case of simply fitting everything you want into a small display area. With the Palm VII comes two additional factors: speed of retrieval and cost to the user. The more data you send over the wireless connection, the longer the user has to wait for your content. Perhaps more importantly, the user (at least with the subscriber plan currently in effect) is paying by the byte.

As a rule of thumb, you should not return more than 500 bytes on any individual page. (Palm recommends even fewer.) Also, keep in mind that if you use the default Palm font, you have about 11 lines of text to work with before you force the user to scroll.

HTML

A subset of HTML version 3.2 is supported by Clipper. In general, you want to stick with the simplest HTML you can possibly use to create an acceptable page on the Palm. This means limiting text effects such as bold, underline, font variations, and so on.

Beyond the recommendations, some elements and extensions of HTML are just not supported. Palm.net will either strip out these elements or return an error to your users. Some of these are frames, nested tables, large or color-based images (see the next section), scripting extensions such as JavaScript, and dynamically loaded applets such as those created using Java or ActiveX.

Images

Graphical images (both JPEG and GIF) are permitted on both local and remote content pages; however, they are limited to the same 153 pixels wide limitation. (Your user will receive an ugly error message if the Palm VII receives an image that is too big.) They also are limited to a maximum two pixels of color depth (in other words, simple grayscale).

Palm recommends that you strive to reduce the number of images returned by your Web site because they dramatically increase the number of transmitted bytes.

You can embed images in your local PQA by defining a meta tag in the `<head>` section of your HTML as follows:

```
<head>
<meta name="localicon" content="myimage.jpg">
</head>
```

In the body of your HTML, you then refer to the image in the same way you normally do:

```
<img src="myimage.jpg">
```

To get the Palm to understand and accept remote images, you must identify your HTML as "Palm-friendly" via the meta tag:

```
<meta name="PalmComputingPlatform" content="true">
```

If this tag is not present, remote images will not be downloaded and rendered. Also, your text will be truncated after 1,024 bytes. If you are in control of your content, however, there is no reason not to include this tag.

Hyperlinks

You define hyperlinks just as you do in "normal" HTML, using the `<A HREF= "linkname">` tag. Things are slightly more complex in that you are permitted to bundle multiple HTML pages and images in your local PQA, so Palm provided a way to distinguish between remote and local links, as follows:

Following is a remote link:

```
<A HREF="http://www.bachmannsoftware.com/index.html">
```

This is a local link:

```
<A HREF="file:myapp.pqa/index.html">
```

The `file:` designation clues Clipper into the fact that it must look in your .PQA file for the desired HTML.

When partitioning your application into local and remote content, you should carefully consider what portions of the content might change over time. Web-based content can obviously be changed as needed with no action from the user. If you need to change the content on a local PQA, however, you will have to get the users to obtain a current version of your PQA and install it on their Palms.

If you have a significant amount of information that must be returned, you should structure your query so that it does not return all the information on the first query. Instead, allow the user to progressively ask for more levels of detail via a "More" link.

History

Mainstream Web browsers support a "history" list that offers a convenient way for users to quickly access recently visited sites.

The Palm VII has a somewhat limited history-tracking capability. The recent pages accessed are tracked, but on a per-PQA basis. The overall Palm VII environment does not track this; each PQA is responsible for designating what should be shown in the history list, and only the history for the currently running PQA is available to the user.

To enable history tracking, you add another meta tag to your HTML:

```
<meta name="HistoryListText" content="My Page">
```

`"My Page"` is replaced by the text you want to see in the history list to represent that page.

Customizing the User's Experience

As you might know, HTTP is a "stateless" protocol and as such does not offer the opportunity for either the host or the Web site to "remember" who the other person is from page request to page request. It is a challenge to customize Web content based on who you are from page to page and session to session. For example, a bookstore might find it useful to remember that you prefer mysteries and display ads and special offers that reflect that preference.

Some sites employ "cookies" to get around this problem. Cookies are small bits of information stored on the user's local computer. This information helps the Web site track the identification of the users and their preferences from session to session. The specific cookie mechanism is not supported, but Palm does support a special variable named `%deviceid`, which you can pass to the host via CGI. This is the Palm unit's physical device ID, and it can be used by the Web site to uniquely identify the users and match them to sets of preferences.

The Palm offers another way to customize the content returned to the user by supporting another variable called `%zipcode`. When passed via CGI, this variable contains the zip code of the nearest wireless base station to the Palm's location. PQAs that provide weather information, traffic reports, and such can support special features that "know" who and where you are.

Launching Other Applications

You can employ special tags to launch and interact with other applications resident on the Palm. For example, the following line launches another PQA-named helper:

```
File:helper.pqa
```

The following line launches the Address Book application:

```
Palm:addr.appl
```

The following line invokes the iMessenger application with the address specified:

```
mailto:glenn@bachmannsoftware.com
```

Steps Involved in Creating a PQA

Creating your first PQA is actually simple. You need only a couple of tools:

- HTML editor—A plain-text editor is best: You definitely do not want to litter your HTML with vendor-specific tags. You also want to have tight control over the HTML so that the minimum number of bytes is transferred. Keep in mind that you will also need to manually insert Palm meta tags.
- Query Application Builder—This is provided in the Palm SDK and converts one or more HTML files along with linked images to a PQA.

As I said before, the Builder will convert not only your "main" HTML file, but will also convert "local" HTML files referred to by the main HTML page's links. All the pages, images, and links are stored in the final PQA.

A Sample PQA: *Palm Programming Information Kiosk*

The current documentation from Palm includes some basic examples of how to create a "hello world" PQA. I take that one step further and create something that might be considered more useful.

I will show you how to create a PQA that is an information resource for this book. The local portion of the application will be a single main page that provides links to information on *Palm Programming*, including an overview, a table of contents, and (most importantly) information about me! Theoretically, the remote portion could be hosted on Sams Publishing's Web site and provide a dynamically updated portal into

Palm Programming's table of contents, corrections and revisions, other sources of information, and so on. You can easily imagine extensions to this kiosk to let a visitor purchase the book and even submit comments, questions, and reviews to the publisher.

The first step in creating our PQA is to develop the HTML. Look at the HTML for the main (local) page in Listing 23.1.

LISTING 23.1 HTML SYNTAX FOR THE MAIN PAGE

```
<html>
<head>
<meta name="PalmComputingPlatform" content="true">
<meta name="localicon" content="sams_sign_left.gif">
<title>Palm Programming</title>
</head>
<body>
<img src="sams_sign_left.gif">
<BR>
Presenting <B>Palm Programming</B> by Glenn Bachmann
<BR>
<a href="http://www.bachmannsoftware.com/pp_overview.htm">Overview</a>
<BR>
<a href="http://www.bachmannsoftware.com/pp_toc.htm">Table of
 Contents</a>
<BR>
<a href="http://www.bachmannsoftware.com/pp_me.htm">About
 Glenn Bachmann</a>
<BR>
<BR>
Glenn Bachmann's Palm Programming is a straightforward tutorial that
teaches developers how to create fully functioning Palm applications
using the CodeWarrior development environment.
<BR>

</body>
</html>
```

If you are familiar with HTML, you know this looks like the source for a normal page. Only two elements here are new. As I described earlier in the chapter, the following line is a meta tag that must be present for the Palm to process images correctly:

```
<meta name="PalmComputingPlatform" content="true">
```

The following line was also covered earlier, and you will recall that it identifies an image that is embedded in the PQA itself:

```
<meta name="localicon" content="sun.gif">
```

23

CREATING PALM
QUERY
APPLICATIONS

Without this tag, Clipper would not be able to properly handle the main page's icon (which is a standard Sams Publishing image).

There are three remote links in the HTML, and all three reference HTML files on the public Internet.

How do I create a PQA from this file? Enter the Query Application Builder! Launch qab.exe, and you will be greeted by a simple utility, shown in Figure 23.1.

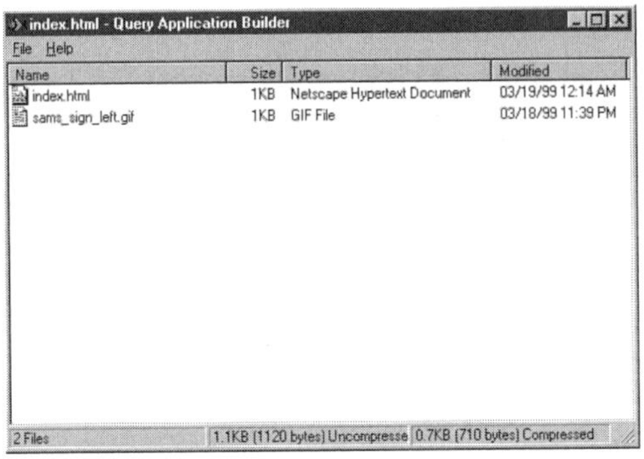

FIGURE 23.1

The Query Application Builder main screen with the HTML and image loaded.

From the File menu, choose Open Index, and locate your main HTML file (often called index.html). The Builder parses your HTML, identifies any local links (not remote links), and automatically adds them to the Builder main window. In this case, it located and loaded the Sams .GIF image.

Choose Build PQA from the File menu, give your PQA a filename (such as Palm Programming.pqa), and click the Build button. You now have a Palm Query Application ready to load onto the Palm VII.

The other three HTML files are all similar, so look at Listing 23.2 to examine the only one that has a small twist: the About Glenn Bachmann page.

LISTING 23.2   HTML SYNTAX FOR THE ABOUT THE AUTHOR PAGE

```
<html>
<head>
<meta name="PalmComputingPlatform" content="true">
<meta name="HistoryListText" content="About Glenn Bachmann">
<title>Palm Programming - About Glenn Bachmann</title>
</head>
<body>
```

```
<BR>
<B>Glenn Bachmann</B> is president of <B>Bachmann Software and
Services, LLC</B>.
<BR><BR>
Founded in 1993, Bachmann Software and Services provides
software products and professional software development
services for the mobile computing and wireless communications industries.
<BR>Bachmann Software has developed products for the industry's
leading corporations and is the creator of <B>Bachmann Print Manager</B>
and <B>Bachmann Report Manager</B> for the Palm Computing Platform.
<BR><BR>
<A HREF=mailto:glenn@bachmannsoftware.com>Send email to the author</A>
</body>
</html>
```

Note two lines of interest. The following line is a meta tag that identifies this page as one that belongs in the History list and gives it the proper text to display:

```
<meta name="HistoryListText" content="About Glenn Bachmann">
```

The following is a link to the built-in mailto tag, and when clicked, it will launch the iMessenger application on the Palm VII, telling it to open a new message with my email address in the to field:

```
<A HREF=mailto:glenn@bachmannsoftware.com>Send email to the author</A>
```

Installing the *Palm Programming* kiosk is a two-step process. First, use the Palm Install tool to load your PQA during the next hot-sync operation, just as you would with a .PRC file. Second, store the remote HTML files in the location referenced by the PQA's remote hyperlinks.

Figures 23.2 and 23.3 show the main *Palm Programming* kiosk page as well as the About Glenn Bachmann page.

FIGURE 23.2

The Palm Programming *main PQA page.*

FIGURE 23.3

That's me!

Summary

With remarkably little effort, I've created a useful application that uses the built-in wireless Internet capabilities of the Palm VII. Although much more sophisticated applications are possible, of course, this chapter demonstrated what you can do with only a little knowledge of HTML and some guidelines on PQA design.

I anticipate (and hope) that we will see a marvelous variety of new and genuinely useful PQAs after the Palm VII's release. When that happens, the vision of the connected mobile computer user will be on its way to realization.

CHAPTER 24

Conduits

Conduits provide a facility for transferring data and applications back and forth between Palm Computing devices and host platforms such as a desktop PC, corporate server, or Internet location.

Conduits lie both at the heart of the Palm computing platform and on the periphery of the world of Palm programming. Without conduits and Palm's hot-sync technology, data could not flow to and from the Palm, applications could not get installed on the device, and the synchronization of data between desktop-based applications and their Palm equivalents could not occur. Yet the Conduit Software Development Kit is a completely separate set of developer tools from the Palm OS SDK, in terms of how it is packaged and distributed by Palm Computing.

Further, conduits are not programmed using the same CodeWarrior tools you use for normal Palm development. In fact, it is impossible today to use CodeWarrior to create a conduit under Windows: You must instead use Microsoft's Visual C++ under Windows.

Many—perhaps most—applications will never require the development of a custom conduit. I've managed to get through 23 chapters containing sample applications with nary a mention of the topic of conduits. In addition, a quick scan of the commercial software, shareware, and freeware available for the Palm indicates that most of them do not include a custom conduit either.

Nevertheless, the rise of the Palm as a legitimate business tool for use in deploying corporate applications and providing access to corporate data is driving the need to deliver non-PIM data to the Palm. Many of these applications will require conduit components to help transfer or even synchronize that data. Third-party tools are available that minimize the need for you to resort to the Conduit SDK for these applications, but there will still be situations where a custom conduit will be preferable.

This chapter covers

- What a conduit is
- How the hot-sync facility interacts with conduits
- How to obtain the Conduit SDK and what it contains
- The development tools and environment

When I was researching this book, I realized that the topic of conduit development could fill a book of its own. I originally had ambitious plans to create a fully functional sample conduit, but I scaled back these plans as I began developing an outline for the conduit material; it quickly became obvious that the topic demanded 100 or more pages and had grown beyond the confines of a chapter or two in the book.

What I ultimately decided would be best is to give developers the information necessary to help them decide whether a conduit is needed in their applications and, if so, what tools and concepts they need to pursue such an endeavor.

What Is a Conduit?

Unless your Palm is equipped with a modem (wired or wireless), conduits are a Palm's only means of communicating with the outside world, including data and applications residing on other computer systems. Conduits work in concert with the HotSync Manager to perform

- Mirroring and synchronizing with data on other systems
- Backing up data residing on the Palm
- Downloading and installing Palm OS applications
- Importing and exporting data

As mentioned briefly in Chapter 18, "Large Applications," conduits provide a way for you to partition your application so that one piece runs on the Palm device while more processor- and memory-intensive tasks run on more capable host systems. You can then deploy a conduit to exchange database records and other types of information between the two pieces of the application. (You can consider this arrangement a strange kind of form of client/server application!)

Depending on the application requirements, you can design a conduit to take one of four forms:

- A data mirror
- A one-directional conduit
- A transaction-based conduit
- A backup

Data Mirroring

Data mirroring is the "classic" synchronization activity, and it is performed by the default conduits for the address book, date book, and so on. The conduit intervenes and takes appropriate action when data has been modified by either or both the desktop and the handheld application.

One Directional

The one-directional conduit assumes that either the desktop or the handheld will be modifying data, but not both. The synchronization activity is limited to copying the data from one of the platforms to the other. If the Palm is to be used as a read-only front end to corporate data, choosing this type of conduit might be a good strategy. Conversely, if remote data entry is to be performed on the Palm, you can simply transfer the data collected back to the host for further processing.

Transaction Based

Transaction-based conduits perform additional processing on the host computer for each record synchronized. If an order record was added from the Palm, for example, and the host system required that a customer order number be generated for each new record, the number might be generated at synchronization time. This type of activity can significantly impact how long the conduit will take to run to completion, so it is recommended that you use it with caution. There are usually other ways to accomplish the same goals using multiple passes.

Backup

The backup is perhaps the simplest kind of conduit in that it only needs to transfer the data from the Palm to the host computer. Most situations that call for a backup conduit will not require a custom-developed conduit but can instead rely on the backup conduit supplied by Palm.

24

CONDUITS

How Does Hot-Sync Interact with Conduits?

A conduit is not a Palm application at all, but rather a Windows dynamic link library (DLL) that plugs into a special interface in the HotSync Manager so that it is invoked when the user performs a hot-sync. This DLL uses Conduit SDK interfaces to access data managed by the desktop application and transfers data to and from the target Palm application.

You can perform a hot-sync via cable, modem, or network connection. Third-party vendors have also provided infrared synchronization utilities. The HotSync Manager handles all these connection types, hiding the details behind a standard communication interface.

The HotSync Manager runs as a background task on your PC. (You've no doubt seen the icon appear in your Taskbar system tray.) It monitors a designated serial communications port, waiting for a notification that a hot-sync is being requested by the Palm device.

When a hot-sync is initiated, the HotSync Manager receives the creator ID for each database installed on the Palm and checks whether there is a conduit registered to handle that creator ID. If there is, the HotSync Manager then calls the conduit and asks it to perform whatever tasks it was designed for.

This level of coordination with the HotSync Manager is possible because there are standard programming entry points that your conduit must support. These entry points are called as functions by HotSync Manager when a hot-sync is being performed. The primary entry point is OpenConduit, in which all the synchronization activity takes place. Inside your DLL, you call functions in the HotSync Manager API in order to communicate with the data on the Palm device.

With multiple versions of the Palm in the field, there are also multiple versions of the HotSync Manager and other Palm desktop software. You are responsible for coordinating versions of your conduit with versions of the HotSync Manager and responding correctly when the HotSync Manager asks your conduit for its version number.

Once created, conduits must be installed on your desktop so they can be recognized by the HotSync Manager. This is done by inserting a number of Registry keys and values in the Windows Registry, one of which is the target creator ID for your conduit (which must match the creator ID of the database to be synchronized). Current versions of the Conduit SDK provide a sample InstallShield script that you can use as a basis for your own installation program.

How to Obtain the Conduit SDK

The Conduit SDK is available for downloading from Palm Computing's Web site at `www.palm.com/devzone`. A copy of the SDK is included with CodeWarrior's toolset, but it is a good idea to frequently check the Palm Computing Web site because the SDK has undergone frequent revisions in recent times.

The Conduit SDK comes with several useful components:

- *Programmers' Guide*: An overview and introduction to conduit concepts and the hot-sync mechanism.

- *Programmers' Reference*: A detailed reference to the HotSync Manager and other conduit-related APIs.

- Sample conduit code: The code for the built-in conduits as well as a skeleton conduit.

- Condmgr.exe: A utility for quickly adding a conduit to the Registry without having to write an install script.

- Headers and libraries: These are required in order to build a conduit in Visual Studio.

Development Tools and Programming Environment

As of this writing, the most current Conduit SDK is version 3.0, which requires the Microsoft Visual C++/Visual Studio environment as well as the Microsoft Foundation Classes version 5.0 in order to create Windows-based conduits. There have been reports of Visual Studio version 6.0 working with the Conduit SDK, but 5.0 is the recommended environment. Specifically, there are problems debugging conduits using version 6.0. Until these issues are sorted out, you should use Visual Studio version 5.0 for conduit development.

To make it easier to get up and running with conduit development, Palm has provided a conduit wizard that plugs into the Visual Studio Project Wizard. Creating a basic conduit shell is now easily done by choosing File, New from the Visual Studio menu, choosing Conduit from the Project tab, and answering a series of questions regarding how your conduit will be used. Visual Studio then proceeds to create an entire project complete with source code, ready for building.

24

CONDUITS

Other Conduit Development Options

If you want to create a conduit suitable for users who perform hot-sync to a Mac OS host, you'll find support in the Mac OS version of Metrowerks.

Also, a Java version of the Conduit SDK works with tools such as Symantec's Café development tool, which allows you to create Windows-based conduits.

Summary

In this chapter, I introduced Palm conduits. I explained what you can use conduits for, and you reviewed the hot-sync process in detail in order to understand where the built-in conduits (as well as the conduits you develop) fit in with the hot-sync mechanism. I also described the contents of the Conduit SDK and the development environment.

I stopped short of actually creating a conduit in this chapter, primarily because of the large amount of detailed information that you'd need in order to understand what is happening in the code. If, after reading this chapter and examining your application's requirements, you decide you need to develop a conduit, I encourage you to download the Conduit SDK, read through the *Programmers' Guide*, and begin examining the source code for the built-in conduits. Although it is tempting to immediately create a conduit skeleton using the Visual Studio Conduit Wizard, in my opinion it is best to understand what you are doing first.

There is a Palm-support discussion forum dedicated to those brave souls who dare to develop conduits. Visit the Palm Computing Developer Zone Web site to subscribe to this list, or browse past messages at `www.egroups.com`, which hosts the discussion group `conduit-dev-forum`.

Appendix

Part VI

IN THIS PART

APPENDIX A

Directory of Palm Development Resources

Following is a list of helpful Internet resources for Palm developers:

www.palm.com/devzone

The home of Palm Computing. You should regularly check this site for news, announcements, and general information. You should also take the time to join the Solution Provider Pavilion, which is Palm's developer program. The pavilion offers access to special programs and higher levels of developer support. Palm also hosts several mailing lists devoted to Palm development. I highly recommend that you join at least the Palm Developer mailing list. Palm's own development support engineers monitor this list. Find the lists at ls.palm.com.

news.massena.com

Darrin Massena runs a news host for Palm programming newsgroups. pilot.programmer, pilot.programmer.gcc, and pilot.programmer.codewarrior are among the active groups. Aside from the Palm Computing mailing lists, this site is the best source for peer support in Palm development.

www.roadcoders.com

Contains an extensive list of articles, sample code, and developer tools. Highly recommended.

www.wademan.com

One of the first (and still most useful) comprehensive sites devoted to Palm programming information.

www.qpqa.com

Quality Partners is the official Platinum Testing resource for the Platinum Certification of Palm products.

www.cdpubs.com

Creative Digital Publishing until recently published *Handheld Systems Journal*, the only periodical I know that is devoted to handheld (and Palm) programming. Many of the archived articles on the Web site are still essential reading. It offers a CD-ROM of the archives for a nominal charge.

www.drdobbs.com

Home of *Dr.Dobbs Magazine*, a general-purpose programming magazine. Lately, Dr.Dobbs has featured articles on various aspects of Palm programming.

Where to Find Development Tools and Helpful Utilities

These are Web sites for vendors offering development tools and utilities for the Palm computing platform:

www.metrowerks.com

Home of Metrowerks, the publisher of CodeWarrior, the official programming environment for the Palm computing platform.

www.pendragon-software.com

Publisher of Pendragon Forms, a wonderful forms-oriented development tool that is useful for both prototyping and full product development.

www.pumatech.com

Home of Puma Intellisync, and creator of Satellite Forms, which is a widely used development tool for the Palm.

www.avantgo.com

Home of AvantGo Corporation, publisher of the popular offline browser for the Web.

www.bachmannsoftware.com

My company's Web site. This is where you will find information on our line of Palm development tools, including printing from the Palm using Bachmann Print Manager and our new reporting tool, Bachmann Report Manager.

`www.pilotgear.com`

Probably the most well-known Internet source for downloading and purchasing Palm Pilot software.

`www.palmcentral.com`

Formerly known as "Ray's Archives," this is one place to go to obtain the GCC GNU compiler for Palm development. The site has expanded quite a bit and now offers hundreds of links to information on the Palm for both end users and developers.

`www.hewgill.com`

Development tools for the Palm Pilot, including CoPilot (the original name for POSE) and Jump (a Java development environment for the Palm).

INDEX

Other Related Titles

Sams Teach Yourself Palm Programming in 24 Hours
0-672-31611-0
Gavin Maxwell
$24.99 USA /
$35.95 CAN

Sams Teach Yourself C in 21 Days, Fourth Edition
0-672-31069-4
Peter Aitken
$29.99 USA /
$42.95 CAN

Sams Teach Yourself C++ in 21 Days, Third Edition
0-672-31515-7
Jesse Liberty
$29.99 USA /
$42.95 CAN

Sams Teach Yourself C in 21 Days: Complete Compiler Edition
0-672-31260-3
Peter Aitken and Bradley Jones
$49.99 USA /
$70.95 CAN

Sams Teach Yourself C++ in 21 Days: Complete Compiler Edition
0-672-31261-1
Jesse Liberty
$49.99 USA /
$70.95 CAN

Sams Teach Yourself Visual C++ 6 in 21 Days
0-672-31240-9
Davis Chapman
$34.99 USA /
$50.95 CAN

C++ Unleashed
0-672-31239-5
Jesse Liberty
$39.99 USA /
$57.95 CAN

Sams Teach Yourself C in 24 Hours
0-672-31068-6
Tony Zhang
$24.99 USA /
$35.95 CAN

Sams Teach Yourself C++ in 24 Hours, Second Edition
0-672-31516-5
Jesse Liberty
$19.99 USA /
$28.95 CAN

SAMS

www.samspublishing.com

All prices are subject to change.

Get FREE books and more...when you register this book online for our Personal Bookshelf Program

http://register.samspublishing.com/

SAMS

Register online and you can sign up for our *FREE Personal Bookshelf Program...*unlimited access to the electronic version of more than 200 complete computer books—immediately! That means you'll have 100,000 pages of valuable information onscreen, at your fingertips!

Plus, you can access product support, including complimentary downloads, technical support files, book-focused links, companion Web sites, author sites, and more!

And you'll be automatically registered to receive a *FREE subscription to a weekly email newsletter* to help you stay current with news, announcements, sample book chapters, and special events, including sweepstakes, contests, and various product giveaways!

We value your comments! Best of all, the entire registration process takes only a few minutes to complete, so go online and get the greatest value going—absolutely FREE!

Don't Miss Out On This Great Opportunity!

Sams is a brand of Macmillan Computer Publishing USA.

For more information, please visit *www.mcp.com*

What's on the CD-ROM

The companion CD-ROM contains a lot of useful third-party software, plus all the source code from the book.

Windows 95/98 Installation Instructions

1. Insert the CD-ROM disc into your CD-ROM drive.
2. From the Windows 95 desktop, double-click the My Computer icon.
3. Double-click the icon representing your CD-ROM drive.
4. Double-click the icon titled START.EXE to run the program.

NOTE

If Windows 95 is installed on your computer, and you have the AutoPlay feature enabled, the START.EXE program starts automatically whenever you insert the disc into your CD-ROM drive.

Windows NT Installation Instructions

1. Insert the CD-ROM disc into your CD-ROM drive.
2. From File Manager or Program Manager, choose Run from the File menu.
3. Type `<drive>\START.EXE` and press Enter, where `<drive>` corresponds to the drive letter of your CD-ROM. For example, if your CD-ROM is drive D:, type `D:\START.EXE` and press Enter.

GNU GENERAL PUBLIC LICENSE

Version 2, June 1991

Copyright © 1989, 1991 Free Software Foundation, Inc.

675 Mass Ave, Cambridge, MA 02139, USA

Preamble

The licenses for most software are designed to take away your freedom to share and change it. By contrast, the GNU General Public License is intended to guarantee your freedom to share and change free software—to make sure the software is free for all its users. This General Public License applies to most of the Free Software Foundation's software and to any other program whose authors commit to using it. (Some other Free Software Foundation software is covered by the GNU Library General Public License instead.) You can apply it to your programs, too.

When we speak of free software, we are referring to freedom, not price. Our General Public Licenses are designed to make sure that you have the freedom to distribute copies of free software (and charge for this service if you wish), that you receive source code or can get it if you want it, that you can change the software or use pieces of it in new free programs; and that you know you can do these things.

To protect your rights, we need to make restrictions that forbid anyone to deny you these rights or to ask you to surrender the rights. These restrictions translate to certain responsibilities for you if you distribute copies of the software, or if you modify it.

For example, if you distribute copies of such a program, whether gratis or for a fee, you must give the recipients all the rights that you have. You must make sure that they, too, receive or can get the source code. And you must show them these terms so they know their rights.

We protect your rights with two steps: (1) copyright the software, and (2) offer you this license which gives you legal permission to copy, distribute and/or modify the software.

Also, for each author's protection and ours, we want to make certain that everyone understands that there is no warranty for this free software. If the software is modified by someone else and passed on, we want its recipients to know that what they have is not the original, so that any problems introduced by others will not reflect on the original authors' reputations.

Finally, any free program is threatened constantly by software patents. We wish to avoid the danger that redistributors of a free program will individually obtain patent licenses, in effect making the program proprietary. To prevent this, we have made it clear that any patent must be licensed for everyone's free use or not licensed at all.

The precise terms and conditions for copying, distribution and modification follow.

GNU GENERAL PUBLIC LICENSE

TERMS AND CONDITIONS FOR COPYING, DISTRIBUTION AND MODIFI-CATION

0. This License applies to any program or other work which contains a notice placed by the copyright holder saying it may be distributed under the terms of this General Public License. The "Program", below, refers to any such program or work, and a "work based on the Program" means either the Program or any derivative work under copyright law: that is to say, a work containing the Program or a portion of it, either verbatim or with modifications and/or translated into another language. (Hereinafter, translation is included without limitation in the term "modification".) Each licensee is addressed as "you".

Activities other than copying, distribution and modification are not covered by this License; they are outside its scope. The act of running the Program is not restricted, and the output from the Program is covered only if its contents constitute a work based on the Program (independent of having been made by running the Program). Whether that is true depends on what the Program does.

1. You may copy and distribute verbatim copies of the Program's source code as you receive it, in any medium, provided that you conspicuously and appropriately publish on each copy an appropriate copyright notice and disclaimer of warranty; keep intact all the notices that refer to this License and to the absence of any warranty; and give any other recipients of the Program a copy of this License along with the Program.

   You may charge a fee for the physical act of transferring a copy, and you may at your option offer warranty protection in exchange for a fee.

2. You may modify your copy or copies of the Program or any portion of it, thus forming a work based on the Program, and copy and distribute such modifications or work under the terms of Section 1 above, provided that you also meet all of these conditions:

   a) You must cause the modified files to carry prominent notices stating that you changed the files and the date of any change.

b) You must cause any work that you distribute or publish, that in whole or in part contains or is derived from the Program or any part thereof, to be licensed as a whole at no charge to all third parties under the terms of this License.

c) If the modified program normally reads commands interactively when run, you must cause it, when started running for such interactive use in the most ordinary way, to print or display an announcement including an appropriate copyright notice and a notice that there is no warranty (or else, saying that you provide a warranty) and that users may redistribute the program under these conditions, and telling the user how to view a copy of this License. (Exception: if the Program itself is interactive but does not normally print such an announcement, your work based on the Program is not required to print an announcement.)

These requirements apply to the modified work as a whole. If identifiable sections of that work are not derived from the Program, and can be reasonably considered independent and separate works in themselves, then this License, and its terms, do not apply to those sections when you distribute them as separate works. But when you distribute the same sections as part of a whole which is a work based on the Program, the distribution of the whole must be on the terms of this License, whose permissions for other licensees extend to the entire whole, and thus to each and every part regardless of who wrote it.

Thus, it is not the intent of this section to claim rights or contest your rights to work written entirely by you; rather, the intent is to exercise the right to control the distribution of derivative or collective works based on the Program.

In addition, mere aggregation of another work not based on the Program with the Program (or with a work based on the Program) on a volume of a storage or distribution medium does not bring the other work under the scope of this License.

3. You may copy and distribute the Program (or a work based on it, under Section 2) in object code or executable form under the terms of Sections 1 and 2 above provided that you also do one of the following:

a) Accompany it with the complete corresponding machine-readable source code, which must be distributed under the terms of Sections 1 and 2 above on a medium customarily used for software interchange; or,

b) Accompany it with a written offer, valid for at least three years, to give any third party, for a charge no more than your cost of physically performing source distribution, a complete machine-readable copy of the corresponding source code, to be distributed under the terms of Sections 1 and 2 above on a medium customarily used for software interchange; or,

c) Accompany it with the information you received as to the offer to distribute corresponding source code. (This alternative is allowed only for noncommercial distribution and only if you received the program in object code or executable form with such an offer, in accord with Subsection b above.)

The source code for a work means the preferred form of the work for making modifications to it. For an executable work, complete source code means all the source code for all modules it contains, plus any associated interface definition files, plus the scripts used to control compilation and installation of the executable. However, as a special exception, the source code distributed need not include anything that is normally distributed (in either source or binary form) with the major components (compiler, kernel, and so on) of the operating system on which the executable runs, unless that component itself accompanies the executable.

If distribution of executable or object code is made by offering access to copy from a designated place, then offering equivalent access to copy the source code from the same place counts as distribution of the source code, even though third parties are not compelled to copy the source along with the object code.

4. You may not copy, modify, sublicense, or distribute the Program except as expressly provided under this License. Any attempt otherwise to copy, modify, sublicense or distribute the Program is void, and will automatically terminate your rights under this License. However, parties who have received copies, or rights, from you under this License will not have their licenses terminated so long as such parties remain in full compliance.

5. You are not required to accept this License, since you have not signed it. However, nothing else grants you permission to modify or distribute the Program or its derivative works. These actions are prohibited by law if you do not accept this License. Therefore, by modifying or distributing the Program (or any work based on the Program), you indicate your acceptance of this License to do so, and all its terms and conditions for copying, distributing or modifying the Program or works based on it.

6. Each time you redistribute the Program (or any work based on the Program), the recipient automatically receives a license from the original licensor to copy, distribute or modify the Program subject to these terms and conditions. You may not impose any further restrictions on the recipients' exercise of the rights granted herein. You are not responsible for enforcing compliance by third parties to this License.

7. If, as a consequence of a court judgment or allegation of patent infringement or for any other reason (not limited to patent issues), conditions are imposed on you (whether by court order, agreement or otherwise) that contradict the conditions of this License, they do not excuse you from the conditions of this License. If you cannot distribute so as to satisfy simultaneously your obligations under this License and any other pertinent obligations, then as a consequence you may not distribute the Program at all. For example, if a patent license would not permit royalty-free redistribution of the Program by all those who receive copies directly or indirectly through you, then the only way you could satisfy both it and this License would be to refrain entirely from distribution of the Program.

If any portion of this section is held invalid or unenforceable under any particular circumstance, the balance of the section is intended to apply and the section as a whole is intended to apply in other circumstances.

It is not the purpose of this section to induce you to infringe any patents or other property right claims or to contest validity of any such claims; this section has the sole purpose of protecting the integrity of the free software distribution system, which is implemented by public license practices. Many people have made generous contributions to the wide range of software distributed through that system in reliance on consistent application of that system; it is up to the author/donor to decide if he or she is willing to distribute software through any other system and a licensee cannot impose that choice.

This section is intended to make thoroughly clear what is believed to be a consequence of the rest of this License.

8. If the distribution and/or use of the Program is restricted in certain countries either by patents or by copyrighted interfaces, the original copyright holder who places the Program under this License may add an explicit geographical distribution limitation excluding those countries, so that distribution is permitted only in or among countries not thus excluded. In such case, this License incorporates the limitation as if written in the body of this License.

9. The Free Software Foundation may publish revised and/or new versions of the General Public License from time to time. Such new versions will be similar in spirit to the present version, but may differ in detail to address new problems or concerns.

Each version is given a distinguishing version number. If the Program specifies a version number of this License which applies to it and "any later version", you have the option of following the terms and conditions either of that version or of any later version published by the Free Software Foundation. If the Program does not specify a version number of this License, you may choose any version ever published by the Free Software Foundation.

10. If you wish to incorporate parts of the Program into other free programs whose distribution conditions are different, write to the author to ask for permission. For software which is copyrighted by the Free Software Foundation, write to the Free Software Foundation; we sometimes make exceptions for this. Our decision will be guided by the two goals of preserving the free status of all derivatives of our free software and of promoting the sharing and reuse of software generally.

NO WARRANTY

11. BECAUSE THE PROGRAM IS LICENSED FREE OF CHARGE, THERE IS NO WARRANTY FOR THE PROGRAM, TO THE EXTENT PERMITTED BY APPLICABLE LAW. EXCEPT WHEN OTHERWISE STATED IN WRITING THE COPYRIGHT HOLDERS AND/OR OTHER PARTIES PROVIDE THE PROGRAM "AS IS" WITHOUT WARRANTY OF ANY KIND, EITHER EXPRESSED OR IMPLIED, INCLUDING, BUT NOT LIMITED TO, THE IMPLIED WARRANTIES OF MERCHANTABILITY AND FITNESS FOR A PARTICULAR PURPOSE. THE ENTIRE RISK AS TO THE QUALITY AND PERFORMANCE OF THE PROGRAM IS WITH YOU. SHOULD THE PROGRAM PROVE DEFECTIVE, YOU ASSUME THE COST OF ALL NECESSARY SERVICING, REPAIR OR CORRECTION.

12. IN NO EVENT UNLESS REQUIRED BY APPLICABLE LAW OR AGREED TO IN WRITING WILL ANY COPYRIGHT HOLDER, OR ANY OTHER PARTY WHO MAY MODIFY AND/OR REDISTRIBUTE THE PROGRAM AS PERMITTED ABOVE, BE LIABLE TO YOU FOR DAMAGES, INCLUDING ANY GENERAL, SPECIAL, INCIDENTAL OR CONSEQUENTIAL DAMAGES ARISING OUT OF THE USE OR INABILITY TO USE THE PROGRAM (INCLUDING BUT NOT LIMITED TO LOSS OF DATA OR DATA BEING RENDERED INACCURATE OR LOSSES SUSTAINED BY YOU OR THIRD PARTIES OR A FAILURE OF THE PROGRAM TO OPERATE WITH ANY OTHER PROGRAMS), EVEN IF SUCH HOLDER OR OTHER PARTY HAS BEEN ADVISED OF THE POSSIBILITY OF SUCH DAMAGES.

END OF TERMS AND CONDITIONS

Appendix: How to Apply These Terms to Your New Programs

If you develop a new program, and you want it to be of the greatest possible use to the public, the best way to achieve this is to make it free software which everyone can redistribute and change under these terms.

To do so, attach the following notices to the program. It is safest to attach them to the start of each source file to most effectively convey the exclusion of warranty; and each file should have at least the "copyright" line and a pointer to where the full notice is found.

> <one line to give the program's name and a brief idea of what it does.>
>
> Copyright © 19yy <name of author>
>
> This program is free software; you can redistribute it and/or modify it under the terms of the GNU General Public License as published by the Free Software Foundation; either version 2 of the License, or (at your option) any later version.
>
> This program is distributed in the hope that it will be useful, but WITHOUT ANY WARRANTY; without even the implied warranty of MERCHANTABILITY or FITNESS FOR A PARTICULAR PURPOSE. See the GNU General Public License for more details.
>
> You should have received a copy of the GNU General Public License along with this program; if not, write to the Free Software Foundation, Inc., 675 Mass Ave, Cambridge, MA 02139, USA.

Also add information on how to contact you by electronic and paper mail.

If the program is interactive, make it output a short notice like this when it starts in an interactive mode:

> Gnomovision version 69, Copyright © 19yy name of author
>
> Gnomovision comes with ABSOLUTELY NO WARRANTY; for details type 'show w'.
>
> This is free software, and you are welcome to redistribute it under certain conditions; type 'show c' for details.

The hypothetical commands 'show w' and 'show c' should show the appropriate parts of the General Public License. Of course, the commands you use may be called something other than 'show w' and 'show c'; they could even be mouse-clicks or menu items—whatever suits your program.

You should also get your employer (if you work as a programmer) or your school, if any, to sign a "copyright disclaimer" for the program, if necessary. Here is a sample; alter the names:

Yoyodyne, Inc., hereby disclaims all copyright interest in the program 'Gnomovision' (which makes passes at compilers) written by James Hacker.

<signature of Ty Coon>, 1 April 1989

Ty Coon, President of Vice

This General Public License does not permit incorporating your program into proprietary programs. If your program is a subroutine library, you may consider it more useful to permit linking proprietary applications with the library. If this is what you want to do, use the GNU Library General Public License instead of this License.

By opening this package, you are agreeing to be bound by the following agreement:

Some of the programs included with this product are governed by the GNU General Public License, which allows redistribution; see the license information for each product for more information. Other programs are included on the CD-ROM by special permission from their authors.

You may not copy or redistribute the entire CD-ROM as a whole. Copying and redistribution of individual software programs on the CD-ROM is governed by terms set by individual copyright holders. The installer and code from the author(s) is copyrighted by the publisher and the author. Individual programs and other items on the CD-ROM are copyrighted by their various authors or other copyright holders. This software is sold as-is without warranty of any kind, either express or implied, including but not limited to the implied warranties of merchantability and fitness for a particular purpose. Neither the publisher nor its dealers or distributors assumes any liability for any alleged or actual damages arising from the use of this program. (Some states do not allow for the exclusion of implied warranties, so the exclusion might not apply to you.)

NOTE: Before using the CD-ROM, read \readme.txt.